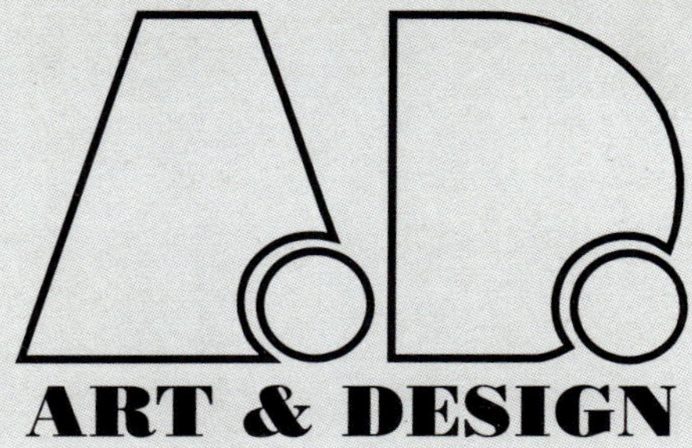

ACADEMY GROUP LTD
42 LEINSTER GARDENS, LONDON W2 3AN
TEL: 0171-402 2141 FAX: 1071-723 9540

EDITOR: Nicola Kearton
SUB-EDITOR: Ramona Khambatta
ART EDITOR: Andrea Bettella
CHIEF DESIGNER: Mario Bettella
DESIGNER: Toby Norman

SUBSCRIPTION OFFICES:
UK: VCH PUBLISHERS (UK) LTD
8 WELLINGTON COURT, WELLINGTON STREET
CAMBRIDGE CB1 1HZ
TEL: (01223) 321111 FAX: (01223) 313321

USA AND CANADA: VCH PUBLISHERS INC
303 NW 12TH AVENUE DEERFIELD BEACH,
FLORIDA 33442-1788 USA
TEL: (305) 428-5566 / (800) 367-8249
FAX: (305) 428-8201

ALL OTHER COUNTRIES:
VCH VERLAGSGESELLSCHAFT MBH
BOSCHSTRASSE 12, POSTFACH 101161
69451 WEINHEIM
FEDERAL REPUBLIC OF GERMANY
TEL: 06201 606 148 FAX: 06201 606 184

CONTENTS

ART & DESIGN **MAGAZINE**
*Marina **Abramović**, Places of Power, from **Cleaning the House**, Academy Editions, 1995*

ART & DESIGN **PROFILE** No 42

THE IDEAL PLACE

*Philip **Peters** • Henk **Oosterling** No(w)here as the Ideal Place • David **Elliott** After Omega • Andrew **Wilson** Making the Viewer Present • **Art & Language** • John **Blake** • Ricardo **Brey** • Patrick **Corillon** • Georges **Descombes** • Alfred **Eikelenboom** • Daniel **Faust** • Renée **Green** • Jan **Van Grunsven** • Thomas **Huber** • Mark **Lewis** • Pieter **Laurens Mol** • Matt **Mullican** • Jan **Van de Pavert** • Urs **Pfannenmüller** • Norbert **Radermacher** • Ulf **Rollof** • JCJ **Vanderheyden** • Lawrence **Weiner** • Stephen **Willats** • Robin **Winters** • Marcel **Zalme** • Rémy **Zaugg** • Mirjam **de Zeeuw***

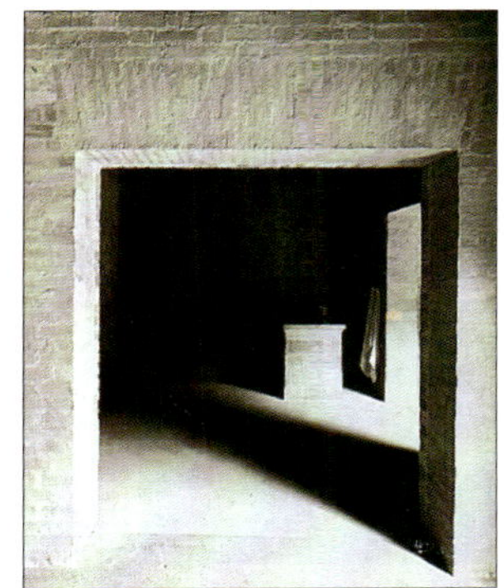

Marina Abramović, Dom Van der Laan, Washing Hands Before Going to Eat

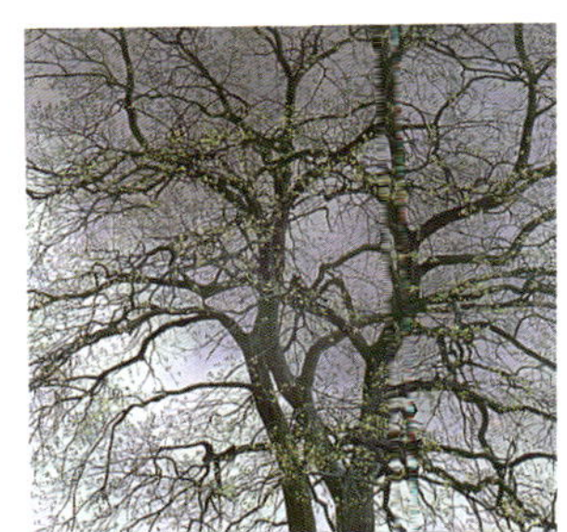

Alice Stepanek and Steven Maslin, Eiche, 1993, oil on canvas, 55 x 55cm

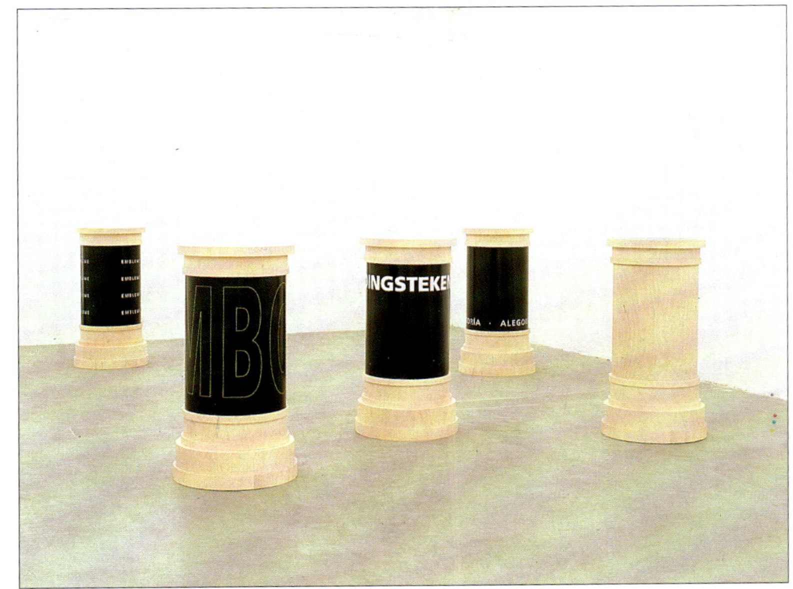

Mirjam de Zeeuw, HCAK 1993-94

MARINA ABRAMOVIĆ

Cleaning the House

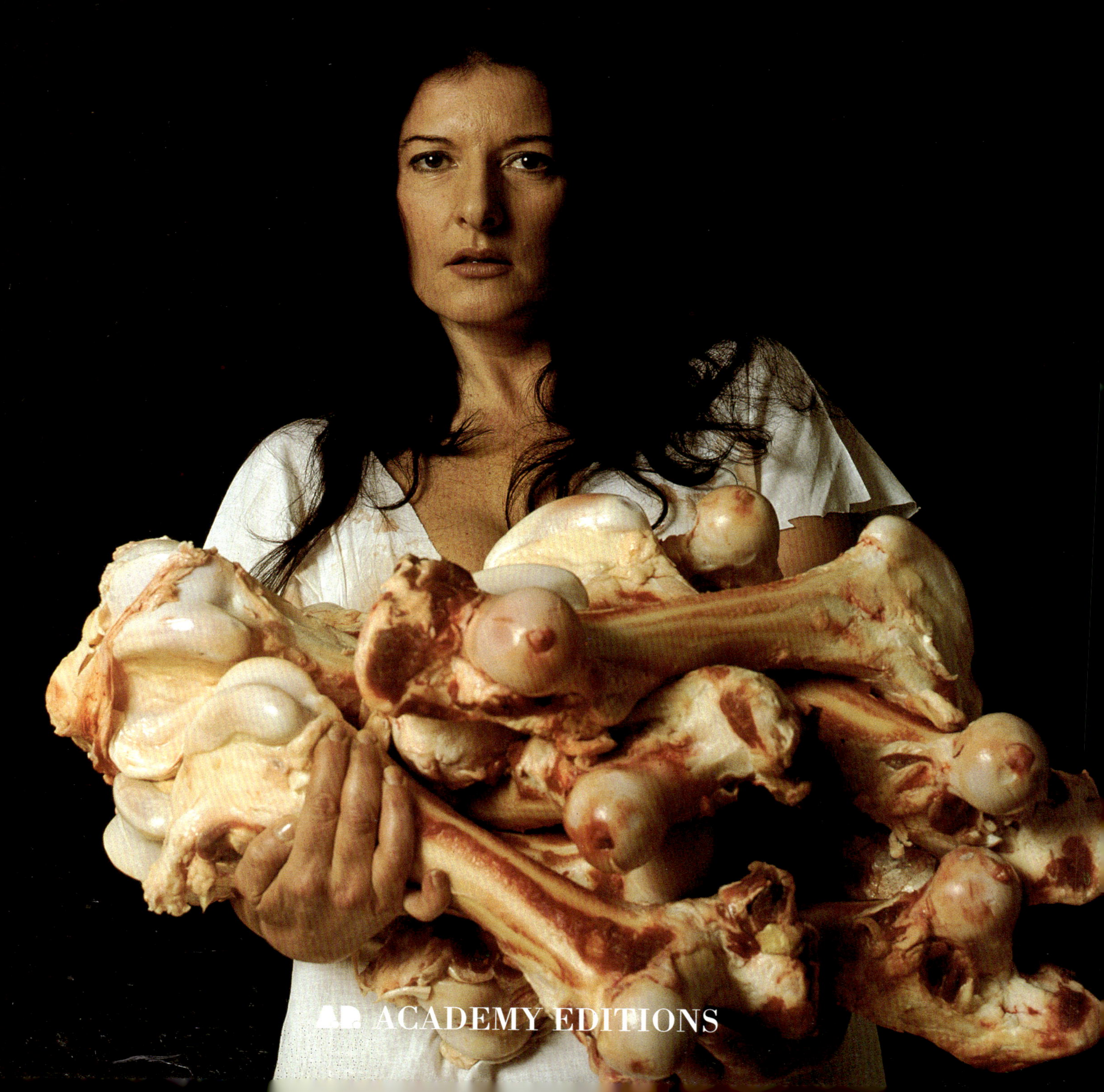

ACADEMY EDITIONS

Places of Power

I am one of those nomadic artists, just travelling from place to place. In the time I have been travelling, there have only been a few places on this planet which have drawn me to them again and again throughout many different stages of my life. And I call them places of power. There are some places which have certain energy and being at these places is sufficient to feel that course of energy. And those places are open for you. Sometimes somebody else can come to the same place and nothing happens. So

very person in their life has their own place of power.

There are also some places where you can never go, but where you have a desire to go.

There is a kind of mystery about the place and it haunts you for years and years. You will never get there for whatever reasons there might be on the way.

These places are also very important because you can travel to them through your own mind and you don't have to be physically present.

Extract taken from *Marina Abramović, Cleaning the House*, Art & Design Monograph, Academy Editions, London, Publication Date June 1995, ISBN 1 85490 399 5. Images courtesy The Artist and Sean Kelly, New York.

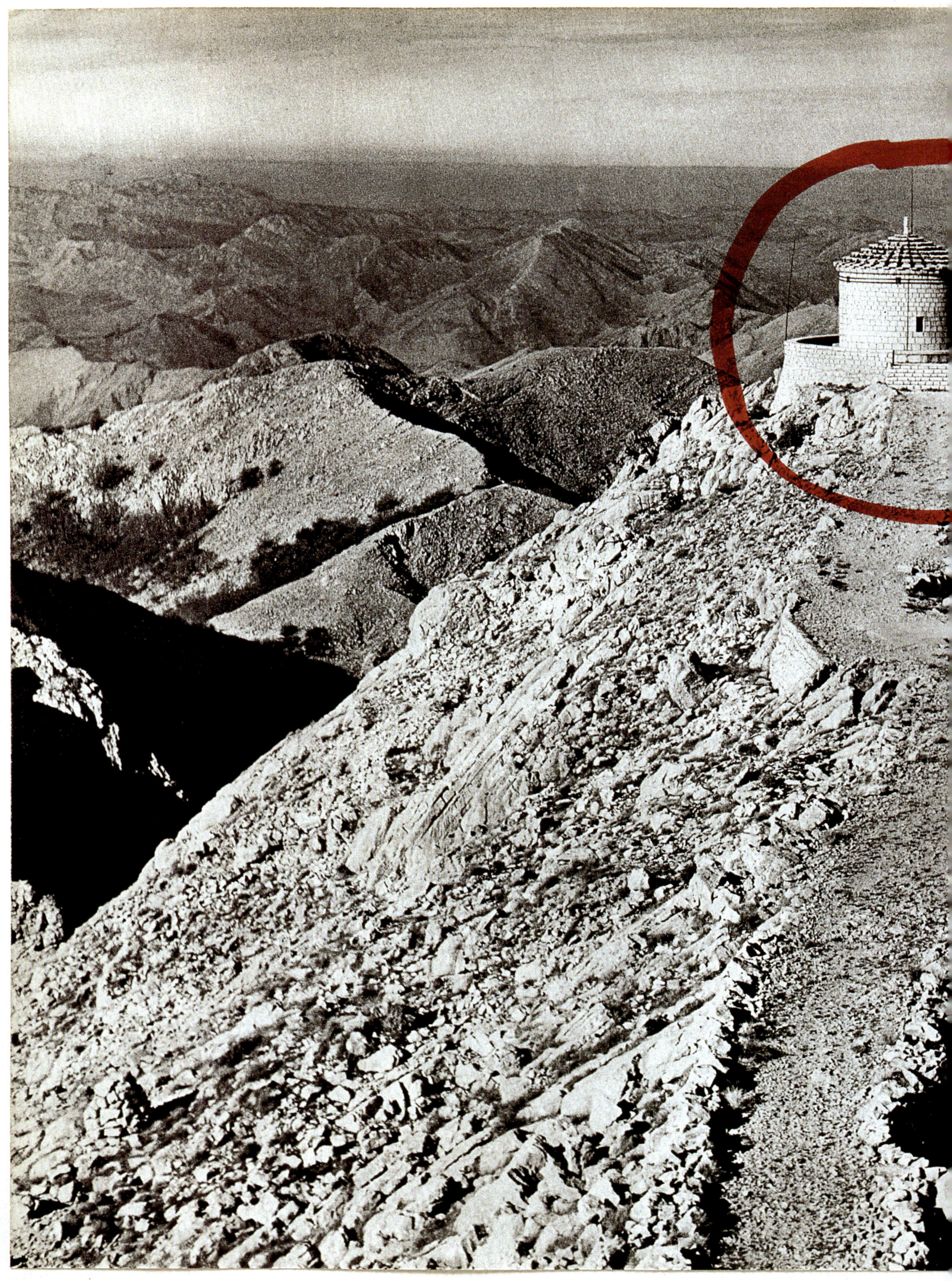

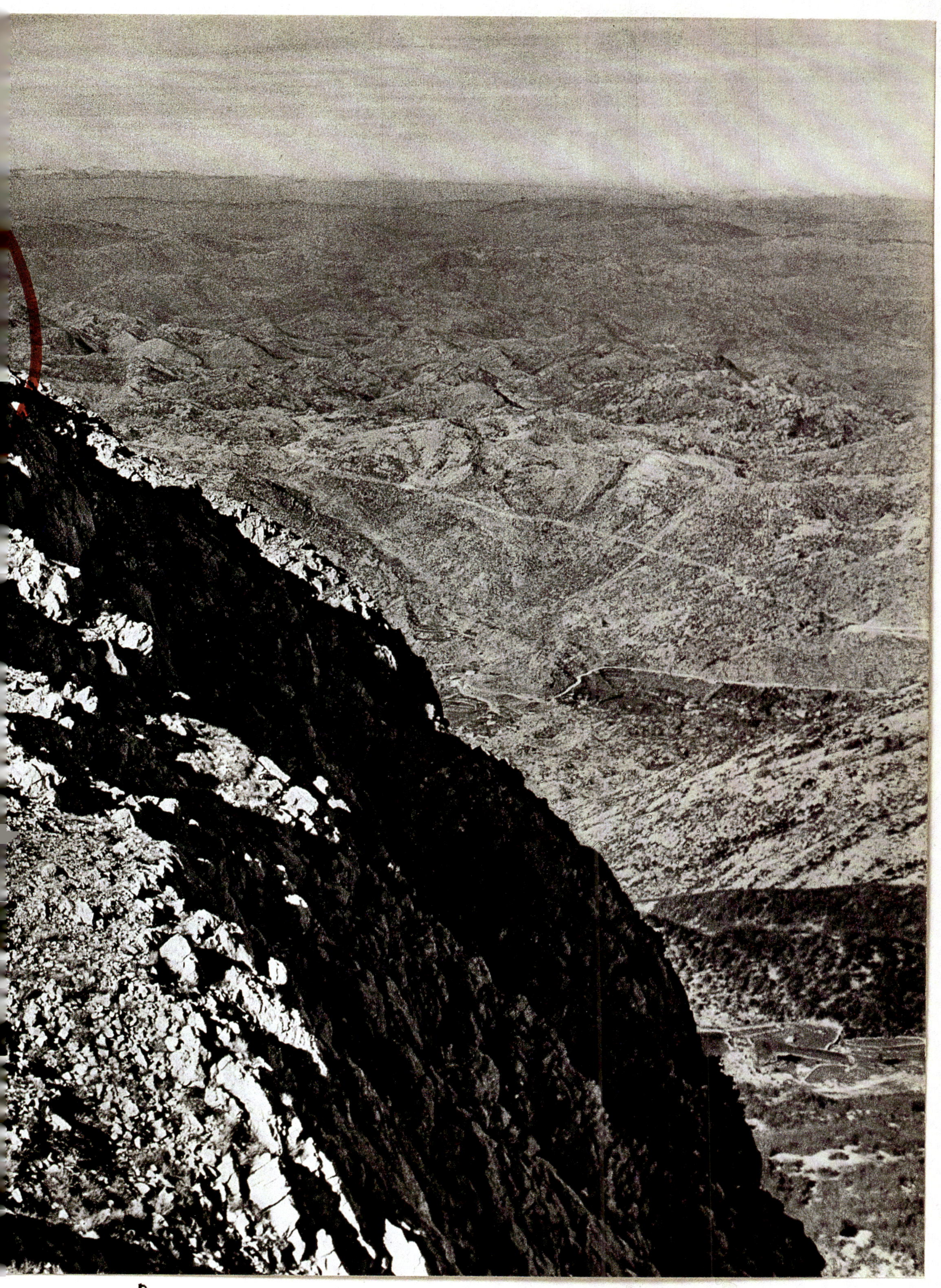

MONTENEGRO - FORMER YUGOSLAVIA

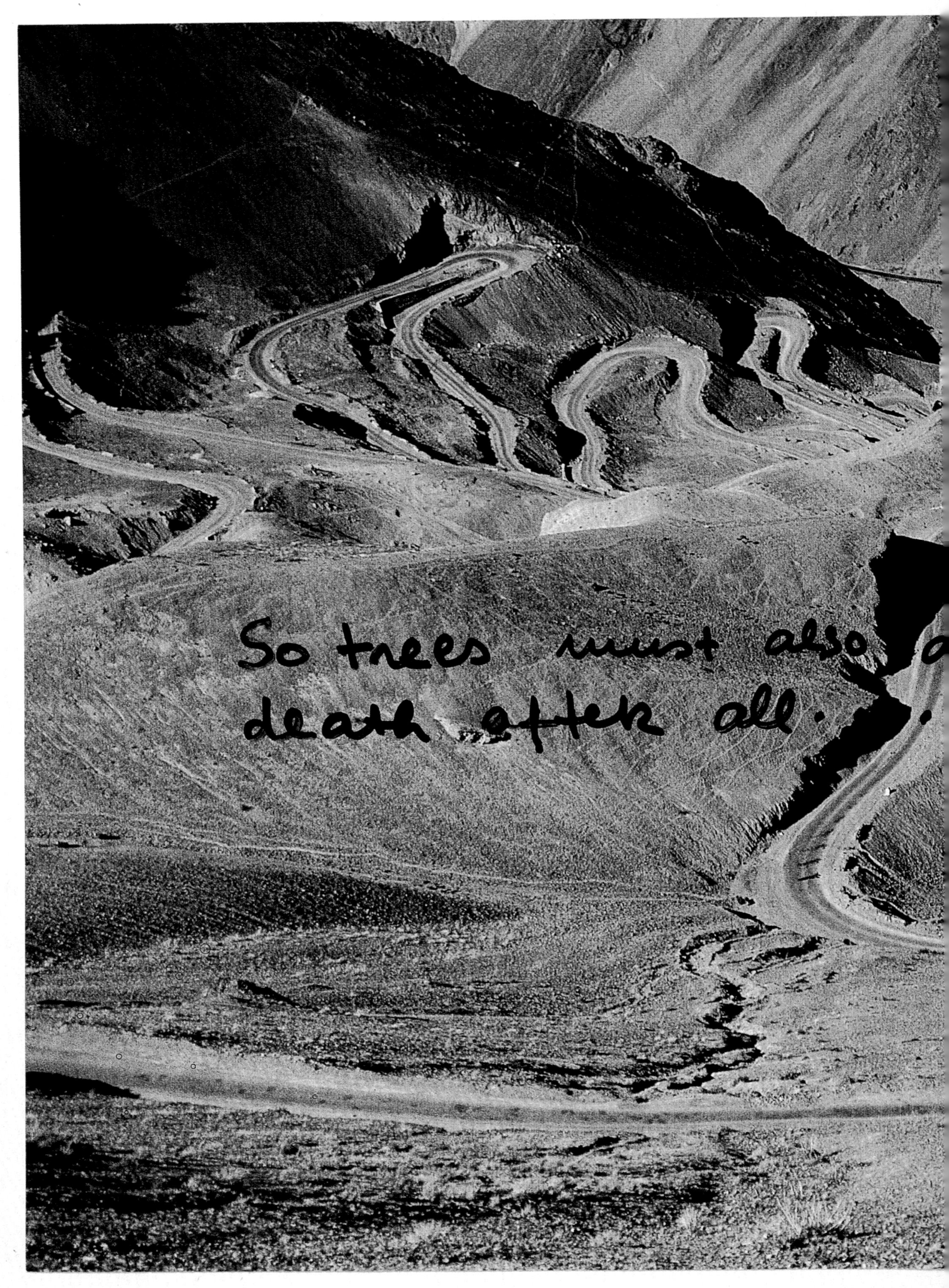

High Plateau - 6000m. Tibet

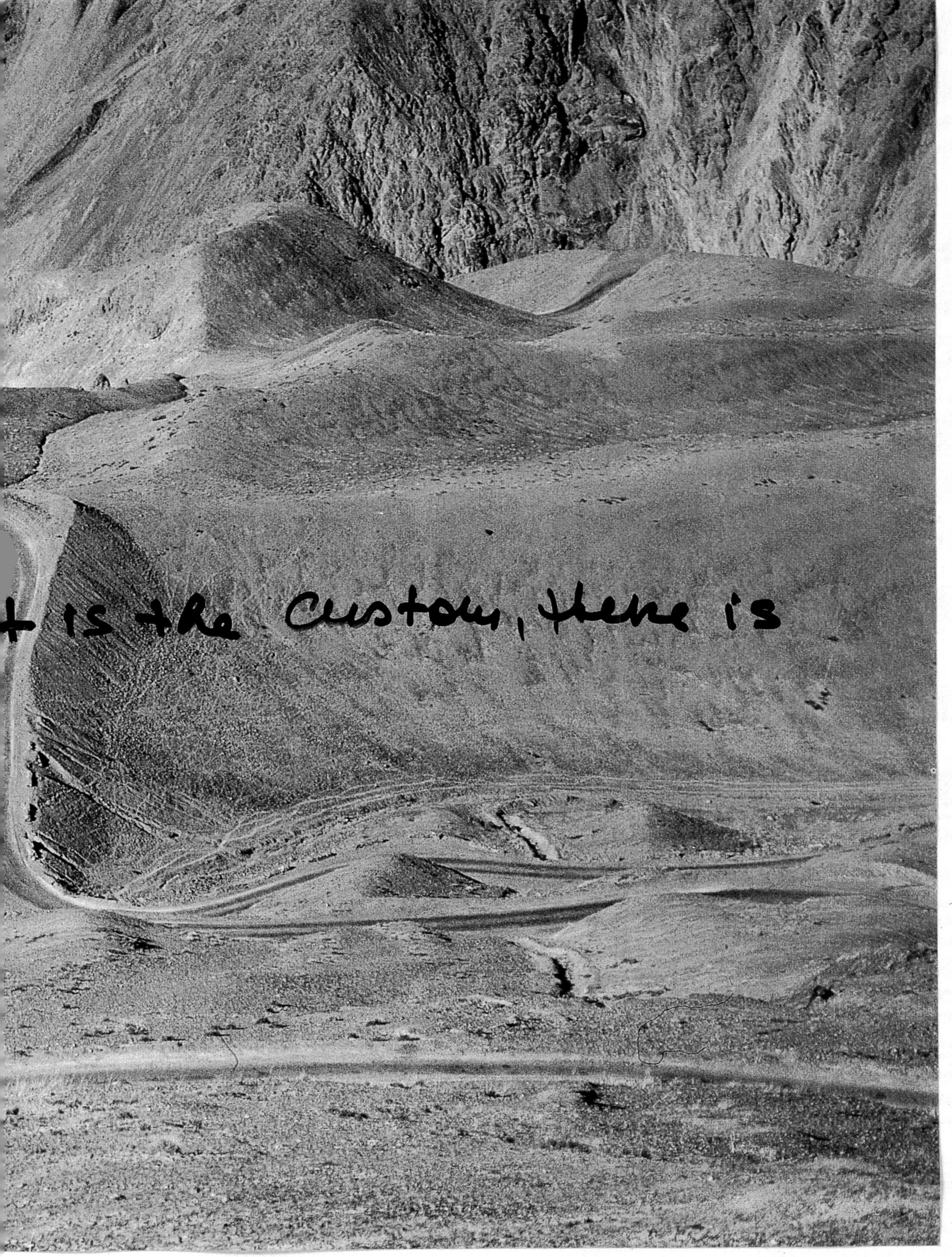
t is the custom, there is

ALEXANDER ADAMS
CHRISTOPHER BAENNINGER
THOMAS BETTS
FRANCES CLARK
KRISTIAN COOMBES
SALLY DAY
ANDREW DRUMMOND
IAIN FORSYTH & JANE POLLARD
CHLOE GRIMSHAW
LIZ HALKON
JILLIAN HASLAM
MARY HONEYSETT
ELISA HUDSON
STEPHEN McCOUBREY
KYOKO MIZUNO
JAMES NEWTON
WILL PENNY
THALIA RIED
ANNA SAUNT
IAN TAYLOR
JOHN PAUL THURLOW
OLIVER VARNEY

Private view: Thursday 29 June, 6-8pm
Exhibition open: Friday 30 June to Monday 3 July, 10am-5pm
(Sunday , 10-4pm)

GOLDSMITHS COLLEGE

Fine Art (Studio Practice) & Theory

Lewisham Way . London SE14 . For further information telephone or fax +44 (0)171 252 8609

THE IDEAL PLACE

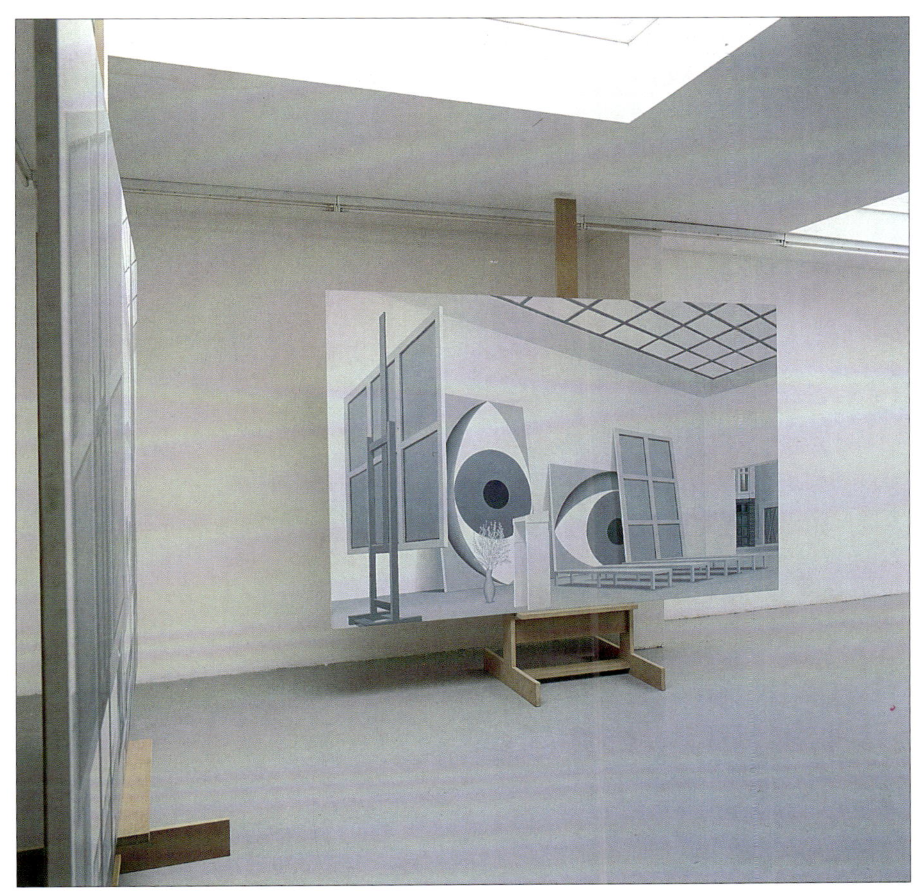

Thomas Huber, HCAK, 1993-94

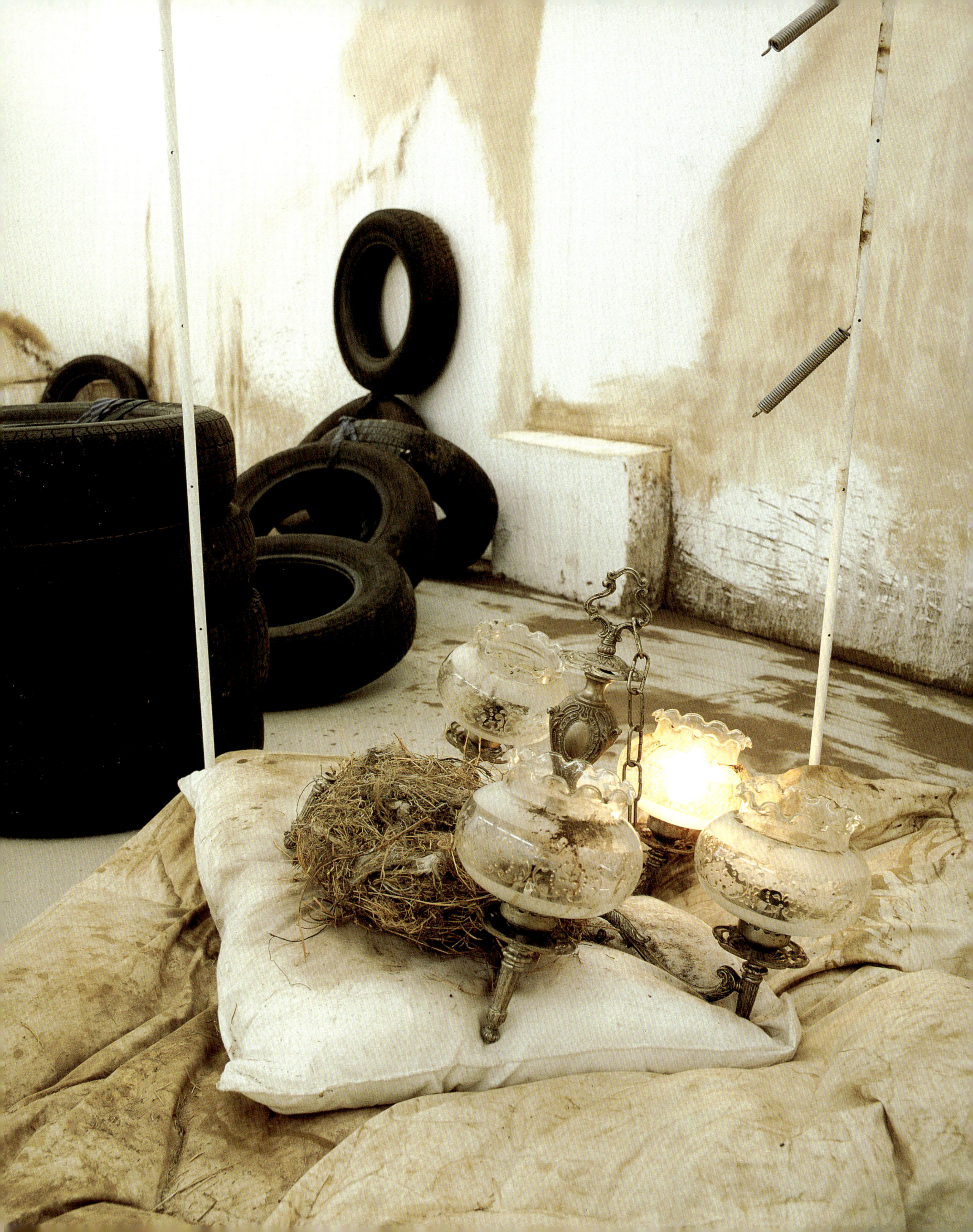

Art & Design

THE IDEAL PLACE

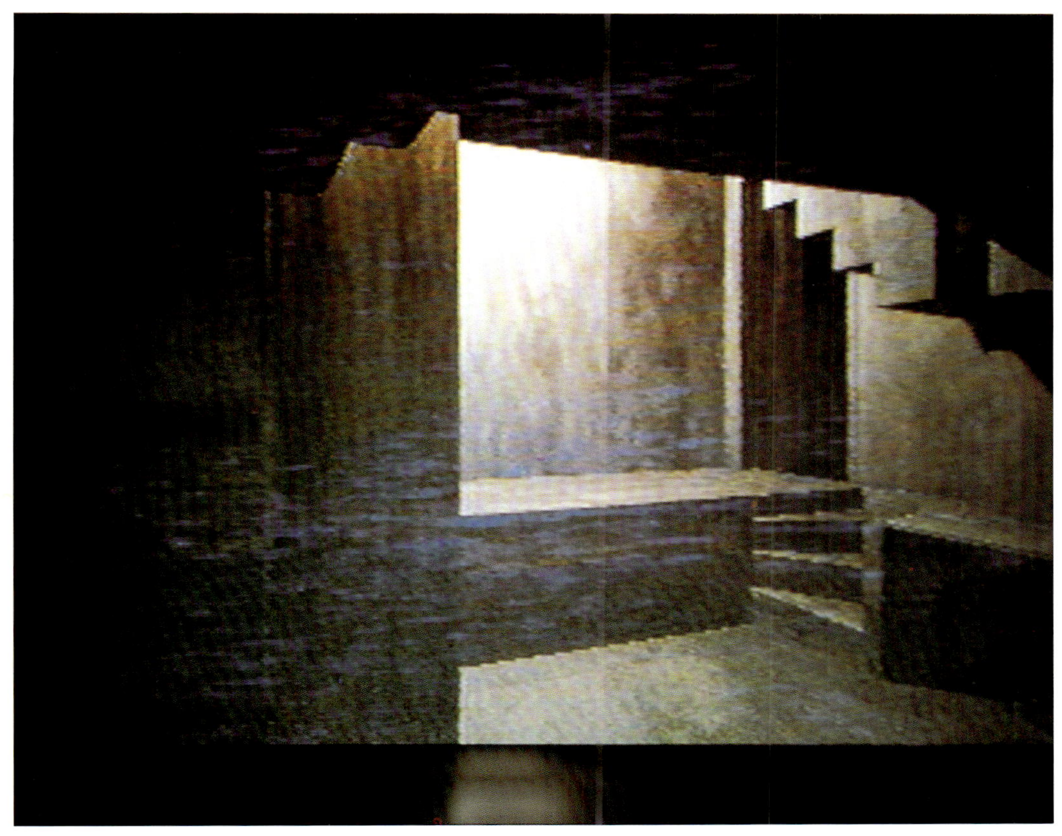

OPPOSITE: Ricardo Brey, HCAK, 1993-94; ABOVE: Jan Van de Pavert, HCAK, 1993-94

ACADEMY EDITIONS • LONDON

Acknowledgements

This issue of Art & Design, produced in collaboration with HCAK (Haags Centrum voor Aktuele Kunst), The Hague, was based on the project 'The Ideal Place' which took place in 1993-94. We would like to thank Philip Peters, Director of HCAK for being our Guest-Editor and Johan Pijnappel for initiating this collaboration. All Translations by Ulrica Vrijman. Unless otherwise stated, all images are courtesy of HCAK, The Hague; pp30-37 the artists; p30 (below) Victoria Miro Gallery, London; p35 (left) Maureen Paley/Interim Art, London; p64 (below) photo Peter Cox. HCAK Would like to thank The British Council and The Goverment of Canada, Department of External Affairs.

FRONT COVER: Urs Pfannenmüller, HCAK, 1993-94
INSIDE COVERS: Jan Van de Pavert, HCAK, 1993-94

EDITOR: Nicola Kearton SUB-EDITOR: Ramona Khambatta
ART EDITOR: Andrea Bettella CHIEF DESIGNER: Mario Bettella DESIGNER: Toby Norman

First published in Great Britain in 1995 by *Art & Design* an imprint of
ACADEMY GROUP LTD, 42 LEINSTER GARDENS, LONDON W2 3AN
Member of the VCH Publishing Group
ISBN: 1 85490 225 3 (UK)

The Publishers and Editor do not hold themselves responsible for the opinions expressed by the writers of articles or letters in this magazine
Copyright of articles and illustrations may belong to individual writers or artists
Art & Design Profile 42 is published as part of *Art & Design* Vol 10 5/6 1995
Art & Design Magazine is published six times a year and is available by subscription

Distributed to the trade in the United States of America by
ST MARTIN'S PRESS, 175 FIFTH AVENUE, NEW YORK, NY 10010

Printed and bound in Italy

Contents

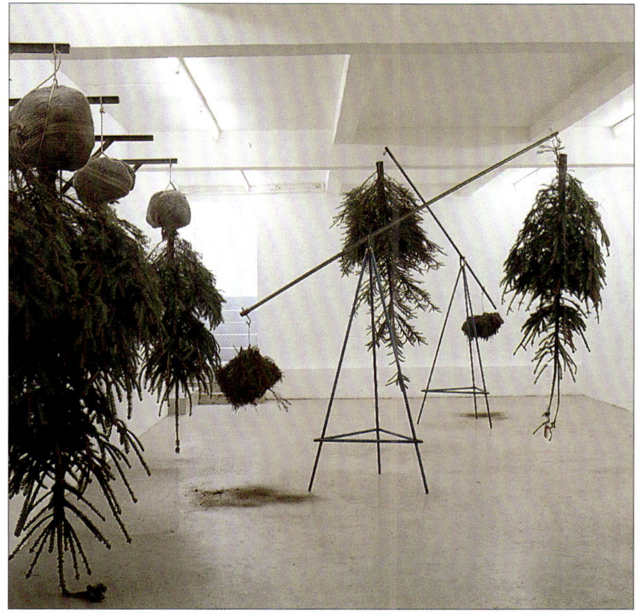

Ulf Rollof, HCAK, 1993-94

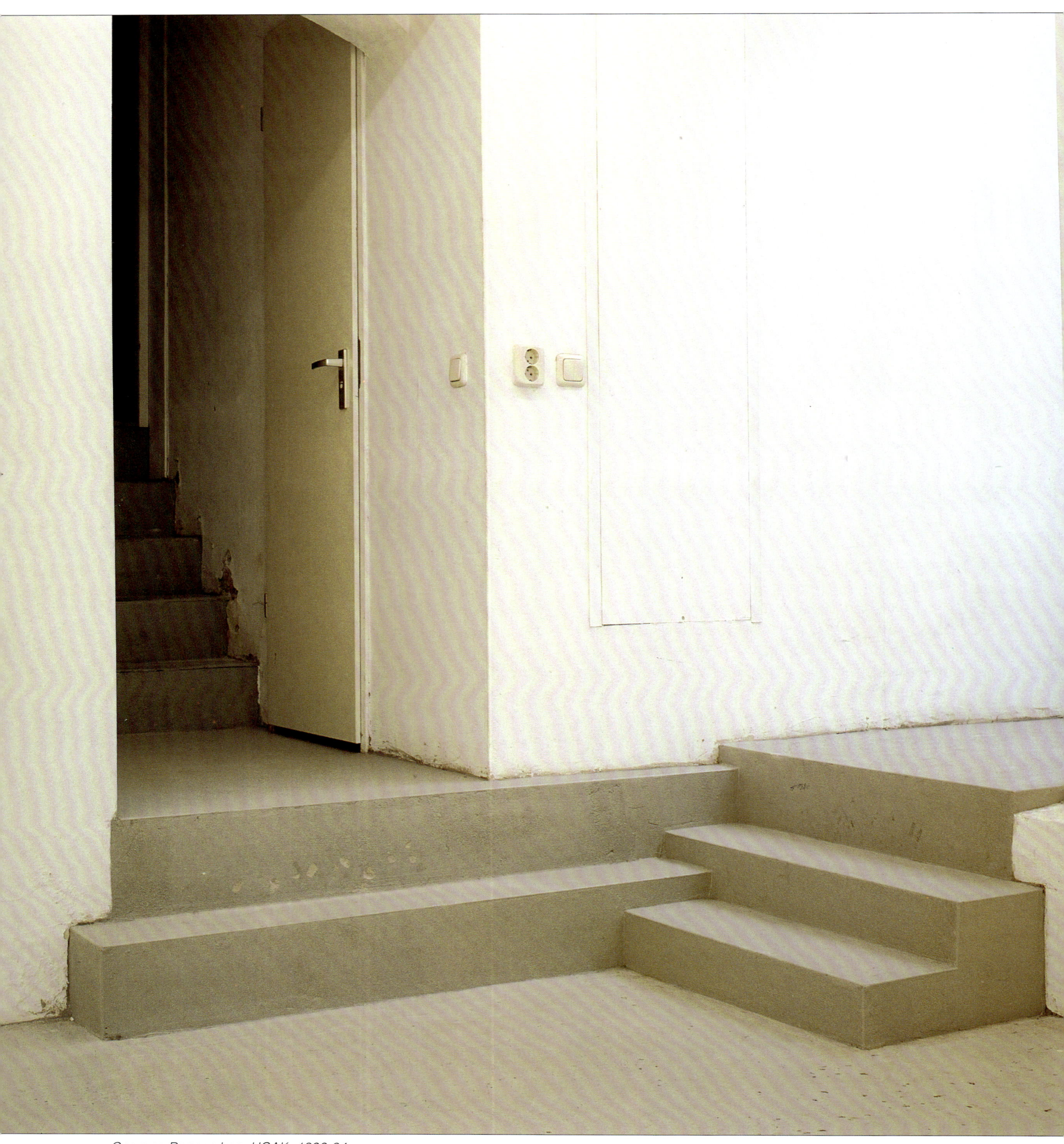

Georges Descombes, HCAK, 1993-94

INTRODUCTION
Philip Peters

This publication documents a project in the Hague Center for Contemporary Art HCAK, in The Hague, Holland, which took more than a year to realise under the title 'The Ideal Place'. Apart from full colour reproductions of the 24 artworks involved, there are texts concerning the topic by the participating artists, short analyses of the works and independent essays on the theme of 'The Ideal Place' written on invitation.

The introductory text which follows is a revised version of texts previously published by the HCAK as bulletins alongside the eight shows of the project. It covers some ideas about the ideal place as time passed and the project developed. It is the intention that the reader will hence be able to see the photographs of artworks in their finished state of exhibition objects in an art show, as well as how a long-term project can lead to various reflections on the subject at hand and on the different works involved. In this way one can, so to speak, experience the way the project developed.

Gratitude is due to the generosity of the 24 artists with whom we worked in such close harmony. Furthermore, I am indebted to the staff members of the HCAK whose tireless efforts have made it possible for the whole project to be realised, especially Carolien van der Donk, Sanny Overbeeke and Mark de Weijer, themselves artists of no mean quality. The same, *a fortiori*, to my friend Marcel Zalme, who was responsible for the idea of 'The Ideal Place'. Without him there would never have been such a project. I also wish to thank Johan Pijnappel and Nicola Kearton for generating the possibility to issue this publication, which for the moment constitutes the final stage of the project as a whole.

The Ideal Place: Another Model

Over the past ten years, the HCAK has constantly been occupied with the organisation of more or less long-term projects centred on specific themes. The first and foremost aim has always been to give art and artists an opportunity. The second objective is to encourage practice by means of themes, through content, discussion – whether public or not – and numerous publications. The third aspect is to examine presentation models.

These objectives create an impression of a programme, but this is not the case: the policy adopted has invariably, step by step, developed from practice, one project generating the next, and so on. Looking back, a logical – or at least arguable – line can be perceived. What emerges as a coordinating theme of all HCAK activities is the place – the position – of art.

In my experience, this type of art presentation is not initially realised rationally. Sometimes an idea suddenly forces itself upon you, which is so appealing that you feel compelled to further examine it. I regard such an idea as a gift. A phase of thinking and talking follows, of analysing its provisional meaning and possibili-

ties. If the idea still persists, it is presented to artists who interest us and when there are positive and interesting responses, it is carried out. At the HCAK the outcome of such a project is always uncertain – we do not know (nor wish to know) exactly what is going to happen. After the project, when the participating artists have finished their work, we have an idea of what we have started. It is only later that various pieces of the puzzle fall into place and the wider context becomes clear, mistakes are realised, and new policy options emerge. With respect to the present project, 'The Ideal Place', we never quite knew what could be expected next. The manner in which it came into being illustrates the process I described above.

One evening in early 1992, Marcel Zalme and I were buying drinks at the bar of a café for the rest of our company, and in this spiritual setting Marcel said, 'I may know of something we could do at the HCAK: the ideal place as destination', and I immediately replied, 'That's what we'll do'. I am convinced that at that moment neither of us knew what we were talking about, but were both quite sure of the fact that we had to do it. Now, after ample discussion, we have found arguments proving that our intuition did not deceive us.

Since the policy of the HCAK has concerned itself in various outflanking movements with the problem of 'the place of art'. Several models were brought up over the years and it seemed to be an obvious next step to ask questions on the 'ideal place'. Just as in the early 80s the concept of 'quality' had to be re-examined (as the HCAK did in the first long-term project, 'Describing Quality', a project which lasted a year from 1984-85), it appeared to us that now, more than ever, the time had come to raise the concept of 'place'.

Right now 'place' and 'placement' play an important part in the practice of a great many artists of various characters and of different generations and backgrounds. However, meaning changes with context, and the passage of time. This is not the place for a detailed art-historical discussion, but it does seem useful to sketch a few contours which are important for our time (it would also be possible to enter into the 'ideal' landscapes of Poussin or the neo-Platonic ideals in the work of Botticelli, but I will let this pass – such references may yet emerge in the writing of others).

The concept of 'place' in a metaphorical sense can probably best be traced back to Duchamp: the meaning of an object changes according to a change of context, which in turn reveals something about the meaning of the context. Another starting-point can be found in Carl Andre's definition of his sculpture as 'place'. As a counterpoint (and forerunner of much of present-day post-modernism) one could point to Robert Smithson's 'non-sites'.

A lot of contemporary art is in line with the concept of 'place'. Often the work literally 'is' a place, in other cases its meaning is metaphorical in all sorts of ways and it also happens that the subject of the work is at the same time its own presentation. When we add the influence of the curator to this (with as an excess the stardom attributed to some of them), a wide field exists, which has not been defined as a theme before.

Consequently, the concept of 'place' did not occur to the organiser just because something has to be thought up again: we perceive it in the art of our time, we single it out, define it as a theme, and on the basis of this, hand it to a (both exemplary and unique) number of artists with the purpose of receiving it back in a transformed state (for instance, although not necessarily so, in the form of an artwork) and exhibiting it. We consider this movement in the project elegant. It is the way we have always worked.

The utopian addition, 'ideal', has several aspects in regard to meaning. On the one hand it evokes 'utopianising', on the other hand it has a provocative touch. Utopia is no longer the most customary attitude in this day and age, of which it is sometimes said that there is no meaning to attribute anymore. The very addition 'ideal' creates the opportunity of taking up and formulating the strongest antithetic stand conceivable. But the time may have come to stimulate Utopia once again in a different way, a way we are not familiar with at the moment. With such a formulation of the theme you can thus kill two birds with one stone.

Is there an 'ideal place'? Could or should such a place exist? We do not know the answer, but we have made it our objective to exchange ideas on this question with a number of artists, with the aim of realising a number of works of art, in most cases (but not necessarily always or by definition) 'in situ'. One can imagine that there could be 'proposals' which cannot be executed in the HCAK or which are not at all workable; such contributions may be realised elsewhere and/or be represented in the HCAK in another manner, by means of documentation, sketches and so on.

We are of the opinion that a presentation of the question such as this one cannot or need not result in solutions. In art, questions do not lead to solutions – that is not the reason why they are asked. A field of meaning is opened up, on which further questions may be asked and where one question evokes another. What we expect of this project beforehand (naturally without being acquainted with any kind of concrete 'result') is a new series of interesting presentations of questions, which may lead to further questions (and possibly to further policy in the HCAK and beyond it). It is the formulation of the question (which question is asked and how?) that will determine the sense and meaning of the project. The idea of a series can be taken literally here: the project took place over a period of more than a year and therefore unfolded gradually, like a flowering rose.

The structure of the project was as follows: 24 artists of different ages and geographical backgrounds were invited to produce work. The HCAK has three exhibition rooms: per period (two in 1993 and six in 1994) one work was exhibited in each room, hence 24 works with each exhibition period lasting one month. The artists were selected on the basis of their affinity with the theme – in many cases the theme was already explicitly or implicitly inherent in their work.

The HCAK is not a museum and does not have more than three exhibition rooms available. For that reason it was physically impossible to present all the works simultaneously in order to represent a group exhibition. That suited us, for we did not want to turn this project into such an event. We wanted to organise a serious, intense project which would contribute over a longer period of time to the discourse on one of the central themes of art in our time.

What we tried to avoid (although this is not a simple task), was the umpteenth contribution to the performances of the international travelling circus of artists – numerous artists are invited to all sorts of places time and again, to do 'their thing', often resulting in similar works strewn all over the world in all kinds of variations, recognisable as just numerous 'trademarks'. In principle, this only serves to confirm a status quo (frequently with commercial overtones).

The HCAK asked all the participating artists to rethink their entire praxis all over again, as it were, within the framework and perhaps as a part of 'The Ideal Place' and, as far as possible, to make a new start on the basis of the given theme. We also invariably stressed the point that it was not necessarily our aim to generate ready-made works of art. The emphasis was primarily on the formation of the idea, but different types of contributions were also conceivable: suggestions, sketches, text and so on.

No attempt was made to group the contributions in terms of content. The diaries of the participating artists were the only norm in programming this project. Moreover, in the present architecture of the HCAK (which we change according to what seems appropriate at the time of a certain project) the works in one exhibition room are not visible from the other two; each work has to make its own statement, the HCAK does not organise any dialectics.

Preliminary to each exhibition, a bulletin appeared in the form of a kind of newsletter, with texts by the HCAK (such as this statement of intent) and the participating artists (written on the basis of talks with us, but before their visual contribution had been formulated). During the exhibition openings, discussions were organised and structured between participants and the public under varying chairmanship.

I would like to express our gratitude to the participating artists for their loyal efforts to contribute to a project which, though evidently interesting to them content-wise, was definitely not so from a financial point of view. It is comforting that artists are prepared to accept the challenge of tackling complex subject matter for little or no financial compensation.

'The Ideal Place' or 'The Ideal Place as Destination?'
Often a programming, and particularly thematic programming, is initially made intuitively, as I have already suggested. In this particular case, at a certain moment something peculiar also happened to the name of the project. For a long time it was called 'De Ideale Plaats Van Bestemming'. The English translation of this, 'The Ideal Place As Destination', caused problems. In American English, such a construction may be passable, but in English it is hard to defend from an idiomatic point of view. Moreover, the word 'destination' gave rise to rather too comical and persistent associations with trains and stations ('Destination: The Ideal Place', if we were to switch the words of the original title). Other solutions were even less satisfactory.

As a result, we started to wonder what would happen if we dropped 'destination'. In English it seemed to be purer, in Dutch we felt we were missing something. Eventually, we decided to call the project 'The Ideal Place' after all, but were uncertain of this as a title.

Our conduct may have been somewhat confused and arbitrary, too much based on vague norms such as 'sound', 'word picture' and 'linguistic feeling'. Had anything essential changed now or not? We had no clear notion of this. It could be argued that the abbreviated title implied a widening of the theme, as in this context the concept of 'destination' is a further specification of the concept of 'place'.

One could say that a place, even when it is ideal, may be a 'destination', but undoubtedly also all kinds of other things/concepts. 'Destination' implies a direction, an arrival even – the destination is the place where everything is 'in its place', the destination is the place the direction is meant for, the place the road leads to. Of course one may sometimes arrive at the 'wrong destination', but in that case a mistake has been made which was not an integral part of the concept: a destination is a goal, for which something is destined. In the (consequently paradoxical) event of a 'wrong destination', it is not the destination that is to be 'blamed', but the direction. To put it more clearly, if there is to be a destination in the true sense of the word, the direction will have to be correct, the direction will have to be the only correct direction – the ideal direction. Consequently, the destination gives purpose to the ideal direction and is the consequence of the ideal direction, that is, the ideal place, whether attainable or not.

Evidently, this meant that a tautology had crept into the original title of our project, making the word 'destination' a rather redundant word, which could possibly be aborted.[1] Besides, the concept of 'destination', and hence the ideal place in this formulation, seems to be a static piece of information – there can only be one single destination, particularly if we deal with an 'ideal destination'. This is precisely the chief characteristic of destination as we have seen. Another related difference in nuance connected with the above, as has been briefly indicated, is the suggestion of a goal evidently worthy of pursuit, implied in the very use of the concept of 'destination', which is made even more emphatic by the combination of 'ideal' and 'destination'. It is almost as if a decree has been formulated: this is the way it must be, in that direction, and nowhere else. Artists of all countries, unite, on the way to the Ideal Destination! And obviously, this is about the last thing we wish to achieve.

Naturally, the concept of 'place' in itself, alone, is easy to interpret as static: place 'is' (and is 'somewhere'). And does not the combination of 'ideal' and 'place' suggest a similar goal worthy of pursuit, as does 'ideal' combined with 'destination'?

Before developing this point, we first need to consider the tautology in the original title and the subsequent removal of it. After all, the tautology is a respected stylistic figure that may be 'in its place' under particular circumstances – not just for the sake of specific types of definitions, but also on account of its rhetorical power. Insofar as a tautology can be regarded as an 'augmentation', or as extra stress due to its cumulative effect, its removal obviously is an improvement when such a stress does not serve a useful purpose. This indeed appears to be the case here: in the objective of the project there is no reason to add any stress, which might easily be taken for an attempt to give it direction, thus closing off all kinds of possibilities in advance. On the contrary, the aim was to create a structure as open as possible, the actual meaning of which was only to manifest itself after this framework had been filled in by the works produced for the purpose. We did not wish to make any pronouncements in advance. Consequently, the tautology as a stylistic figure seems to be less desirable in this context. 'Double' is too much, 'single' will do. The word 'destination' had to be removed.

Hence, 'The Ideal Place'. Is the concept of 'place' really a static concept? Of course. A place is where something *is*. But it is not as specific as 'destination' – that is, the identity of the place is less clearly defined, and not necessarily as 'destination'. And what if this place has been further defined in another way, as 'ideal'? Even then it seems to me, that 'destination' is more specified than 'place' in itself, even if this place is 'ideal'. For a destination is the form of place that is at the same time a goal, a finishing point. Therefore the 'ideal destination' in itself can again be regarded as a tautology. But 'the ideal place' cannot. A place may be anything and anywhere, and this also applies to an ideal place. Thus we have arrived at the core aim of this project: our ignorance on the subject. We do not know what or where 'the ideal place' is, nor if something like it exists, or even whether this should be necessary or desirable. Consequently, we cannot link it up with any rules regarding destination or whatever else. This means that eventually the concept of 'place' in the project can hardly be defined as purely static. We do not even know if it exists and therefore we are not able to define it in any way. As long as the 'ideal place' is unknown, no characteristics, such as static or the opposite or whatever else, can be attributed to it.

But surely the addition of 'ideal', by definition, makes this place – no matter what or where it is – a goal worthy of pursuit? Is not 'ideal' an addition giving direction to 'place'? After all, 'ideal' expresses something about the place we are going to deal with. And is such a thing possible at all, in view of the above? We might just be flirting with this concept of 'ideal place' and with our own ignorance. On the one hand, we claim not to know what it is or could be, but on the other, we do give it the predicate of 'ideal', at the same time as coming to the conclusion that something – the existence and quality of which are uncertain, or at any rate unknown – is not to be defined in any way whatsoever. Asked another way, is this not a contradiction in terms? Are not we caught in our own trap?

I think that this is essentially a linguistic problem. 'Ideal' and 'place' are two words. If there had been one word to indicate 'ideal place' (and possibly there are languages in which this is so) there would not be a problem. The word 'ideal' would not have been regarded as a predicate of 'place', just as 'place' is not a predicate of 'place'. Something cannot be a predicate of itself, as it *is* itself and a predicate may or may not be attributed to it. The world would otherwise solely consist of crazy tautologies, where each meaning would only consist of repetition, a closed circuit in which communication is impossible, least of all through language. In fact, in certain circles it is argued that this is true, but on the strength of different kinds of considerations which are not to the point here.

So it is evidently a linguistic misunderstanding, or at least a matter of interpretation, to make a distinction between 'ideal' and 'place'. At any rate, we have decided to depart from the notion that an 'ideal place' is a non-compound concept. It is concerning this concept that we admit our ignorance – we do have a few ideas on what 'place' is, or could be, and we are also able to manage 'ideal' somehow, although this is a lot more complicated. But we do not have a clue about 'the ideal place'. Of course there are a lot of things we could say about it and go round and round the subject in circles, but we have not arrived at a watertight definition, certainly not if this definition is to be relevant in, and to, visual art. That is not the purpose we have been hired for by ourselves. If we knew everything, we would not organise art projects (and besides, the world would look different, though by definition we do not know how). Consequently, the reason for the project continues to be ignorance and curiosity with respect to 'the ideal place'. For that reason we invited 24 artists to share our ignorance, and possibly to learn something from them, even if only from other forms of ignorance.

Obviously, the ideal is something worthy of pursuit in the sense that it presents itself as something to be preferred to the status quo. On the other hand, the fact that it is unattainable is a (if not *the* outstanding) characteristic of the ideal – if it were attainable, it would no longer be the ideal; once attained, it would itself have turned into the status quo. In this respect, the ideal is to be compared to the horizon, forever moving up and thus preventing attainability. The ideal is a Utopia, something to be referred to and to be argued over in all sorts of ways, without ever becoming 'tangible reality'. The ideal is 'the other'.

In other words, if we were in an 'ideal place', we would not even be able to conceive of the formulation 'ideal place'. Intrinsically, the concept of 'ideal place' implies that we are not there or at least that we do not realise that we are. Consequently, from this point of view 'the ideal place' does not exist as actual fact and can therefore hardly be a goal worthy of pursuit.

This does not alter the fact that 'the ideal place' as mental or spiritual construct could indeed have the right to exist, but it is doubtful, to say the least, whether this would be a goal worthy of pursuit, if only because it is simply impossible – two fields of meaning (concrete factuality and mental concept) are confused here and melted into a paradoxical relationship. A goal worthy of pursuit (at least a goal that stands a chance of being attained) implies a factuality, a situation, something which can actually be attained – a 'destination'. The concept of 'ideal place' is no such goal, as we have just concluded.

[Unexpectedly, another aspect of the relation between 'ideal place' and 'destination' is raised here. These are possibly not synonymous concepts after all, and their 'interdependence' is, most paradoxically, not mutual. 'Destination' does indeed imply that this destination is 'the ideal place', but 'ideal place' in itself need not be a destination and, strictly speaking, even this is out of the question, since 'destination' does or can exist as a fact and 'ideal place' evidently does not or cannot. Therefore, it is best to express it thus: 'destination' and 'ideal place' may apparently coincide under particular circumstances or be similar in a particular sense, but obviously it is not a case of A = B and therefore automatically B = A. A 'destination' can be reached, and what is more, that is the very meaning of the concept, but 'the ideal place' is by definition unattainable. Possibly, destination and ideal place are two sides of the same coin. In that case they are polar (or at any rate complementary) concepts belonging together, but at the same time, 'in practice' largely (at least unilaterally) excluding one another. According to this line of reasoning, the original tautology turns into a paradox and one might almost consider restoring the first title. The final word has not been said on this issue yet and the name of the project may have to be changed a few more times if there should be reason to do so in the course of time and on the basis of the contributions made. Since we do not know what we are dealing with, the project may give rise to constant change: that is the point of it.]

Returning to the subject of 'the ideal place': insofar as 'the ideal place' is to be regarded as a goal worthy of pursuit, this pursuit is doomed to fail, at least as far as its 'factuality' is concerned. Likewise, the 'ideal landscape' of Poussin only exists as a painting, as a spiritual concept, as a visualisation or, at worst, an attempt at visualisation but not as a 'real' landscape. In this respect Poussin's landscape bears every resemblance to the metaphysical monochrome. God cannot be identified by His name. What we can say about God is especially what He is not. All that can be said about Tao is that we do not know what it is. We call it Tao because it has to have a name so as to be able to discuss it, but this name in itself again belongs to the 'ten thousand things' and hence not to Tao, except in the sense that the ten thousand things are also manifestations of Tao, but without being identical to it. And so on and so forth.

The pursuit of the ideal is therefore like a finger pointing at the moon. In a sense the ideal is becoming more and more distant due to the very pursuit of it. On the other hand, one might also say that 'the goal is to be found in the path'. In that case the pursuit itself has become 'the ideal place'. But if it is true that 'the ideal place' does not exist 'in reality', this means that we have to make do with an exclusively symbolic or even ritual pursuit. Maybe that is what art, in the final analysis (and in its initial origin) is: a ritual.

The Function of the Literal Place

It is clear that when we speak of 'the ideal place', we do not necessarily mean a physical place. This may be possible but it is certainly no more than one of numerous possibilities. At least, this applies to the thematisation of the literal place, for on the other hand it is also impossible to leave the literal aspect of the concept of 'place' completely outside consideration. Implicitly, this issue always comes up: of all artistic disciplines visual art is the only one having a presentation problem. Literature is to be found in books, and the design of these books – apart from a few rare exceptions – is irrelevant for reading the contents, assuming that these remain legible. As far as the performing arts are concerned, the problems can largely be controlled: if certain conditions (such as the size of the stage, acoustics, lighting and the like) have been met, any text, score or choreography can be performed. Visual art, however, depends on the nature of the presentation for an adequate communication of its meaning. This implies that contents and the meaning of a work depend on the manifestation of that work, which does not only mean that the work must have a visible form (or indication of form, any sign of existence), but also that the context, the place where the work is (and possibly the company of other works within this same context) is part of this manifestation. Then presentation (showing the work in any context whatsoever) automatically turns into interpretation and, according to some, manipulation. There is no such thing as clean hands here.

This is a problem for the organiser. At the same time it is also his field of activity: the organiser arranges, whether it is his intention or not. This is often carried out consciously and passionately – after all, the organiser contributes his share to the meaning, to the history of ideas. Thus, he is not just an instrument present in a role subordinate to art, in a sense the roles are reversed as the organiser determines which meanings are given to which works, regardless of (and sometimes in conflict with) those attributed by the artist.

The HCAK has always tried to play as neutral a role as possible within this paradoxical framework, letting the work make its own statement. We even went so far in this particular project as to present one single painting per exhibition room, and consequently eliminating direct, concrete context as much as possible. But it is hard to maintain that we as organisers are not present at all in our projects and other exhibitions, particularly when, as in this case, we put forward a thematic suggestion.

When we announce that we are going to present 24 works on the theme of 'The Ideal Place', it is evidently to be assumed that each work has something to say on this subject. This is indeed so, for we invited the participating artists to make works under a common denominator. But suppose that at some point in this series we should present a more or less random work which was not made according to this denominator; in such a case the visitor is likely to take it for granted that it was. After all, that is what we have persuaded him to believe. The work in question, regardless of its original meaning, will then comply with the context and *nolens volens* make a statement on 'the ideal place'. At most, one could conclude that this statement is inadequate or difficult to analyse for its merits in this context, but it is hard to doubt that it refers, or wishes to refer to, the theme.

This appears to be an academic problem as we must not forget the artist, and undoubtedly he will see to it that his work is not abused for an aim it has nothing to do with. In this case this was easy to achieve, for our project did not concern work from existing collections to be used by the organiser more or less as he pleases. (Whether this can actually be done in practice is, in my opinion, a matter of perception and consultation, and besides, of copyright.) All the work presented in the HCAK is and continues to be the property of the artists, both in a literal and spiritual sense.

To put it differently: in a case like this the artist is an 'accomplice', he is co-responsible for the thematic context in which his work is shown and has consented to it. If he should send in a still life or a descent from the cross, this will be a statement on what he considers as the 'the ideal place'. The work may have been made with the intention of saying something about 'the ideal place' by making use of the theme 'still life' or 'descent from the cross'. On the other hand, it is also conceivable that the work existed prior to this, and had another meaning in its original autonomy.

What gave rise to thinking this over again, is the fact that in the series of 24 presentations there are some which have not been made specifically for this occasion, for example the contributions of Art & Language and Pieter Laurens Mol. In these two cases, somewhat inconsistent with our own starting points, we agreed to present existing work. In the case of Art & Language it was made clear that a work existed which comprised this very theme (as, in a sense, all the work of Art & Language occupies itself with the positioning of art). Pieter Laurens Mol also assured us that he had a work available which had not been shown before, complying with the conditions of the theme.

Now we were confronted with a peculiar dilemma. On the one hand, one might say that each work is the artist's view making a statement on 'the ideal place', and for that reason is suitable for presentation in a project with this theme. On the other hand, we had made up our minds not to include existing work in the project. We wanted the project not just to yield products (results), but also to be an expression of a process that we, the organisers, wished to instigate by using the concept of an 'ideal place' as a theme. The optimum effect would be achieved if the artists involved were to reconsider their entire practice and start from zero in their contributions, insofar as such a thing is actually to be realised.

Hence we have returned to the organiser's role. What is it we want? Do we want to highlight a theme which in our view is important, or do we want to play a part in generating practice? In all honesty we ought to reply that we would actually prefer to do both. Eventually, we opted for a compromise, especially from the point of view that any dogma leads to the devil and hence, we should be sufficiently flexible to acknowledge and accept any 'chance hits' we might run into at face value. In the case of Art & Language it could be maintained, in view of the nature of their practice, that almost every work was suitable for our project. I am quite sure that Mol's work was not originally made with the thought of any kind of 'ideal place' in mind. Due to the specific context in which it is now presented, this work – which can indeed be interpreted within the framework set – undergoes a certain change or shift in meaning.

Thus the literal place invariably plays a part in this project in two respects. In the first place, in a physical sense, because it is the place where the work is shown (although we have always left the possibility open to solve this in another way, the artists have not deviated from the principle of a work of art to be presented in the HCAK building) and in the second place because of the meaning the space has been charged with for the duration of this project – the meaning of 'the ideal place'. In art presentation neutrality has always been a fiction (for instance, there is no one who still believes that the classical white exhibition rooms and grey floor found in the HCAK are in any way 'neutral') but in this case it is evident that the metaphorical tension the rooms have been charged with, due to the present theme, gives everything in those rooms a meaning which for the greater part has already been coded in advance.

This does not detract from the sense and meaning of the project and besides, within the framework set, it is art and artists who have the final word; however, what it does make clear once again is that presenting art is almost by definition a paradoxical affair and that the relation between place and artwork is an indissoluble double bind. The organising hand, the presentation, the context, is like a kind of gravity which, as far as I know, is difficult to escape from.

The Ideal Place and the Public

In a number of ways the theme of 'place' plays an important part in contemporary visual art. The specific formulation of the theme of this project was controversial and provocative. The participating artists guaranteed international quality and a variety of lines of approach. Without lapsing into exaggeration we may therefore state that the HCAK was the ideal place to find out more about the ideal place.

Who was supposed to find out more about it? What was the 'target group' of the organiser? Why did we do all this in the first place?

If we are honest, our first aim as organisers was to satisfy our own curiosity. In other words, we ourselves were the first target group. I do not see how this could be any different. Just as a work of art, programming has to arise from an obsession of the organisers, as otherwise there would be nothing at stake, resulting in exhibitions which are a dime a dozen and therefore unnecessary. Although initially programming is a rather personal affair, it should not degenerate into solipsistic navel-gazing either, with, as a result, a totally hermetic construction. Programming also involves communicating and mediating, so the organiser should have something to say, or rather, has to find ways to have art say what it has to say. The programme should have more general relevance than a chance individual hobby. The programming needs form and preferably a somewhat clear form. However, the programme must not wish to prove a proposition nor should works of art be dragged in as illustrative material. This cannot be stressed often enough.

The second target group consists of the artists invited, and of the people directly around us – in short the people we work with and with whom there is a continuous exchange of thoughts. Without doubt, these people have a certain influence on the policy of the HCAK, although usually this influence can not be specifically traced on a long term basis.

A third concentric circle is formed by colleagues from 'outside', those who in any capacity whatsoever occupy themselves professionally with contemporary visual art and who sometimes express their opinions during encounters in or out of the HCAK, or in writing.

Finally, the fourth circle, the visitors – those who are evidently interested in art and in the special problems formulated by the HCAK. This is the group who in a restricted sense is usually referred to as 'the public', which one must quantify in order to be eligible for subsidy, nowadays quite often determined by the viewing rates as well. For a small institution, the HCAK has seen a reasonable number of visitors who have displayed great loyalty and shown continuous interest in its activities over the years.

In addition, a fifth circle is yet to be distinguished: this group covers those who rarely, if ever, visit the HCAK exhibitions, but who have expressed a desire to keep receiving the publications. This group can hence be classified as the readers – those who are interested in the theoretical treatment of the problems stated, without wishing to, or being able to, see the art works within the framework of the practice offered by the HCAK. Undoubtedly, the HCAK publications operate within a network of publications in the experience of this group, and in most cases probably in combination with visits to exhibitions elsewhere (closer to home, for instance, for not all of us are professionals who can travel the world at the expense of others).

In a sense, a sixth group is to be distinguished as well: those who are led by rumours (as a norm) of what is happening, a group that holds all sorts of opinions without participating (or wishing to participate) in live practice or theory, or without ever betraying an original – let alone hazardous – point of view; a group that seldom makes an effort to investigate something at its source; a group 'watching with its ears'. They are the hangers-on, the parrots, the parasites. They have no genuine interest in, or love for, art, and have no need for intellectual debate. Their priority is the weighing of interests in which their own interest comes first and foremost. Unfortunately one can also come across them in museums, commissions and government institutions. They always visit places where they need to be seen, never to places where this has less or no effect. They are therefore rarely seen in the HCAK. For this type, the HCAK is not the ideal place.

Consequently, we have always been aware of the fact that the HCAK, with its three small exhibition rooms in a city like The Hague – apart from the Gemeentemuseum with the best collection of Mondrians in the entire world – is so ill-equipped in the field of art that it can hardly make claims to large quantities of art tourism. It is obvious that this has its advantages as well as its disadvantages. If we should have a museum or Kunsthalle with 24 exhibition rooms at our disposal, a project like 'The Ideal Place' would no doubt have attracted a much larger, international public; the media would have paid much more attention to it and so on. On the other hand, the project would then have been an exhibition among many others, a media event of the type that does attract a large public, but unfortunately often for the wrong reasons. Of course it may be argued that such a patronising attitude with respect to the motivation of the public does not befit the organiser – he ought to see to the supply and for the rest, keep his mouth shut. This is an obvious, but also rather easy point of view that is not indisputable.

The stadium attracts more people than the theatre does and no wonder, for supply and objectives have little in common. The Tate Gallery attracts the public more than the HCAK does – this is also obvious, as it is larger and for that reason there is more to be seen; it has an international collection of historical interest; its situation is more central; and it has a certain reputation. Consequently, there are obvious reasons why a large museum is visited more frequently than a smaller, more distant institution. However, many people visit the museum as an attraction among other attractions, and run through all the exhibitions rooms at a high speed, so as to be able to go to the market or whatever else afterwards. A visit to a museum easily turns into a neutral kind of pastime, the museum into an atmosphere among many atmospheres, the meaning of which remains totally submerged. There is no objection to any of this – each of us has the right to do as we please (and larger numbers of visitors yield higher receipts) but this is not the kind of attention art deserves and is meant for.

Everyone is welcome, but this is not the kind of public the HCAK is really interested in. When you have a small type of institution like the HCAK, where only a few works can be presented simultaneously (in our case three, during the course of 'The Ideal Place') a kind of condensation of attention is bound to take place in a more or less responsible programming – a kind of concentration which is less easily achieved elsewhere. This is something anyone can observe for himself: when I visit a large exhibition I want to see all of it. I may go back once more, but even upon a first visit I do not intend to miss anything. If I pay too little attention to each separate work, I will not do justice to the art. I have already written about this subject in greater detail, on the occasion of our earlier project, 'The Single Painting', in publications of the HCAK and the Dutch magazine *Kunst & Museumjournaal* (of which I am the current editor-in-chief) and I shall not repeat it all here, but I have maintained my conviction that more attention is now being paid to the single work of art as fewer works (and therefore fewer causes for distraction, fewer incentives) are present. Travelling to a distant location and the effort it takes to see a work, easily becomes more or less directly proportional to the intensity of the resulting interaction. In a sense, one is better off in the little chapel at Monterchi with nothing but Piero della Francesca's Madonna del Parto for miles around, than in the Uffizi. It does go without saying, however, that this little chapel attracts only a fraction of the number of visitors of the Uffizi, as an effort has to be made and viewing rates do not like effort.

Even without referring to the old derogative idiom of the 'alternative space', smaller institutions such as the HCAK are frequently referred to as 'side tracks' in comparison to the 'main road' of the museum. They are places without a collection, so that no collection errors can be made, hence the responsibility is smaller and at the same time the legitimising power (which after all largely consists in the power of money) is minimal or even non-existent. Consequently, risks can be taken and experiments can be made. Such a place has a 'laboratory function', which cannot be expected (anymore) of a museum. It is a kind of sanctuary without many consequences.

I have never quite understood what is meant by all this, but these kinds of formulations always clearly involve a quantitative hierarchy (and consequently, wealth, and consequently, power). From this point of view an institution like the HCAK (and of course I can mention others more or less similar to it), in my opinion, is mainly ascribed the function of a lightning rod Anything that should not take place in the museum will have to take place there, for then not only is it conveniently disposed of, but there is a place for it to be exhibited as well. Meaning and quality are no longer at issue.

What – let us stay close to home – is in fact the function of the HCAK? Despite recent signs of change, the museum is still partly an exhibition machine just as fast as, or even faster than, the art trade, bringing 'new' (or neglected) art with the possibility that it can subsequently be included in a more prestigious circuit, although one of the tasks the HCAK has ascribed to itself from the very beginning, has long ceased to be a first priority. In any case, this business of 'discovering' new artists is rather silly, and seldom extends beyond the surface.

The HCAK occupies itself with themes which, distilled from the practice of contemporary art, are given greater depth in the form of projects. This means that through a thematic approach, new practice is being stimulated and theory evoked. The common denominator covering all HCAK projects is the place of art, both in the sense of pure contents 'within the work of art', and in the sense of presentation method – the way in which the artwork is dealt with in a mediating function directed towards the public. What struck me in connection with this is that in our practice a development is noticeable in the direction of ever-increasing economising – more than one single work per exhibition room was almost never shown over the past years.

Returning to the original subject, this implies that the public come to the HCAK in order to see a maximum of three works. In my opinion this is a fortunate and in a sense, even 'beautiful' situation. One will have to do one's best, but one can be sure that something special will be exhibited, and moreover in a place where there is no opportunity for anything else but concentrated attention. As an example of this I can mention the recent visit of an internationally acclaimed museum director and curator to The Hague. We wanted to take him to the HCAK. Despite the pressures of time, he was eager to visit us – after all, we were exhibiting one of Lawrence Weiner's works. But then why should one be set on seeing that, we all know it inside out, don't we? This reaction may be regarded as symptomatic. People think in terms of names, not works, for the issue is not whether there is a work by Weiner, but which work it is and what it means in this particular location. The Weiner happened to be an extraordinarily good one and can be counted amongst the finest Weiners conceivable, which within the framework of 'the ideal place' moreover constituted an unexpected counterpoint to the other contributions. Eventually, our honourable friend was very pleased with having seen the work, as it had added something worthwhile to what he already knew (and this also applied to the other two works in the exhibition at the time). This kind of confrontation ought to take place more often, but in that case officials will have to abandon their expectations and, just as everyone else, take the required time over it and do their best. Lack of time obviously plays a fatal role here.

The HCAK offers the public a certain reflective atmosphere far away from the world of glamour and stardom – a studious climate with a concentrated programming. This is rather modest and at the same time terribly pretentious: on the one hand we do not compete with anything or anyone, and on the other hand we do claim to arrange exceptional confrontations with exceptional art which contributes to art practice itself, and to the theoretical perception of this practice. This is most definitely a high claim and we are convinced that we are living up to it.

Obviously we are not anti museums, nor perhaps the large and well-attended exhibitions of various characters. The HCAK does not oppose them. However, we do offer a different context: the museum has long ceased to be the island of tranquillity and intellectual reflection it is sometimes taken for being, and the question is whether its format is suitable for this. The museum has evolved directly from the collection, it has been built for it, and the combination of a great many dissimilar objects continues to be the foundation of the existence of the museum. The collection *is* the museum.

The HCAK wishes to be a studious, but also changeable place, directed inwardly, but dynamic too, without losing sight of its place in the world – a place of quiet, care, attention, concentration and reflection as well as a place of criticism. This does not detract from the canvassing by means of extensive mailing and advertisements, and the monthly public symposiums where a public is definitely sought and involved in the debate. However, maybe for that very reason, it is not the mass public we refer to here; it concerns the people who want to take an active part in the debate and want to make an effort for it. We – and the art world in general – could use more of their kind.

The Ideal Place: An Ideal Place for Contact
As far as I know Mondrian and Kirchner, for example, never talked to each other. I would have liked to peep through the keyhole had such an encounter taken place.

I have no idea of who talks to who in this day and age; now that the possibilities for contact have expanded due to the increase in international mobility, oddly enough the art world gives the impression of becoming more and more autistic. I am not referring to the officials (although quite a few remarks could be made on the subject) but to the artists themselves. There are no, or hardly any, 'movements' or 'groups' and 'manifestos'. Everyone seems to have packed it in. Evidently there is no cause left to dedicate oneself to.

On the other hand there are indeed numerous causes to be

supported, but these tend to be individual causes. The common seems to have disappeared from art. Even though a few art researchers or organisers may from time to time notice a common denominator, in reality these are usually artificial constructions, possibly forms of wishful thinking. I am not saying (what is sometimes said, and partly for that very reason) that the quality of art has deteriorated since the end of the 'epoch of heroes' (which of course was and is just as much a construct) and that we are now living in a period of decline. I do not think so at all and besides, I do not think I would know how to measure this. But what I do witness around me are great contactual problems (I may be wrong of course – it has happened before, but in this case I would be surprised if it were so).

Neither am I saying that there is no longer a relationship among artists regarding contents or artistic approach, nor that the complete individuality of the various works therefore automatically results in contactual problems. After all, if this were so, it would be hard to interpret any work of art or even to recognise it as such. There are sufficient similarities and conflicts to be grasped. The artists themselves, however, do not seem to be particularly interested in them. A general discourse hardly exists anymore. Each does his job and takes his own course. Naturally, this is characteristic of a culture without a centre and it does not take much effort to release all the clichés of this type of thinking in order to explain it. However, I happen not to consider this particularly interesting and in this context it is probably also somewhat beside the truth. It may just have to do with taking an interest in, being keen on, and doing your best with respect to what happens around you.

I simply want to describe what I see and taking our project, 'The Ideal Place' as an example, we developed a system where every two weeks (at the most) three artists would occupy one exhibition room each, in order to create their work and/or to install it. On the day of the opening there was a forum discussion with a chairman and the public. From the HCAK we regularly organised informal evenings at somebody's home – after all, one should try and entertain one's guests. Usually it concerned three artists who definitely did not see each other every day, if they knew each other personally at all. They had come to occupy themselves with one and the same theme, 'the ideal place'. And what place could possibly be more ideal for an exchange of thoughts on the subject of the ideal place or any other subject regarding art, for that matter? So why is this so rarely done?

Practice has shown that each artist works for himself and that in most cases, whether the meeting is spontaneously arranged or pre-organised, the encounter ends up in small talk, or at best in talking at cross-purposes. This is pleasant enough, but in a sense it is probably a missed opportunity. However, the people of the HCAK are no talk-show hosts or therapists wishing or having to see to it that the participants pay attention to the lesson. But essentially it is of course completely ridiculous to see three artists formulate an 'ideal place' (or a representation of it, or a view on it) on a minimal territory, all of them pretending that the others do not exist at all. This lack of interest borders on arrogance or has actually already amply exceeded this border. I am not implying that we as organisers have not maintained friendly relations with by far the greater part of the artists, for this has nothing to do with it. But in my opinion, a culture such as the art world, in which there is no communication among colleagues, presents a serious problem.

I admit that being an artist is a solitary profession: one is alone with one's work and all decisions have to be taken in solitude. This, and the route followed by the artist perhaps contributes to making the artist a monomaniac and often egocentric kind of person. When talking to an artist, it is always best to talk about his own work, although occasionally a few other reflections may be uttered, or perhaps the artist may have read the occasional book which can be discussed, or he may have a fancy for canaries, or even a remarkable sense of humour. But (difference in) views are not discussed, unless in a casually and often bantering tone.

The monthly talks in the HCAK show a similar pattern: the artists talk about their own work, answer questions asked by the chairman and the public (which can be very interesting) but an essential exchange of ideas is never or rarely effected, despite all sorts of attempts on the part of the chairman. Most of these talks consist of separate monologues. It appears that it is no longer possible for artists to communicate with one another in any field other than through their work.

A few years ago the HCAK organised 'Metamorphosis', which was a thematic project in which artists responded to each others' work. When this project had ended – which in fits and starts had yielded very good works of art – a private discussion took place among participants and people involved in the HCAK, later published in book form. Whoever reads the text will notice that a greater confusion of tongues has seldom occurred: the artists were simply unable or unwilling to understand one another's work. Without wishing to assess this in a similar manner, more or less the same thing seems to happen in the case of 'The Ideal Place'. At the end of this project, 24 proposals with respect to 'the ideal place' (often of a high quality) have passed in review, but the artists will not or hardly have been aware of the points of view and considerations of their colleagues. I find this hard to understand.

The quality of the project does not suffer from the lack of contact between artists (the works will not be any worse for this) but it is still peculiar and unsatisfactory that the discipline of visual art almost seems to have degenerated into hyper-individual navel gazing. All those navels, in fact, *do* have quite a lot to offer, so there is not much need for us observers to complain, but the phantom-like idea, that of no common 'reality' regarding content, no artistic interaction, seems to exist, causing a feeling that something important is lacking.

Although the artist of course 'speaks by means of his work', he is in principle also a kind of intellectual, seeking his place in the history of ideas, who should be deemed capable of more than just monosyllabic comment. Every day this is proved again and again, but nearly all this comment (often polysyllabic) only encompasses their own work.

Art does not exist in a vacuum: it originates from the world, the world is its subject and it is returned to the world as (art) product. A work of art is a phenomenon in the world. This applies to all works of art, not only to those made by you or me who do not (wish to) know of each other's existence. In my opinion, the phantom-like character of the situation partly arises from the fact that although all works are 'reality' (in their concrete materiality as well as in the sense of facts that can be interpreted) they are at the same time denied to be so by those who, besides their creator, should be closest to them. That is, in terms of contact among artists the works do exist as objects, but on the other hand they do not, because no one bothers with them. And it appears to be so that objects (and possibly this applies even more to art objects) need love, attention, care and reflection. If this is lacking, their presence becomes dubious and phantom-like. It is therefore fortunate that the work of artists is not just made for their colleagues. The question is whether in that case we would still have a public deserving that name.

As regards work by others (and in a sense this also applies to his own work, though in certain respects to a lesser degree and in a somewhat different way) the artist is an observer among observers. This implies that he, just as everyone else, will have to do his best and will have to make an effort to get in touch with what someone else wished to express. Possibly (or obviously) this is more difficult for the artist-observer than for another, 'ordinary' observer, because he is so tied up with the expression of his own opinion, his own point of view, his own world view, that faced with a different approach he cannot detach himself from his own. But for that very reason the artist could make use of someone else's work for an even greater articulation of his own assertions (and there is no reason why this interaction could not contribute something on a verbal level as well, since we are all able to express ourselves in language). But an effort is needed to achieve an idea of what that other work wishes to address, for otherwise there can be no relationship whatsoever. In order to achieve an optimum effect in this respect, I am firmly convinced that we should keep talking. Then we can say there is a discourse, and otherwise just a disjointed account. A disjointed account may be fine, but a sound culture also requires a discourse held by the bearers of culture (whoever these may exactly be, but artists are at any rate included in them).

After all, we as organisers also talk to all those artists about their work and, apart from possible benefit to themselves, for us it is an instructive occupation. That is one of the reasons why this kind of contact takes place at all. Of course the work should do the job, but a living artist can be asked questions in order to achieve a further exchange of thoughts. I would like Vermeer or Botticelli to explain one or two things, but unfortunately it is too late for that. However, as long as a live exchange of thoughts is possible, it is incomprehensible if this should not be effected, notably among artists. After all, they are all occupied with the same issues, or are at least, when we look upon art in relation to the rest of the world, all operating in the same field. A lack of interest may also imply plain, simple laziness.

In my opinion, all this may also have to do with the exaggerated status of the artist – celebrated as a star, but after all just an ordinary human being capable of doing something that not everyone else is capable of, or at any rate making an effort to do something not aspired to by everyone else. There *are* a lot of people who are making a similar effort, just as in every other professional group, but it is no reason to refer to this group as an elect group of genius elevated above the level of their fellow creatures (let alone above their just as privileged colleagues). Besides, the circuit is getting increasingly nervous nowadays – the artist travels back and forth all around the world at high speed to make works everywhere, quickly disappearing again on his way to the next place. Although there are exceptions, what we often experience these days is that in order to keep in touch with artists, we have to chase them by phone or telefax across several continents. From time to time an artist is here to install his work in one or two days, briefly taking part in the forum discussion, and immediately leaving again to do the same thing elsewhere. This could be so that his colleagues do not have a chance to alter their perception of his position, but in the long run (and due to this very fact) it also involves the risk of jeopardising concentration on his own production (and those who are malicious could easily mention examples of 'victims' already). In spite of contradicting myself, the risk of art and culture in general not meeting its potential and falling into decline because of this sort of nervous lack of concentration, might not be completely imaginary.

I am glad I am not an artist myself. Restricting ourselves to the example of the project at hand, I can give my whole-hearted attention to all 24 proposals for 'The Ideal Place', and all the time they require. There is a lot to be learned from this project: I think we (and our public) have learned more from it than the participating artists, however highly their contributions may be assessed.

The Ideal Place: Soundless, Invisible

As soon as a work of art comes into being, it is inevitable that the question of material will become an issue. Art needs form in order to make its presence known and form consists of material. In this respect a piece of paper of 2 x 2cms is not much different from oil paint, nor an adhesive letter from reinforced concrete. This material aspect, shared by all visual art, implying that 'form' and 'content' are identical (or that in and/or through form, content manifests itself) resulting in an object that can change its meaning when it is brought in connection with other objects, is the cause of the presentation problem. As I said earlier, this problem is actively and exclusively restricted to visual art and does not play a part in any of the other arts, if particular basic conditions (size of stage, acoustics, legibility etc) have been met.

It transpired that not everyone was willing to agree with, or accept this. Notably, from various quarters it was pointed out that the same thing applies to performing music (and mutatis mutandis drama or ballet could also be mentioned, but for the sake of convenience I will use music as an example here). This music is, after all, dependent on interpretation and consequently each presentation will be different, just as visual art may undergo fluctuations in meaning due to changes in context. From this point of view, performing music has a presentation problem like visual art (incidentally, in a sense the sound produced could then be regarded as 'material').

My opinion is that this point of view is somewhat debatable and that in a remarkably roundabout way, part of the essence of the project 'The Ideal Place' is thus touched upon and posed as a problem once again.

Nowadays it is true that we have museum directors who call an exhibition of work from the permanent museum collection 'the material' (as was the case with Rudi Fuchs' first exhibition at the Amsterdam Stedelijk Museum), suggesting that evidently they are (wish to be) the 'players' of this material, *casu quo* that visual art should not be considered 'autonomous', but a means to an end – the end being the statement or interpretation by the curator on the basis of his 'material'. However, in such a case the curator uses the inherent presentation problem as an alibi for blowing up the problem even further or, if you like, for making a virtue of necessity. The presentation problem then turns into a kind of playground for the ideas of the curator, he takes possession of the work as if it were a free-for-all.

In doing so, the curator takes up the position expected – and indeed required of the performing musician if he is to practise his trade – but this same conduct shows an extraordinary (and to my taste usually incorrect) view of dealing with visual art. After all, in this question the only real material is the material of which the artwork has been made and the artist is (was) the 'player' of that material. In this sense, each work of art can comprise its own interpretation within the limits of the possibilities for presentation. Strictly speaking, no other work of art is required for this, no exhibition room or complete museum full of works and definitely no public interpreter. The work of art is material and final, and often it is probably best to keep our hands off. Apart from this, everyone naturally carries his own 'musée imaginaire' and all sorts of other texts with him in his head, forcing him in his capacity of observer to come to his own interpretation. But this is a relation of dialogue between the work and its observer, which need not bother anyone else; it is not a statement to the public, nor is it a way of showing the object which is the work. An interpretation actually written down for the public no longer affects the way in which the work was presented under the circumstances in question.

Consequently, the curator only needs to be the provider of an interpretation to a very limited extent – if at all – so as to show the work of art to advantage (or rather, to have the work come into its own). Basically, his interference with content is often undesired, although sometimes it may be hard to avoid; or there are the times when the explicit need for interpretation by the curator is necessary, producing fascinating results. However, there is a price to be paid for this, for in such cases the separate works of art are suddenly asked all sorts of questions which they cannot or need not answer, or all sorts of functions are attributed to them which intrinsically they do not possess, but which due to change in context they suddenly prove to (have to) perform, often to their own surprise. It is obvious that here we are faced with an unlimited market for manipulation, particularly when we include excesses in our considerations such as those brought about by characters like Peter Greenaway and later Robert Wilson as 'guest curators', both of whom were given free rein to use the collection of the Museum Boymans-van Beuningen in Rotterdam for all kinds of purposes for which the works in question were definitely not intended.

Now we will reverse the matter. The role of the performing musician, compared to the role of the composer, is also limited: unlike the exhibition-maker he can, and apparently must, communicate various self-made interpretations, but in each case this will have to be done on the basis of a score which is fixed. Should the performer significantly deviate from the score in any sense whatsoever, he will create new music or at any rate a partly new score, and at that precise moment his role changes from performer to composer. Visual art is quite different as the work of art is its own interpretation – it does not have a score, it is both score and performance simultaneously. From this point of view the presentation problem of visual art could be reduced from an interpretation problem to a simple problem of 'influencing through literal context'. In a manner of speaking there is no need for any thought at all as at that stage no 'interpreter' is required for the problem. This is

inherent in the fact that here matter is necessarily presented in the company of other matter, whether similar or not (whether of an artistic nature or not, even the heating pipe or the skirting-board may play a decisive role in this) causing the various visual elements to affect each other, as a purely physiological fact alone, with all its consequences. This is what I call the primary, ever-existing and inevitable presentation problem of visual art: it is in the first place a problem of a purely physical or physiological nature – the problem of arranging and classifying by the curator only transpires later to make matters more complex.

The performing musician 'performs music'. We may safely assume this without much chance of contradiction. This implies that this music already exists (namely in the form of a score) and that the musician's interpretation is an added value. One person thinks this of a particular piece of music, the next has a different opinion and a third may also have his own thoughts about it – no performance of one particular piece of music sounds the same. The composer is treated to all sorts of added opinions, views and ideas concerning his work, which do not necessarily have much to do with the score as such. Thus there are 'free' and 'less free' interpretations (we may, for instance, agree that Glenn Gould's interpretation of Brahms's *op. 10 Ballads* is considerably 'freer' than those of all other well-known performers). The problem of assessment in this sector, however, is that 'free' and 'less free' eventually are categories of little importance, since no one knows how a piece 'ought to' sound, particularly not if the composer is no longer alive and increasingly so if the music was written even longer ago. In this context the rapidly-changing fashions in the so-called 'authentic' practice of performing old music is almost amusingly illustrative.

Music is something that can be heard and visual art something that can be seen. Apart from a few exceptions, visual art cannot be heard (and if visual art can be heard, hearing it is always subordinate to some kind of visual aspect), but music can definitely be seen and even read: that is the score. Beethoven can be read. Besides, this is even a necessary condition for the existence of a practice of performance – if Beethoven could not be read, his music could not be played at all. This implies that there is an 'Urtext' – the score – which is the starting point for the sounds produced on the basis of it, but in no way synonymous to it. The status attributed to the score is of essential significance to our problem. If we actually wish to hear the music with our ears, we need an intermediary, the performing musician, the interpreter. We may be partly hearing Beethoven, but partly also Gould or Schnabel or Kempff or Solomon or Brendel, and this creates a world of difference. What we do not know is how Beethoven himself would have liked to hear this score played, for in his time there was no recording equipment, hence nothing to serve as a frame of reference. We obviously cannot query him as to his true intentions (which from a certain stage in his life he would not have heard anyway. He himself could not even hear the performance of his later scores, a fact which will prove to be not without importance to our problem). Finally, we might also think that there is no reason why we should accept the composer as the ultimate authority on his own work. So we are faced with a problem: how should Beethoven sound? However, is this actually a presentation problem in the sense in which we come across it in visual art or is it a problem of a totally different nature? To solve this we shall have to decide what the essence of the music is and which status should be attributed to which component.

In order to get more information on this subject I want to present an example, which in this context I can only discuss briefly, but which is not without complexity. I possess two recordings of the *Preludes* and *Fugues op.87* of Shostakovich. One of them (on which part of the work is performed) is played by the composer himself, and the other by the great, recently deceased Tatjana Nikolajewa. Much to my regret, I have not been able to find out which of these two recordings is older. This is a pity, because the sleeve of Nikolajewa's record explicitly states that it has been made under supervision of, and authorisation by, the composer. On the other hand, this lack of knowledge also results in nice additional matter for discussion. At the moment when Nikolajewa was playing the work (and apparently when she had finished playing, at any rate until the moment when the record with the authorisation by the composer was released) Shostakovich was evidently of the opinion that this was the 'official' performance – this was the way in which the piece should be played. But in the meantime he also recorded it himself (and here we are only talking about recordings, facts that can be verified afterwards, for naturally the piece has been performed many more times without having been preserved). Suppose that Shostakovich's recording preceded Nikolajewa's, then his view of his own work was evidently substituted by another view, namely Nikolajewa's, for various rather fundamental differences to be pointed out, which definitely were not just caused by the fact that Nikolajewa may have been a better instrumentalist than Shostakovich (who had a reputation to uphold). Those differences are also to be found in the field of tempo and the like: deliberate choices, opinions.

As a comparison, in visual art we can hardly imagine Baselitz appreciating the interpretation of one of his paintings by Johannes Gachnang more than his own performance – this is nonsense, because these categories do not apply at all here. Baselitz's painting had long been finished before Gachnang started meddling with it. The latter did not paint it and therefore an interpretation of the work as such is out of the question – at most there is an 'increased presentation problem', consisting of the question in which context Gachnang is going to hang this Baselitz, and which undesired and possibly undesirable meanings he will thus add to Baselitz's in itself already final statement.

Back to music: we may wonder to what extent, under the circumstances indicated, Nikolajewa is actually the (co?)-composer of that particular moment in the history of Shostakovich's *op.87*, when this piece evidently went through a significant and considerable number of changes. But if Shostakovich's own performance is of a later date than Nikolajewa's, what is his earlier authorisation of her interpretation worth in that case? What is more, in a sense he may have composed the piece once more, as it were, in the manner evident from his own recording. Obviously Shostakovich had no fixed idea about how *op.87* should sound. This shows how closely 'interpretation' and 'composition' adjoin or even overlap one another. Earlier 'compositions of the same piece' by Shostakovich himself or by whoever else, may thus have been cancelled out and at any rate they were 'different pieces'.

In order to complicate matters even further, Nikolajewa recorded *op.87* twice more after the death of Shostakovich, evidently twice in the conviction that at that moment she knew better than before and that subsequently these new views also had greater validity, irrespective of the authorisation of the first recording by the composer. In addition, one might also argue that all performances/interpretations, independent of a vague criterion like 'quality', simply exist next to each other and all have their own validity, but if one wishes to maintain this (and in itself there is a case for it) one is bound to meet problems in determining the identity of 'the piece itself', which is our concern here. Anyway, there is an accumulation of interpretations of Shostakovich's *op.87* (and this applies to any piece of music) with the one thing in common being that they deviate from each other in various manners as well as claim to be Shostakovich's *op.87*.

Is this possible? Can things so widely different claim the same identity? Are all these performances indeed *op.87*? Or are they no more than different views, implying that in an ontological sense they are not the work, but represent it, are reflections of it, and on the basis of this express an existential opinion on something that need not at all be Shostakovich's *op.87*; but for instance, to put it blandly, the temperament or problem of the musician in question or whatever else? If this is so, no interpretation is the work. All the interpretations are, at best, a personal attempt at communicating something, one could maintain, on the basis of the work. But what then is the work? There is a Shostakovich *op.87*, is there not? Yes, it does exist, and that is the score. The score of *op.87* is *op.87*, all the notes are there and in addition, a number of essential instructions for the practice of performance. The only thing is, however, that it is evidently not possible to perform *op.87* – at least not in a way which everyone agrees that this particular performance coincides with the score, and the score does not lie, it is fixed. Consequently, the score is the music and all interpretations are nothing but representations of it, reflections, points of view, and so on. Apart from the fact that as far as I am concerned there are few things in life that give greater satisfaction than comparing different interpretations of a score, continuing the line of argument consistently we will have to decide that the most 'correct' performance of a piece of music is the performance consisting of a score not expressed in sound.

To put it differently, performing music has no *presentation* problem, as visual art, but a *representation* problem and this is something completely different, although in practice it does not result in fewer possibilities and difficulties. The curator presents a painting, a visible object, and thus introduces it within whatever kind of context that may affect the functions and effect of this painting, but the work itself remains unchanged. The performing musician represents a piece of music which he expresses through his personal input by definition changes (if only because it is translated from one medium into another. Translation always implies change and if it concerns something as complicated as translating one discipline into another, the variables will soon become utterly complex and often obscure).

If we can now agree on the obviously somewhat absurd proposition that the only non-representing performance of written music is the performance, 'the ideal place' in music could be when music is visible and readable in a score, but inaudible. We may also argue that Beethoven could not hear his own works however much he would have liked to. Evidently, this implies that 'hearing' is something that need not necessarily be done with the ears, a reminiscence of sound seems to be sufficient. Most composers do not hear their own work with their ears (that is, in the material of sound) until the moment of its first performance. This does not imply that they do not have an opinion, a view of what their own work should sound like, in advance. The contrary is in fact the case, as otherwise this work would consist of a more or less random collection of 'sounds', *casu quo* 'signs', deprived of any meaning attributed by their maker, in which absurd case composing would not make sense and consequently, there would be no need (or even possibility) for producing music anymore.

Taking matters one step further, we may conclude that the soundless score may be the representationless, 'ideal' music, but that this is immediately amended from the moment when I start looking at this score. I do see those 'neutral' signs, but due to my interference with them (by reading them) these signs at once change into my interpretation, my soundless yet definitely existing representation. The 'purity', the 'ideal' of the score is immediately corrupted. In short, the ideal music is not only the score not expressed in sound, but strictly speaking even the score not opened. It is obvious that in practice this does not help the music lover very much. It is said that the sense of a work of art, in whatever discipline, consists of exchange, of contact between the work of art and the observer/listener. We may put my representation, my immediate interpretation of the score (or of anything I read or hear) on the same footing as the similar phenomenon occurring when one looks at a work of visual art, as mentioned before. It concerns a relation of dialogue, not the form in which a work is brought into the open. Such a relation does not decisively affect the intrinsic status of the work as such.

Nevertheless, we may try out whether the analogy with visual art makes sense on such an extreme level too. Could it be that 'the ideal place' in visual art is invisible, in other words that ideal visual art (if we consider art concretely as an object, as a 'place', which is possible) is art that is not presented? Or could it be so that, because visual art is presented and music represented, the material formality, or rather, the coinciding of matter (that is, the literal presentation of the object as such) and content (the meaning of this presentation) results in that very difference which makes the ideal work of visual art (which after all remains unchanged) literally 'presentable' under any circumstances, whereas ideal music ought to remain 'unpresentable' (that is, 'soundless')?

The Ideal Place: An Immoral Proposition?
It has struck me that in the course of this project, 'the ideal place' has almost always been approached as something positive, something to be aspired to, existent or non-existent, attainable or not attainable, utopian or nostalgic, personal or collective, private or public. Actually, the ideological desirability of it has not or hardly been brought up. It is up to us to call this heart-warming, naive or dangerous (or all three).

On the one hand, man is evidently willing to assume that such a thing as an 'ideal place' does exist or ought to exist, and that we would all profit by it, that we should therefore aspire for 'the good', 'the ideal'. And it does sound tempting: 'ideal place', 'ideal society'. It suggests a world almost beyond space and time, in which everyone is equal (has equal value) or can take according to his own need without the various needs frustrating one another. The ideal place therefore seems to presuppose an ideal structure (of any kind whatsoever) in which ideal people live or at least in which we all become or prove to be ideal creatures as if by magic (of course, one of the conditions of an ideal place is the moral quality of the inhabitants, for they make a place ideal, otherwise the place is defiled by 'non-ideality' and can therefore by definition never be ideal). We can think of it as a paradise, a nirvana, a Valhalla or a 'clean' world without war, hunger or any other injustice, but definitely a mentally possible or at any rate desirable 'place' (regardless of whether this concept is seen as a static place or as a dynamic continuum). Whoever could be against such a thing? Or to put it more strongly, who would not wish to be there forever?

On the other hand, there are also people who believe that there is no such thing as an ideal place, that it cannot exist at all, since man is not 'good' or does not even have any inclination towards 'being good', and that these are irrelevant or non-existent categories in themselves. In this vision, the ideal place is a superfluous fiction and instead of vague escapism of this kind, they would rather deal with the real, tangible daily affairs, with what is going on now, at this moment in time, in whatever field or manner. We tend to believe only what we can touch, that is hard enough in itself and for the rest there is nothing between heaven and earth.

A third suggestion is that the ideal place is here and now, but that we fail to recognise it as such: gold slipping through our fingers without noticing it. Then the ideal place is reduced (or from a reverse point of view, elevated) to a question of perception of the existing reality, to a question of interpretation, introspection, 'spirituality' and mystique.

Besides philosophy and fine art and other disciplines that can afford themselves to reflect on 'the ideal place', there also exists something like the flat history of facts that have verifiably taken place or are now taking place – more a question of ordinary 'schoolbook history' than historical interpretation. I admit that a stuffier example is hard to find, but here it serves its purpose excellently, since on the basis of this it will immediately be unambiguously clear to any pupil that the awareness of any sort of 'ideal place' – and particularly the doctrine that this is something to be aspired after – has resulted in all the disasters mankind has brought down on itself. To put it even more strongly, in practice the awareness (or rather, notion) of an 'ideal place' has usually led to the idea that this notion (and hence the pursuit of it) also had to be made clear to others, *all* others, willy-nilly, for the noble end justifies the means. (And moreover, in the name of transforming the world into an ever more comfortable 'ideal place', we have polluted it and brought it to the verge of chaos.)

In this respect nothing has ever changed in the world: we are still suffering from wars, religious conflicts, class struggle, forced migrations, ethnic purges and so on, clashes of systems and structures resulting from the tendency (often skilfully manipulated by power-mad demagogues) to spread the supposed ideal, and the clashes arising when various ideals (or even similar ideals in different disguises) meet somewhere. This hardly ever has a happy ending.

This brings us to another position, taking our project 'The Ideal Place', to the position of HCAK as organiser of such a project and that of the participating artists. We started the project from the point of view that the concepts of 'place' and 'placement' in contemporary art form a central issue in all sorts of ways. In the first place, of course, as a mental (and we now add, moral) construct. As the HCAK has occupied itself from the very beginning with 'the position of art' (both literally, as presentation of a presence, and figuratively in the sense of representation of meaning in culture), it seemed obvious to seek something we did not know yet: the *ideal* place. In retrospect, this is in itself a deliberately provoking formulation implying a certain naiveté. But this provocation had more to do with the fact that in art 'place' and 'placement' generally present themselves as not very 'ideal', as a genuine problem, rather than as a neutral theme. After all, we are not living in an age marked for its abundance of Utopias. In an earlier instance I already wrote (and we always mentioned this to the artists involved) that we did not know whether an ideal place was desirable at all, but without realising that our proposal to create 'an ideal place' could in a sense also be regarded as *indecent*.

The subjective aspects of the 'ideal place' are obvious: my ideal place is not your ideal place, but for that reason neither is a *real* ideal place in a general sense. At best they are two small islands and it would not come as a surprise to anyone if the inhabitants were to fight each other in the name of their ideals. Consequently, the absolute, ideal place does not exist, yet this is the implicit starting point, for otherwise 'ideal' would only mean: 'what pleases me personally' and that is not an interesting category, for then we are dealing with a private sense of well-being, which is no reason for starting an art project and, for that matter, artists usually do not produce works of art just to express this feeling. This has been evident in this project, in which there has not been any contribution propagating the 'ideal place' in that way (although in my opinion some came dangerously close).

So this implies that an invitation to occupy oneself with 'the ideal place' is almost like a summons to a crusade, like imposing the sharia or throwing bombs at Grozny or Bosnia, exterminating all Tutsis or forbidding headscarves to be worn at schools, to mention a few topical examples of various types.

The ideal has become a contaminated concept and it may be best to distance oneself from it (but in that case one backs out of the ethical discussion and therefore the possibility of taking up a position) or even to contest it (which in its turn leads to the paradoxical situation that the ideal is contested in the name of another ideal that is supposed to be 'against the ideal'). In brief, it seems impossible to have clean hands – it is either Scylla or Charybdis, the classical prototype of a 'double bind'. One is inevitably tainted by, or cursed with, some ideal or the other, and thus 'the' ideal accuires a completely different definition, the definition of being the ultimate manifestation of human failings, 'stuck between a rock and a hard place'.

Thus we could state that our project also has an indecent aspect, an immoral invitation which perhaps one ought to refuse when asked. But that was not what happened: 24 artists have made themselves guilty of complicity by making utopian or pessimistic works, or works which are a denial of the ideal. In brief, they have neatly kept to the assignment as always; they have simply dedicated themselves to the touring, and worn out international art circus (though at a modest and relatively 'unimportant' location). There has not been any rejection on ideological grounds and (actually it was only now that we noticed this) we are beginning to realise that we ourselves should at least have considered that possibility.

But would it have been better if we had *not* executed the project on those grounds? Are we 'suspect' as it were by carrying it out and are all the participating artists no more than little egoists wishing to show their tricks everywhere without taking their ideological and historical responsibility into account?

In my opinion, such a conclusion is not tenable either, I think it is going too far: the indecency of the ideal is, in my view, one more aspect of it, one of the many possibilities of interpretation (or am I trying to argue that what actually is wrong is right, am I trying to justify what cannot be justified by rationalising the larger problem away as no more than just one line of approach to a theme which eventually is 'neutral' again?). By dedicating a project to 'the ideal place' as we have done, this aspect of the matter is bound to be discussed at a certain moment (rather late perhaps) and when we can bring it up it will not remain concealed and, all in all, this appears to be necessary and therefore rather a merit than a flaw of the project. It is a subject to which we hope to return later in a more thorough evaluation of the project 'The Ideal Place' as a whole, in connection with a number of works that (do) point in this direction. May the conclusion suffice, for the moment, that art presentation is an activity in which the most unexpected and seriously ethical dilemmas can crop up without us (of HCAK) being able to immediately achieve a more satisfactory solution than just spotting them.

Note

1 In the light of criticism offered by some people including members of Art & Language, it might be necessary to introduce a further nuance. When I want to go to London (eg when my original destination was London) but end up in Birmingham (eg my actual destination was Birmingham) the idea of destination and that of 'ideal place' cannot be regarded as a tautology because 'destination' applies to my original aim as well as to the actual fact of my ending up somewhere I did not want to end up. So maybe, to be clearer, we could say that my *destination* was London but that it was my *destiny* to end up in Birmingham. Then 'destination' resumes its meaning as the *intended* ideal place, whereas destiny describes something like a twist of fate which might or might not turn out to be 'ideal' in some sense, but 'ideal' certainly is not the first and logical predicate of it.

NO(W)HERE AS THE IDEAL PLACE
ON THE RELATIONS BETWEEN CONCEPTS, PERCEPTS AND AFFECTS

Henk Oosterling

The ideal place constitutes a pregnant void within any culture. Western, democratic tradition has been haunted by it ever since Plato's speculations on Atlantis and the ideal state, which have continued to inspire later generations. For instance, Thomas More translated both elements in his *Utopia* (ou-topos), a 'land of no-where' which is said to have originated from sheer fantasy. With the arrival of modern times these phantasms acquired a more earthly character. As soon as the autonomously acting, rationally calculating individual was developing into the pivot of history, and the political debate, still determining our present time, was gradually taking shape during the Enlightenment at the end of the 18th century, the ideal place became a projection in time. As a picture of the future it gives sense and direction to the collective mission of emancipating citizens and workers. In the course of the 19th century artists also started liberating themselves from the rulers' fetters, eventually resulting in art operating as a critical authority within bourgeois culture.

The Foundation of the Political Ideal: Reflective Self-Consciousness

In view of this background, the question about the relation between the ideal place and art appears to be linked with a political vision regarding man as a rational, critical creature. He controls his own destiny, reforging it into history. It is in the philosophy of Kant – and in a critical continuation of this, in the philosophies of Hegel and Marx – that towards the end of the Enlightenment, the ideal place turned into a historical task. Whereas Plato still conceived the realm of ideas at the foundation of sensory reality as a transcendent world and believed that the 'political' community described in his *Politeia* (*Republic*) was the purest expression of this World of Ideas, Kant believed that the Idea is no longer situated beyond, but within, human consciousness. To Kant, Ideas are functions of the ways in which self-consciousness analyses its effectiveness on a transcendental level: that is to say, it reflects on its conditions of possibility coherently and exhaustively. The Ideas – soul, totality of the world, God, freedom – then prove to be transcendental postulates. As coping stones of thought they have no right whatsoever to exist beyond self-consciousness or reason. According to Kant the Ideas are purely regulative. Projected onto historical reality they present at most a rule by which the course of events in their coherence can be grasped. However, this theory presupposes a conception of history as a process of increasing freedom, as an emancipatory or collective process of awakening. In this progressive vision, the notion of Utopia plays a guiding role.

The modern notion of Utopia or the ideal place is therefore a political extrapolation of the postulates of Reason. Without this postulate, which from a socio-political and economic point of view was interpreted differently in each case by Kant, Hegel and Marx –

and the effective realisation of which also implies the renowned 'end of history' – time as a progressive accumulation of collective learning processes (ie, as emancipation) is inconceivable. It will be clear that the self-consciousness of the critical avant-garde is also fed by this ideality, for the avant-garde conforms to history by seeing its artistic labour as a contribution towards a better world. In this sense its labour is political, because it is community-establishing.

Provisional Position-Finding

How can this political-philosophical concept be linked with artistic imagination? Three possible versions of this relation present themselves: 1) the ideal place *and* art, 2) the ideal place *in* art and 3) the ideal place *of* art. Given the socio-political meaning, the first version aims at an interaction. This is already inherent in the genealogy of the notion of avant-garde, for after 1870 the political meaning was transferred to the cultural-artistic domain.[1] The emancipation of art, however, causes any renewed subordination of artists to political power to be conservative, and possibly even suspect in the 20th century. As soon as modern artists subject themselves to rulers uncritically, the danger arises which Walter Benjamin referred to at the end of his notorious essay on the technical reproducibility of the work of art in modern times: totalitarianism.

In the spectacular conclusion of the epilogue, the aestheticising of politics is connected with fascism and the politicising of art with communism.[2] Both political systems make use of a propagandist, because politically representative art in the form of Neo-Realism. In retrospect, the initial embrace of the avant-garde during the infancy of the Soviet Union has proven to have been no more than growing pains. When revolutionary zest died out, here too, any form of non-representative, autonomous art was declared 'ent-artet' in double respect. So if we are to deal with the relation between the ideal place and art, we should be aware of the fact that this trap is wide open. For that reason, the avant-garde developing in opposition to bourgeois culture is taken as the point of reference. The relation between politics and art is seen as a field of tension never to be resolved, a fundamentally uninhabitable no man's land, a literal *ou-topos*.

The second version of the theme, dealing with the ideal place *in* art, usually refers to the way artists have depicted, expressed or dramatised – in brief, represented – ideal existence in their artistic medium. That this version is related to the first is evident from the distinction that is to be made between confirmative (from an avant-garde perspective conservative) and critical representations. The question immediately presenting itself then is the question about the role of non-representative or abstract art. Due to its flatness, ie the absence of the three-dimensional illusion, the concept of 'place' acquires a fundamentally different interpretation here.

But it is possibly all much simpler and we should not restrict ourselves to the ideal place *of* art. It may be sufficient to give an analysis, whether critical or not, of ritual or institutional embedding – the way in which, in the widest sense of the word, works of art have been ex*posed* in the course of the centuries. This might result in an amusing summing up of the spaces where works of art were placed, so that members of the community could experience them as a literal reflection of their public spirit. The fact that this second version is also linked with the first is again apparent from the *display* of power which usually characterised the exhibition of works of art. But the distinction in the second version is also important: the objective of socio-political power relations, and consequently of demonstrating public spirit – which the representation of heavenly or earthly authorities concretely implied – was initially confirmative and only became critical in more recent times. This history of factual exhibitions ranges from the caves of Lascaux and the scenes of Greek tragedies, through the immense spaces of cathedrals and palaces to the Salons, culminating in the galleries and museums of our time. The being embedded in the mass media, used as a theme by Benjamin, is the last link in this process to this very day.

However, the arsenal of possible interpretations of the theme is by no means exhausted. As soon as we further unravel the rather too general term 'art' systematically, the complexity of the question asked increases exponentially. After all, what aspect of art practice are we actually talking about? About production, reception or about what, in the early 20th century, took shape as the autonomous work of art: that peculiar material substrate which, passing over the intentions of the artist, ignoring the expectations of critics or other viewers, nevertheless offers a coherence that continues to be significant, in spite of constant shifts? In Applying these aspects of art to the first three versions and consequently substituting the term 'art' for 'artist', 'artwork' or 'art viewer', no less than nine options present themselves for the discussion of the relation between art and the ideal place.

Consequently, we are faced with multiple subjects for discussion. It is true that one is more interesting than the other, but because they are mutually interwoven, each subject is significant. For instance, the question whether or how artists are politically committed through and in their art is inextricably bound up with the question regarding the ideal place for viewing art. Questions about the political value of (Neo)Realistic and Abstract art, about the function of the museum as an ideal place for the viewer, about the studio or the canvas itself as ideal place for the artist, merit close analysis, if only because from an art-historical projection each in itself continues to offer a different perspective on the mutual coherence of works of art.[3]

The Hypo-Critical Position of Postmodern Man
Nevertheless the question posed still requires one radical shift. For is it still possible to talk without restraint about the relation between politics and art without determinedly ignoring the recent discussions on politics, art and even history from which we eventually derived categories such as pre-modern and modern? These often technical discussions arising at the end of the 70s and overshadowing the greater part of the debate on the position of art in the 80s, have at least led to the insight that the question about the relation between the ideal place and art is utterly problematic – after all, due to the fact that since the 60s Western civilisation has become increasingly media-directed and aesthetic, the position of art has changed fundamentally.[4] Are opposed concepts such as conservative/revolutionary and bourgeois/avant-garde art still adequate for a 'political' assessment of current art expressions? Does their political impact not lie somewhere else? Is it still a sincere question in a time in which the avant-garde has expired and the avant-garde range of thought has split up into the supposed trans-, neo- or post-avant-garde?

In my opinion, the postmodern condition no longer permits a modernist-critical answer to the question about the ideal place, since with the loss of the actual forms of these places, historical perspective has also dissolved. This is precisely what Jean-François Lyotard points out with his thesis that the Great Narratives have come to an end. The Kantian, Hegelian and Marxist legitimations of political action have lost strength due to their own history. These encompassing conceptual legitimations in which an attempt was made to reduce science, morality and art – the true, good and beautiful – to one common denominator have blown to pieces. The result is a fragmentary multitude of small tales about separate art expressions. All those art historians and art critics who are still focusing on this modernist range of thought, often despite themselves, seem to have ignored this fragmentation. As soon as the temptation to speak in terms of modernist oppositions is yielded to again, the answer to the question about the ideal place loses its succinct meaning and a repetition of moves is all that takes place.

This may be one of the reasons why artists and philosophers – such as Jean-François Lyotard, Jacques Derrida or Gilles Deleuze – are increasingly seeking alliance with each other. The former preferably provide their catalogues with other than art-historical and art-critical analyses, because these are often still focused on modernist categories and a historical perspective. The latter draw a radicalism from art which feeds their self-disruptive insight that thought can no longer comprise reality. Nevertheless – and here lies the paradox of these forms of philosophising – thought ensures that feeling is compelled to make this encompassing movement. It is only by using the medium of thought, or language, in such a way that it allows its own inadequacy to ring through, that thought can preserve its integrity. In a concrete sense this implies an utterly paradoxical sort of language abounding with all kinds of ambiguous expressions and aporetic phrases. In a sense this kind of aporetic philosophising has inherited the avant-gardist intention of showing the obstinacy of its material and its medium in the work itself.[5] This is one reason why Lyotard and Deleuze are concerned with avant-garde art.

With these philosophers, criticism is by definition self-criticism. This is therefore by no means a matter of criticism in the modern sense of the word, but of bending this criticism back towards itself – a kind of hyper-reflection. For instance, from this hyper-critical consciousness they write that any criticism should not only bring up the presuppositions for discussion, but that there is also a blind spot in this way of thinking which can never become visible; a blind spot that was probably the breeding ground for the modern Utopia idea. This is perhaps the reason why philosophers focus on the unruly imagination of the avant-garde, hoping to catch a glimpse of this void in another medium than discursive language. The question about this void, however, is no longer critical. A term introduced by Jean Baudrillard in one of his writings may be more adequate. He derives this term from the idea that the postmodern individual has finally achieved the desirable state of freedom and enlightenment. The ideal place of modernity has been realised in the telematically controlled consumer society and constitutional state:

> Si l'art n'était au fond qu'une utopie, c'est-à-dire quelque chose qui échappe à toute réalisation, aujourd'hui cette utopie est pleinement réalisée: à travers les médias, l'informatique, la vidéo, tout le monde est devenu créatif en puissance. Même l'anti-art . . . [6]

In that sense postmodern man is trans-aesthetic. If the answer to the question about the relation between politics and art is to be meaningful at all, according to Baudrillard's immodest opinion, it ought to be more critical than critical, ie *hypo-critical*.

Self-consciousness of Art as the End of Art

Let me resume the question about the relation between the ideal place (or the Utopia) and art from a hypo-critical perspective. Arthur Danto thinks that 'we have entered a period of art so absolute in its freedoms that art seems but a name for an infinite play with its own concept . . . '[7] The end of art is supposed to be announced in the work of Warhol. Danto sees a form of 'stage-managed philosophy' in this. Modern art, discharged from representation by the medium of film, had already turned its back on reality: 'Modern art is philosophy in the medium that up to then has been treated as transparently as consciousness is supposed to have been in traditional theories of mind'[8]. To Danto, Warhol's *Brillo Boxes* are the turning point in art: they no longer refer to 'real' things, but raise the question about their artificiality. This bending back of the work of art towards itself, this self-reflection is also a sign of the end of art. According to him Warhol's *Brillo Boxes* show an aesthetic self-reflectiveness. Ordinary utensils placed in an aesthetic context immediately raise the question about their artificial status, causing art and a statement on its essence to coincide. Danto does not agree with Lyotard's thesis of postmodernism. He thinks that postmodernism 'as the celebration of openness' eventually becomes posthistorical 'in its explication'.[9]

His thesis on the end of art actually concerns the end of a particular conception of art, notably the Modernist conception. The distinction between 'to stop' and 'to come to an end' is instructive if we wish to grasp this at all. In the latter case it is a matter of attaining a goal according to a logic characteristic of, in this case, art. History has come to itself, and thus to an end: nothing new is to be expected anymore. The benefit art has profited by is an infinite pluralism and a relativism inherent in it. With Danto too, art has realised its ideal place by means of a logic internal to its own history: 'a given movement of art must be understood in terms of a certain historical necessity . . . '[10]

There is a lot to be said against this position and particularly against the Hegelianism attached to it. Danto's thesis loses strength, notably because of his consideration that in the development of art a necessary logic developed, ending up in Warhol's work, and turning Neo-Expressionism into a regressive gesture. Not least because in fact it is an externally legitimising story again, applied to concrete art practices. Or to paraphrase Lyotard: behind Danto's statement on the end of art lies another Great Narrative, namely Hegel's. It is not without reason that Danto himself points out that it is better to refer to the end of art history than to the end of art.

Paul Crowther criticises Danto's thesis of a necessary, internal logic. He indicates similarities between what is usually seen as two competing tendencies within modern art: on the one hand the complexity of fauvism, futurism, expressionism and surrealism; and on the other hand that which has been composed of suprematism, neo-plasticism and abstract-expressionism. The apparent contradiction disappears as soon as we realise 'that the art work receives its ultimate authentification as a vehicle for expression of *feeling*'[11]. Both tendencies derive their legitimation from 'some kind of elevating expressive effect embodied in its creation and reception'.

Crowther calls this point of view 'the "legitimising discourse" of art'. Alluding to Danto's Hegelianism he comments:

> If, therefore, we are to talk of a 'logic' of modernity in the visual arts at all, it can only be in the loose sense of a *radical transformation of the existing legitimising discourse of art*. This, however, should not be seen as a logic of 'necessary' progression; neither must it be viewed as a matter wholly internal to art itself. [12]

Socio-cultural factors also play a part in this. Wholly in line with Lyotard's thesis, according to Crowther, Warhol's *Brillo Boxes* do not so much herald the end of art, but rather 'the transitional point at which modernity begins to pass into postmodernity'[13].

A continuity is therefore definitely to be perceived between Warhol's *Brillo Boxes* – and in line with this, minimalism and conceptualism – and, for instance, the work of Anselm Kiefer and Malcolm Morley, which to Danto are merely moments of pluralism:

> The difference between the two stages consists in the fact that whereas the late Modernists question the logical scope of art and take it to and beyond its limits, the Critical Postmodernists question the social reality of art (ie the status of the legitimising discourse) from within [14].

From these different options it may be evident that the hypo-critical question about the ideal place from a postmodern perspective is not so simple to answer positively. It is an utterly precarious matter to say anything at all about art as such without falling into the wide open trap of the Great Narrators. For that reason I prefer to explore the question about the ideal place on a more limited scale, without abandoning Danto's views completely. Danto's stress on self-consciousness and conceptualising, once they have been stripped of their universalist overtones, seems to be an essential contribution to a new interpretation. His final consideration merits reflection: 'Philosophy too comes to an end, but unlike art it really must stop when it reaches its end, for there is nothing for it to do when it has fulfilled its task'[15]. His philosophical eclipsing of art, however, is something I want to avoid by maintaining this very field of tension between philosophy and art, between conceptuality and representation. In my opinion it is this field of tension with its inconclusiveness that seems qualified for a radically different interpretation of the notion of the ideal place.

Rethinking Kant: Philosophy as Art or Artificial Philosophy?

In order to clarify this I had better first concentrate on this rather carelessly used term 'Postmodern', which obviously is *the* stumbling block. For this purpose I agree with Lyotard's self-criticism of the term 'postmodern', introduced by him in *The Postmodern Condition*. In spite of all appearances, in later texts he states that 'postmodern' is not an epochal but a reflective quality. It does not refer to a period after modernity, but to a hyper-critical, or in Baudrillard's terminology, hypo-critical consciousness of modernity itself.

According to Lyotard, the postmodern is a modus of the modern. However, it is only as a consequence of the fundamentally different socio-economic and political conditions after the Second World War that this vision could come to light, since it was not until 'after Auschwitz'[16] that it became clear that the pretensions of Enlightenment had been belied by their own history. From that moment the realisation of the inadequacy of critical rationality and the uncontrollable technology resulting from it are personally experienced.

Subsequently, Lyotard tried to rethink and rewrite modernity. From his implicit criticism of Hegel, this is done by resuming the Kantian tension between thought and the world of 'Dinge-an-sich' – a subject-object tension which Hegel thought he could solve by the notion of the 'Geist' expounded in history. A rethinking of the problem of the sublime as it is worked out by Kant in his *Kritik der Urteilskraft*, plays a central part in this. I will not pursue Lyotard's position and thoughts any further here, but while adopting his initial idea I will now seize upon the range of thought of Gilles Deleuze, developed in cooperation with Félix Guattari in the course of 25 years, so as to sketch a different relation between philosophy and art in general and between conceptuality, perceptivity and affectivity in particular.[17] Through this account I will interpret the relation between the ideal place and art in a hypo-critical way.

a) Idea: Problemised Conceptuality
In Kant's philosophy, as I already indicated at the beginning of this article, three faculties of the human mind are mutually linked. According to the Kantian outline these are knowing, wanting and feeling, to each of which a critical analysis is devoted.[18] The concept playing such a central part in modern consciousness philosophy after Kant is thus, by way of the affect, connected with the perception characteristic of art. The question in line with the question about the ideal place in art will then be: what is the effect of a combination of concept and representation on individuals? And, as is still claimed among the avant-garde, does this have a community-establishing character or does it just concern a purely individual occurrence here?

In the range of thought of Gilles Deleuze and Félix Guattari, the interaction between concept, percept and affect or emotion are central issues. With Deleuze the concept has already been related to the core of the notion of 'ideal', ie 'the Idea' at an early stage. His criticism of Hegel initiated in his prominent book on Nietzsche of 1962, is concisely conveyed in his dissertation *Difference & Repetition* of 1968: 'dramatise the Ideas'. For this purpose the *experience* of a work of art is stressed: 'The work of art leaves the domain of representation in order to become "experience", transcendental empiricism or science of the sensible'. Deleuze draws attention to a conception of aesthetics which does not start from what can be represented through the senses, but from 'the very being *of* the sensible'.[19]

Deleuze makes a strict distinction between concepts and ideas. In a Kantian manner he believes that the movement of concepts – conceptual or discursive thought – is set and kept moving by the Idea, which is not exhausted in concepts. The difference inherent to things, as that which cannot be grasped by conceptual thought

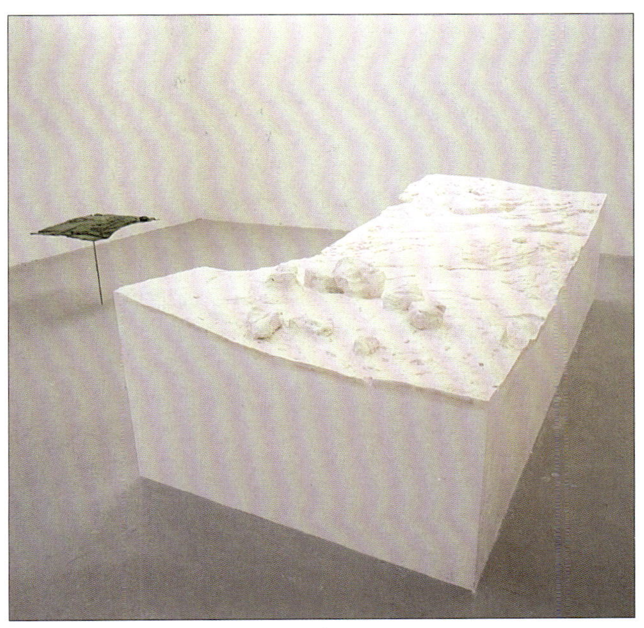

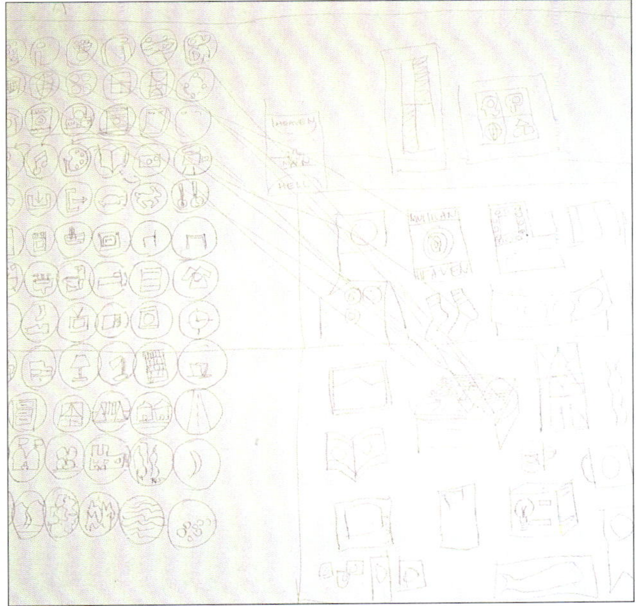

HCAK 1993-94. FROM ABOVE: Marcel Zalme; Matt Mullican

because this is by definition identifying and totalising, has its effect in the Idea: 'the difference is internal to the Idea; it unfolds as pure movement, creative of a dynamic space and time which corresponds to the Idea'[20]. Put differently: 'Difference is here internal to an Idea, even though it is external to the concept which represents an object'[21]. Formulated somewhat more strictly, 'Idea' is the movable core of the concept, in which a non-conceptual differentiation, staying out of vision like a blind spot, resounds. While with Plato, the Idea in Deleuzian terms is still a philosophical concept on account of its transcendental quality, with Kant the concepts are 'problemised' in the Ideas: 'Kant even refers to Ideas as problems "to which there is no solution"'[22]. The core of the Ideas is their problemised and problemising character: 'The "problematic" is a state of the world, a dimension of the system, and even its horizon, its home: it designates precisely the objectivity of the Idea, the reality of the virtual'[23].

If the core of the 'ideal' is this idea and the objectivity of the idea a tension never to be resolved, the reflection of which is rather the field of art than of philosophy, a new interpretation of the relation between the ideal place and art is beginning to take shape here. In philosophy the idea already transcends the conceptual, but once it had been exposed to its own irreality by history, the conceptual descended into the body, into a sensory and affective realm causing its quality to change fundamentally. Deleuze endorses the urge of conceptuality to grasp the absolute in an Idea. 'Die Anspruch der Vernunft auf Totalität', conceptualising aiming at coherence 'wants' to encompass or totalise an infinite fragmentation, started as a result of the power of imagination in the Idea – 'elle a bien un maximum de *compréhension* simultanée', states Deleuze in his book on Kant[24]. But at the same time there is the realisation that this comprehension is a transcendental illusion, a regulative fiction.

b) Paradoxical Conceptuality: The Art of Thinking
What Deleuze eventually advocates is a transformation of the activity of thinking itself. Although philosophy is forced to make use of concepts, these need no longer be regarded as purely identifying, encompassing totalities, as was the case in modern consciousness philosophy. Through reformulation of the concept on the basis of the Idea, Deleuze can gear thought to a task that can never be accomplished: thought of the difference which is characteristic of things. What 'precedes' thought is itself inconceivable. This 'foundation', which gives thought its coherence and in that sense is community-establishing, is of a non-conceptual nature. More than 'a concept that is or can be thought' – as it is defined in the book that due to Guattari's death in 1993 had to be the unwished-for conclusion of a long and intensive cooperation – the (abysmal) foundation of thought is 'the image of thought, the image thought gives itself of what it means to think, to make use of thought, to find one's bearings in thought (s'orienter dans la penser)'[25]. With the term 'image', a perceptual dimension lying 'in', 'behind' or 'underneath' thought – depending on topographical imagination – opens up. These images of thought are a kind of 'metaphors of abyss' which in their cultural-historical definition guarantee the coherence between the concepts.

More and more terms, derived from art practices, are being grafted onto this new interpretation of conceptuality. For instance, an interaction between philosophy and art is indirectly alluded to: on the one hand an aesthetic dimension is arising in thought, on the other hand works of art are becoming more conceptual. This development seems to be in line with the developments in avant-garde art: 'Abstract art and conceptual art are two recent attempts to bring art and philosophy together'[26]. Deleuze and Guattari see thought as activity increasingly as an artistic matter. Philosophy is no longer contemplation, as it was for Plato. Nor is it reflection in the Kantian sense. However, they do not agree with the point of view of Jürgen Habermas either, for whom philosophy pre-eminently is intersubjective communication. Philosophising in the Deleuzian sense is first and foremost creation:

La philosophie consiste toujours à inventer des concepts . . . La philosophie n'est pas communicative, pas plus que contemplative ou réflexive: elle est créatrice ou même révolutionnaire, par nature, en tant qu'elle ne cesse de créer de nouveaux concepts.[27]

To put it in a problematic way, after this transformation the concept of 'concept' appears to have become a very much stratified concept. As the concept can never hope to realise the illusion of a totality, it is 'un paradox, forcement'[28].

c) Sensation: Percepts and Affects
Thought becomes 'artificial' in a literal sense. But what is the relation of this conceptuality to art? The idea from *Difference & Repetition* of 'the very being of the sensible' recurs in later writings in the 'sensations' in the most literal sense of the word. Deleuze describes the work of Francis Bacon in this terminology and thinks that in this remarkable oeuvre a 'logic of sensation'[29] is to be perceived. As soon as these sensations are linked with the concept, it also becomes clear what a hypo-critical discussion of the relation between the ideal place and art implies. The concept is widened by adding two other dimensions, notably percept and affect. The work of art turns into an experience that can no longer be explained as representation of reality, nor reduced to the intentions of the artist or the interpretations of the viewer: 'If resemblance haunts the work of art, it is because sensations refer only to its material: it is the percept or affect of the material itself, the smile of oil, the gesture of fired clay, the thrust of metal . . .'[30]. What remains of the work of art as a thing 'is a bloc of sensations, that is to say, a compound of percepts and affects'[31]. Even if the material, which only forms a factual condition, 'lasts for only a few seconds, it will give sensation the power to exist and be preserved in itself in the eternity that coexists with this short duration'.

Nevertheless, Deleuze thinks that art does more than just supply images, causing viewers to be affected by them. If this was so, our conception of these two dimensions would be too psychological:

Percepts are no longer perceptions; they are independent of the state of those who experience them. Affects are no longer feelings or affections; they go beyond the strength of those who undergo them. Sensations, percepts and affects are beings whose validity lies in themselves and exceeds any lived . . . The work of art is a being of sensation and nothing else: it exists in itself.[32]

In the original French text it becomes somewhat clearer what affects are 'des dévenirs', or 'becomings'. Deleuze's early philosophy of differentiations eventually becomes a thinking of happening, of becoming. This 'happening' is unformed by definition – hence the interest in the experience of the sublime, which defies any form whatsoever. It is an expression of the inconceivable differentiation. This implies that the experience of works of art is first and foremost an experience of the Other and of the Difference. To Deleuze this experience implies that in art reception a change in the viewer or listener is possible: 'ceaselessly becoming-other', or 'Sensory becoming is the action by which something or someone is ceaselessly becoming-other . . . ' He believes it is particularly in the way the unruly work fails to correspond to reality and by turning the materiality of the medium into perceptual reality, that the work can effect a shift in the matter-of-courseness of worldly order:

> By means of the material, the aim of art is to wrest the percept from perceptions of objects and the states of a perceiving subject, to wrest the affect from affections as the transition from one state to another: to extract a bloc of sensations, a pure being of sensations. A method is needed, and this varies with every artist and forms part of the work.[33]

It is not Danto's post-historical pluralism resulting from self-reflectiveness, but the paradoxical consciousness of a fundamental differentiation that is characteristic of our time, which is only postmodern insofar as it implies a resumption of modernity and thus also of the notion of 'history'.

If the relation between philosophy and art makes anything clear at all, it is the impossibility of distinguishing between these three dimensions of experience and maintaining a rigid separation between philosophy and art. For according to Deleuze, art does not think less than philosophy, 'but it thinks through affects and percepts'[34]. This radical reformulation of the consciousness philosophy initiated by Kant and Hegel and of the constitutive opposition of concept and perception within the Great Narratives also implies that 'in any case, and in all of these states, painting is thought: vision is through thought, and the eye thinks, even more than it listens'[35].

From Utopian No-Where to an Utopian Now-Here [36]

Let us return to our original question. In the first place, we may conclude that an interesting shift is to be perceived with respect to both the Modernist vision and Danto's analysis. The ideal place or Utopia has lost its historical quality – and in this I agree with Danto – we have gone beyond art(history). But since it has not become clear from his account what distinguishes one work of art from another and – something that continues to ring through behind the question about the ideal place – where the 'political' impact of a work is to be traced, another, let us call it political, criterion is required. For Danto's pluralism continues to be 'value'less. Besides, we may suspect him of still having a very modern vision of philosophy and conceptuality. Through his still highly metaphysical definition of thought, he continues to be bound to a modern vision of art, even more so as soon as he puts forward self-consciousness and conceptuality as constitutive elements of current art expressions.

With his reformulation of both conceptual philosophising and the experience of the work of art, Deleuze offers an alternative. His insight into the elusiveness of happening, determined by differences, is a point of view from which art and the ideal place can be related in another way. This concerns a post-historical articulation of place. It can no longer be an attainable land of no-where at the end of the horizon. But what it can be is an immediate now-here in which art happens. That is why this is not so much a matter of an ideal place, but rather of an ideal shift from conceptual to perceptual perspectives. The 'political' impact will then lie in the fact that viewers become and continue to be sensitive to the strange and non-reducible difference.

What this means in a panic-stricken world relapsing into xenophobic instincts in order to survive as a community, is not hard to guess. In my opinion it is inevitable that this experience is first of all personal, due to the necessity of consciousness to distinguish itself from others in its critical detachment. Nevertheless, it is not wholly inconceivable that this experience may reinforce public spirit.

Thus avant-garde political resistance has been literally transformed into a postmodern resistance: by means of a minimal shift the public is shown the non-reducible strangeness of things again and again. Given the entertainment culture of art and judging by art tourism, this resistance must obviously be entertaining as well. In Deleuzian terms, creating the subversive aspect of current art expressions may come to light, 'because to create is to resist'[37]. Whether we call this work post-, neo- or trans-avant-garde is insignificant. What is more important is that in art the struggle against power still exists. But now it has become force of habit, it being the power of the matter-of-courseness with which we still objectify the world with modern eyes and manipulate objects with modern hands. It is only in this way that art, just as philosophy, can still be critical. Nevertheless, any philosopher and artist realises – and here lies his hypocrisy both from a psychological and a methodical point of view – that his or her 'subversive' counterproposal also implies a seizure of power.

The post-historical aspect presents itself quite differently: in an undermining of any historicity, ie a resistance against any historicising. According to Deleuze, art and philosophy have 'resistance in common – their resistance to death, to servitude, to the intolerable, to shame, *and to the present*'[38]. This resistance against the Present as a transitional stage between Past and Future, a resistance against the moment and against happening can be heard, what may also be heard is a call for the inestimable value of the here and now as an atopic now-here: 'it is the now of our becoming'[39].

Possibly this is a devious return to the auratic moment of which Benjamin thought that it had dissolved in reproducibility: 'Even the most perfect reproduction lacks one thing: the here and now of the work of art – its unique existence in the place where it is found'[40]. This auratic moment, according to Benjamin, presents itself as 'a once-only manifestation of a distance, however near it may be'[41]. Possibly this is the depth never to be attained, causing the experience of out-of-place works of art to remain abysmal on principle.

Notes

1 Renato Poggioli, *The Theory of Avant-Garde*, Cambridge/London, 1968, p10.

2 Walter Benjamin, *Het Kunstwerk in het tijdperk van zijn technische reproduceerbaarheid*, Nijmegen, 1985 (1973), p42.

3 Thus the last question about the ideal place of the artist results in an iconoclasm kept under control by paintings such as Velasquez's *The Ladies-in-Waiting*, Goya's *Family of Charles IV*, Courbet's *Interior of my Studio*, Picasso's *A Portrait of a Painter, After El Greco*, Bernard Buffet's *Self-portrait* and Richard Schaffer's *Room with Figure*.

4 See Wolfgang Welsch, 'Astherisierung – Schreckenbild oder Chance', *Kunstforum International*, Vol 123, 1993, pp228-235.

5 The thinkers referred to largely derive their inspiration from Nietzsche. For an analysis of his work on the basis of this thought see Henk Oosterling, 'Philosophie als Kunst? Kunst als Poros, Aporie als Kunstgriff', *Die Kunst der Sprache und die Sprache der Kunst*, Roland Duhamel, Erik Oger (eds), Würzburg, 1994, pp55-83.

6 Jean Baudrillard, *La Transparance du Mal. Essai sur les phénomènes extrêmes,* Paris, 1990, p24.

7 Arthur C Danto, *The Philosophical Disenfranchisement of Art*, New York, 1986, p209.

8 *Idem*, p206.

9 *Idem*, p210.

10 Arthur C Danto, *The State of Art*, New York, 1987, p208.

11 Paul Crowther, *Critical Aesthetics and Postmodernism*, Oxford, 1993, p185.

12 *Idem*, p186.

13 *Idem*, p187.

14 *Idem*, p195.

15 *The State of Art, op cit*, p218.

16 This Adornian theme is worked out by Lyotard in a strictly methodical way in *The Differend* (1983). In other writings, such as *Heidegger et 'les juifs'* (1988) this inconceivable event is further elaborated from a political-philosophical point of view.

17 For a more detailed account of Lyotard's thesis see Henk Oosterling 'Het "denken" van de materie. Aporetisch schrijven en esthetiek', *Lyotard lezen*, R Brons & H Kunneman (eds), Meppel, 1995.

18 Kant works out their conditions of possibility in his three criticisms, *Kritik der reinen Vernunft, Kritik der praktischen Vernunft* and *Kritik der Urteilskraft*. The transcendental foundation of truth, goodness and beauty, respectively, is worked out here. In the last criticism, in which an attempt is made at effecting a bridge between knowing and wanting, between science and morality, the focus is on rational art criticism, ie the criterion of taste.

19 Gilles Deleuze, *Difference and Repetition*, London, 1994 (1968), p56/7.

20 *Idem*, p24.

21 *Idem*, p26.

22 *Idem*, p168.

23 *Idem*, p280.

24 Gilles Deleuze, *La philosophie critique de Kant*, Paris, 1963, p73.

25 Gilles Deleuze and Félix Guattari, *What is Philosophy?* London/New York, 1994 (1991), p37. The last phrase once again suggests the analogy with Kant's position. See I Kant, "Was heisst: sich im Denken orientieren?" in *Schriften zur Metaphysik und Logik I*, Werkausgabe Band V, Suhrkamp, Frankfurt a/M, 1977, pp267-283. Whereas Kant was gradually liberating himself from the sensory definition of thought, Deleuze/Guattari show the affective and perceptive integration of thought.

26 *Idem*, p198.

27 Gilles Deleuze, *Pourparler*, Paris, 1990, p186.

28 *Idem*, p187.

29 *Francis Bacon, Logique de la sensation*, Paris, 1981.

30 *What is Philosophy, op cit*, p166.

31 *Idem*, p164.

32 *Idem*, p164.

33 *Idem*, p167.

34 *Idem*, p66.

35 *Idem*, p195.

36 As Samuel Butler, Deleuze and Guattari show, by means of what seems to be just a pun, how attention can be drawn to a hidden aspect in our nihilism from no-where to now-here. (*What is Philosophy*, p100).

37 *Idem*, p110.

38 *Idem*, p110.

39 *Idem*, p112.

40 Benjamin, op cit, pp11-12.

41 *Idem*, p15. If Benjamin's observation that 'human sensory observation changes along with the entire way of life of human collectives' (14) expresses a keen insight, this may well mean that a new reflectiveness has emerged in artistic consciousness, which can no longer be ignored. And if the question about the ideal place means that, being situated in space, we have always observed this ideal, this necessarily implies a different sensory experience of this space.

AFTER OMEGA

David Elliott

Ten years ago any symmetry with a semblance of order – dialectical materialism, anti-Semitism, Nazism – was sufficient to charm the minds of men. How could one do other than submit to Tlön, to the minute and vast evidence of an orderly planet? It is useless to answer that reality is also orderly. Perhaps it is, but in accordance with divine laws – I translate: inhuman laws – which we never quite grasp. Tlön is surely a labyrinth, but it is a labyrinth devised by men, a labyrinth destined to be deciphered by men.

Jorge Luis Borges, *Tlön, Uqbar, Orbis Tertius*
Buenes Aires, 1940

'In the beginning was the idea.' No, these words are not intended to proclaim a heresy, a provocation aimed at Old Testament scholars or at philosophers who believe that the word *is* the idea. They are, if you like, a form of theology. Words and ideas are indisputably linked, and perhaps we may avoid disagreement by regarding the relationship between them as between fleas and dogs, or mice and churches? They need each other and this need is the agent of change. For you, the word may be hard and inflexible: the Law, but for me it is soft, malleable, full of possibilities.

'In the beginning was the mistake.' Is that the blasphemy with which we can all agree? I will rehearse it here for you: time began with a peal of cosmic laughter (which still echoes) and from that moment the history of the universe has been measured out in banana skins: the creation – stars, planets, life, society, conflict, culture, art. Communication is flawed as there is no alternative to misunderstanding; our taste for it can only be explained by its effectiveness as an antidote to loneliness. On the rare occasions we agree, this is as much a mistake as on the multitude of times we disagree, and just as unpredictable. But, knowing this, and in spite of it, we go ahead in the hope that the joke may be explained, the wheel of fortune may turn or, if all else fails, that our demise might raise a laugh by which we might be remembered. The ointments, or opiates, of religion, ethics or aesthetics are powerless to change events; they just help to pass the time in an inhuman world.

Borges, however, leaves us with some shreds of hope: he had imagined that the country, culture and language of Tlön had been invented by men in the image of a Labyrinth. Because men had devised this metaphor, therefore logically, they could also decipher it. But are not all perceptions of country, culture and history constructed by men or women who pull objects and events like rabbits out of a hat to give a direction of meaning to life which corresponds with the needs of the moment in which they are writing?

Thucydides was one of the first. Writing in the fifth century BC, he described the near contemporary events of the Peloponnesian War, using eye-witness accounts and the incorporation of the views and impressions of others, to present a narrative which would be valuable to instruct future statesmen. History has lessons and the lessons have changed according to circumstance. Tacitus celebrated the expansion of the Roman Empire and the civic virtues it brought with it; Saint Augustine saw history as the progress of mankind redeemed by God. Edward Gibbon, writing towards the close of the 18th century, was convinced that a rational and sceptical view of the past and its religions would vindicate the present by showing where mistakes had been made; his *History of the Decline and Fall of the Roman Empire* (1777-88) isolated the causes of decadence in order, he hoped, to innoculate the future from its virus.

After the Napoleonic Wars, the University of Berlin became the centre of historical studies in Europe; here the cult of the *objective fact*, allied with a belief in God and nation, remodelled the past in the reflection of an emergent Prussia. Wilhelm von Humboldt, Leopold von Ranke and, latterly, Friedrich Meinecke believed that a scientific attitude towards establishing fact provided a method by which natural truths such as economic progress and national self-determination could be uncovered, the selection of the former predetermining the latter. As a method, it seemed to work because it was self-prophesying – born out by events – concerned symbolically not with the past but with the immediate present and the future. Of these, Meinecke alone lived long enough to see the certainties of this system fail when the will to power of a single nation foundered on the rocks of inhumanity, fantasy and individual conscience.

Primed by the Enlightenment and the Industrial Revolution, the transformation of Europe throughout the 19th century was fuelled by the conflation of ideal of nationhood, empire, individual and class with the determinist and scientific ideals of progress. The resulting maelstrom led to many conflicts, some obvious, others less so. The history of the competitive wars and revolutions of the 19th and early 20th centuries needs no repeating here, particularly because concentration on what are essentially ideological and economic conflicts masks the irreconcilable tension which characterises the essence of all modern culture – the inevitable and perpetual struggle between the desire of the individual and the communal will.

The cult of the rights of the individual, expounded by Thomas Paine, Jean-Jacques Rousseau, and Romantic poets, writers and painters who followed the Byronic ideal, amongst others – Bohemians and avant-gardists, who followed – had to coexist in logical and irreconcilable conflict with collective ideals of nation and class. Meanings were articulated and imposed from above, but they also perculated from below. In this laboratory, modern culture was formed. Now, like Baron Frankenstein, history may galvanise these ill-matched parts into one living body to give life to the monster we call Modernity. This is the name of that sullen creature that lives in the heart of Borges' labyrinth.

However, time has passed since Borges wrote about Tlön and new empires have fallen into decline. You may rightfully question whether the monster still exists. The immolation of modernity on the pyre of deconstruction has long been treated as fact and the tenuous phenomenon of post-modernity has been regarded as a new doctrine – as a new, pluralistic, eclectic world order. But has reality changed? Are we not, in fact, really experiencing the entropy – the twilight – of the gods of modernity? The style of the contemporary Valhalla is neo-modernity, mock-modernity. During the 1980s, and maybe to the present, the sentimental strains of such Wagnerian muzak have played on while the glowing range of products laid out in the supermarkets of mock-modernism have bought forgetfulness of the state stores of the past. But we still desire and consume them in the same way. In the modern Babylon, where all men try to speak the same language but fail, the game may *seem* different but the rules have not changed; today at the site of the historic tower, there is no rubble, walls or other remains (its fabric was carried away by later villagers), simply a vast hole in which the reeds grow.

Another metaphor from history and mythology – the Labyrinth, with its implications of blindness, confusion and danger – seems seductive in the face of what we perceive as political, social and cultural chaos. But, for me, its determining rigidity, its closure, lack of hope – and single exit – fails to convince.

As we slouch towards the millennium we are tempted to think of ends rather than beginnings and to sink into the warm bath of neo-pathetic sentiment. The death of ideology (with the transient sadness of other *petits morts*) has enabled us to imagine a perspective which has a longer view and to see that between the individual and the collective, in whatever form they may appear, there can be no Hegelian synthesis, no easy fix. Such a dialectical view of history and culture has passed its sell-by date. The rouged corpses of East and West have finally rotted and the mental and physical restraints upon which they depended for their survival are in terminal disarray.

In the West, ideas of progress, tacitly inscribed within the cultural institution of the avant-garde, perished over 20 years ago. At the same time, their deviant brothers in the East – revisions of Stalinist orthodoxy – also ran out of ideological conviction. Both were the offspring of modernity yet, as in all families, there was rivalry and conflict. The plot reads like a TV serial: in the West originality and individual genius predominated, while in the East it was the tyranny of the collective. The pathetic metaphor of soap opera – post-modernist here before its time – hightlights the discrepancy between what artists actually thought and did and how they were perceived and written about. The stereotype of the modernist artist – alienated from the mass – became the apotheosis of individualism, both creative and destructive. In the established histories of modern (Western) art, each -ism supersedes its predecessor in the headlong rush to restructure reality in its own form. Sometimes members of the avant-garde enlisted the political ideologies of right and left to add conviction to their plans.

In those parts of the world where the nirvana of the dictatorships of the proletariat was at hand, the concept of an avant-garde was obsolete. All policy was formulated by the Communist Party, alienation was tantamount to subversion and the only refuge for artists of independence and integrity could be found in ironical perspectives or political dissidence. Sometimes knowingly, sometimes uncon-sciously, art in the East became a parody of itself. Long before sincerity became outmoded as an artistic strategy in the West, the Chinese boxes of quotations within quotations and of creative misunderstandings gave the Eastern bloc artist space in which to live, breathe and work.

What both East and West had in common was the development of an interstitial space between word (law, doctrine, ideology) and image which opened up possibilities for new meanings, new growth. In this *terra incognita* anything was possible; the positivist model of binary opposites could be seen as an illusion because there were no opposites, merely different aspects of the same reality – and space to be explored in between. Progress was dead, to be replaced not by entropy or decline, as Spengler had predicted, but by less ambitious goals of a completely new order.

Liberated from the pessimism which, in a binary system, institutional optimism requires as its nourishment, there may no longer be the need to seem either naive or jaundiced. History, whether we may have regarded it in the past as a glorification of nation, race or progress or as irredeemable proof of absurd or inhuman laws, has had to move on. The disposal of power remains important but, in a world in which an industrial accident in the Ukraine may irradiate the reindeer in Lapland and the sheep in Wales for years to come, the devotion to a limited ideal of progress at all costs seems foolhardy if not suicidal.

If a model of history or culture was to be described in terms of painting, the *grandes machines* of the Academies or hard edge grids and solid masses of a geometric avant-garde would be replaced by skeins of chaotic networks linking dynamic, scattered nuclei of different sizes spread randomly across the picture surface. And where, you may ask, would be the order of logic in this new kind of non-systemic, fuzzy system – an open inversion of Borges' Labyrinth? The answer is the one Borges himself gave at the beginning of this essay: it is there if you think it may be *and* if you are willing to decipher its patterns.

Others may succumb to the allure of the apocalypse, I will not. Doomsday is possible but not inevitable. In a world in which nuclear and chemical pollution, global warming, AIDS and other epidemics run out of control against a background of division and exploitation between rich and poor, north and south, waged and unemployed, housed and homeless, no culture can remain insular. Our individual survival lies in the confrontation of these uncomfortable facts. This is not ostensibly a statement of morality or ethics, merely of self-interest.

There is an undeniable feeling that we have run through the alphabet, that something is at an end. After Omega, do we – like actors in a Beckett play – start again to repeat an inevitable pattern, or is there the possibility of growth, change and greater complexity? Artists see life more clearly than most and, at the edges of the histories by which they have been badly served, have given form to many different kinds of paradise and nightmare. To dream alone, however, is dangerous; the strength of art lies in that it has become a field of action in its own right. Even though the self-destructive agendas of the now defunct, avant-gardes tried to erode the distinctions between art and life, the result was not the long-awaited death of art but its continuation as a *metaphor for life*, with its survival inextricably related to our own. This is the symbolic ground that art and culture now occupy – its practice, its ethics, its aesthetics, its history and its future – all may provide an armature for survival. I can think of no more ambitious aim.

Real heroes often fail to look heroic, and art is not life. But reality and its symbols are related. Outside the Labyrinth, the quality of this relationship is crucial. It not only gives texture and meaning to the patterns of chaos which we must come to respect and trust but also, at best, may be the beginning of a new series of relationships. It is my hope that out of this so far unexploited source of energy, new feelings, ideas, images and languages may appear, creating the space in which the relationships we call art may continue to develop.

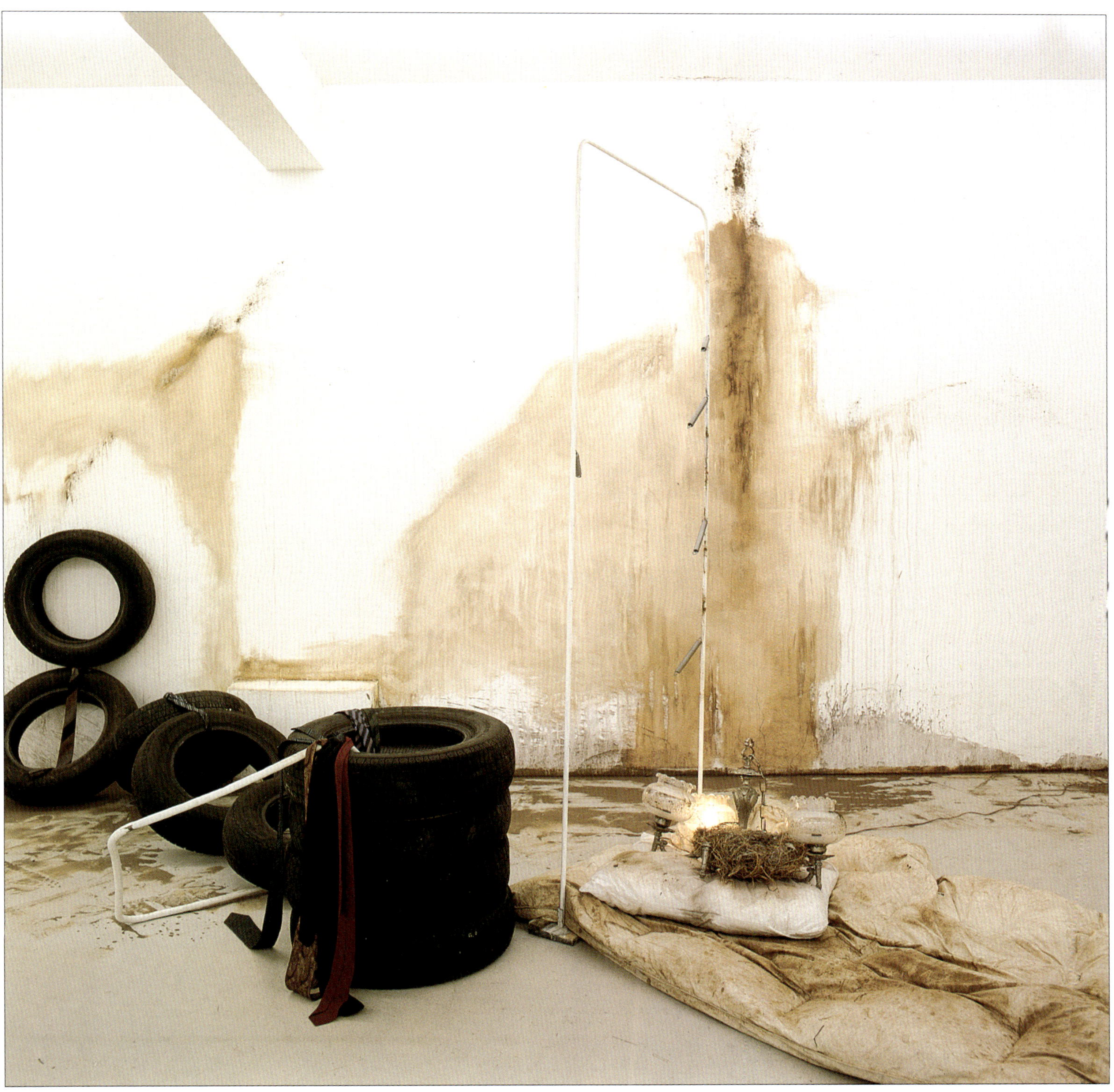

HCAK 1993-94, Ricardo Brey

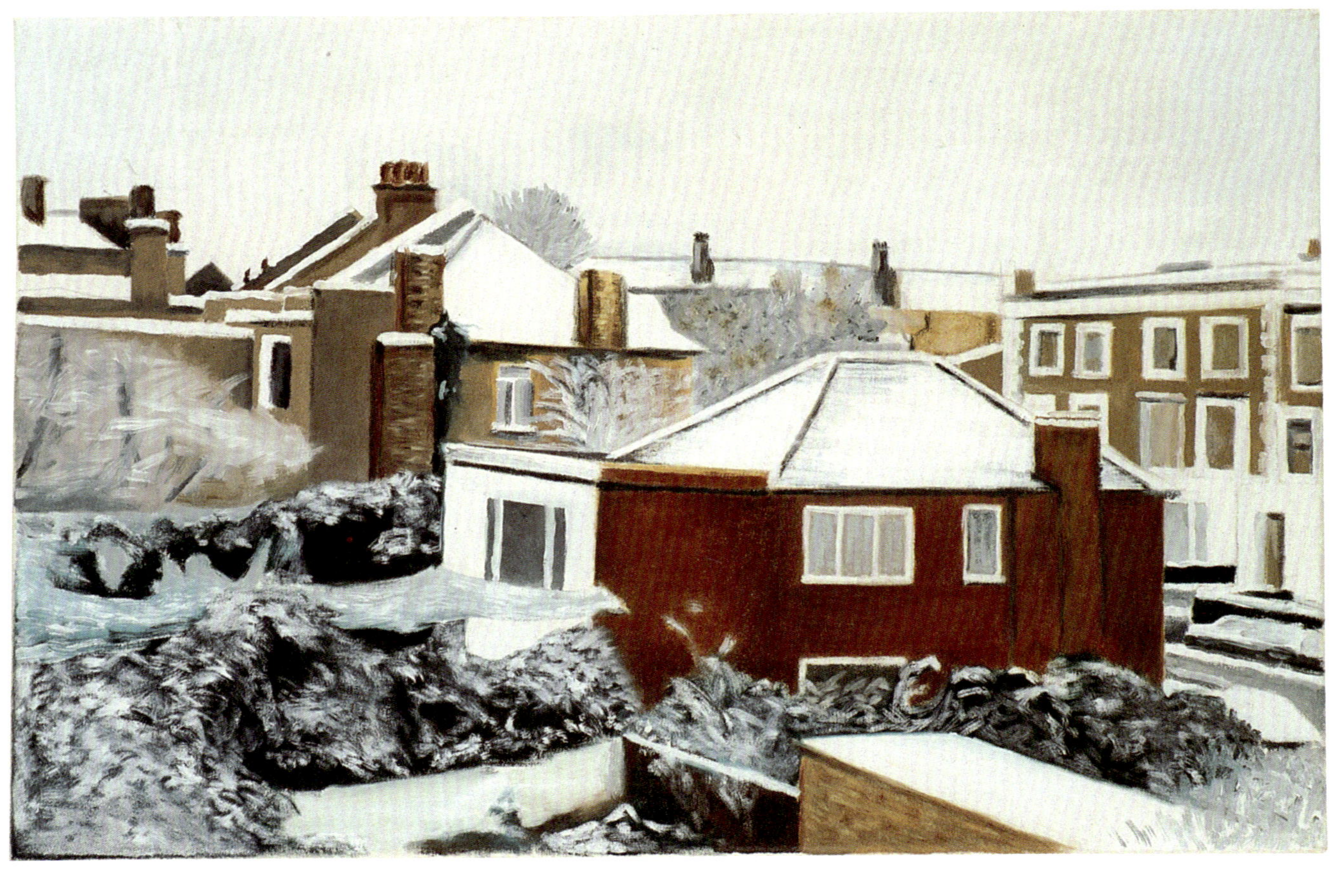

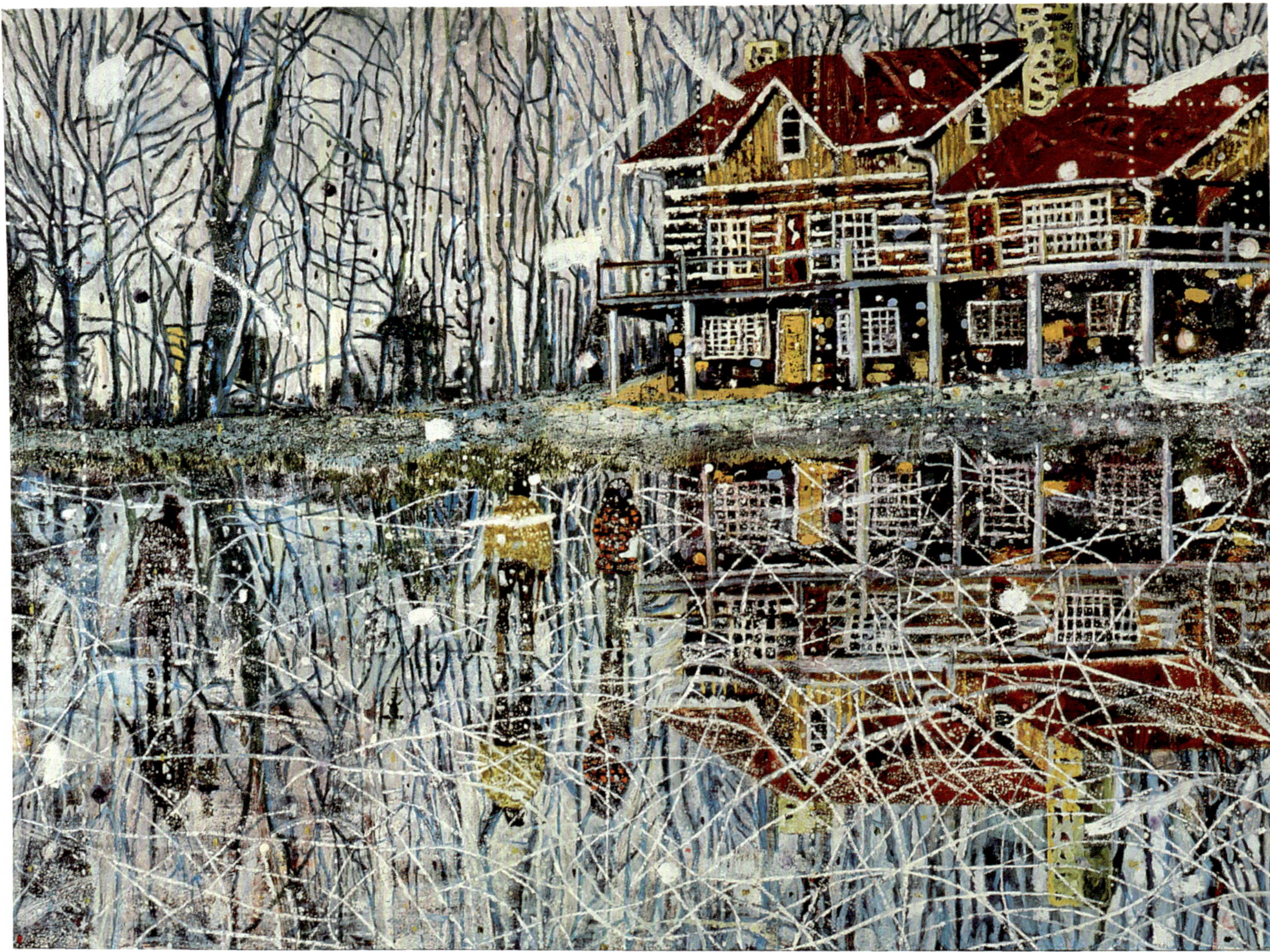

FROM ABOVE: Clair Joy, London (Snow), *1994, oil on canvas, 41 x 61cm; Peter Doig*, Pond Life, *1993, oil on canvas, 185 x 240cm*

MAKING THE VIEWER PRESENT[1]

Andrew Wilson

The sublime is not something to be pictured, nor is it a means towards a description of something. It informs a strategy of becoming which is situated more or less within the conceptual domain as an idea of making meaning, where perception reaches out beyond just a sensing of the limits of an object. If Edmund Burke, in his writing on the sublime, was hampered by an unstated but clear relationship between determining both qualities of reception (affect) and a corresponding objectifying representation of something as an object (through its deceptive presentation as art), this was a prospect that Immanuel Kant, in his *Critique of Judgement*, largely avoided, stating that the sublime could not be represented and that its reception involved an implicit statement about the nature of the perceiving mind (as opposed to the object being perceived). Art, at base, cannot be a source of pure aesthetic judgement in the same way as nature because it is directed, defined, subject to mediating influences, and artificially created. However, if the problem of making art can be sited on the gap between idea and the realisation of idea as image, questions such as 'how do you represent that which cannot be presented?' or 'how do you frame that which is outside the frame, indeed beyond framing?' direct attention not at external formal appearance but at an internal structuring of language where creation becomes predicated by failure.

In August 1824, John James Audubon, the American artist, visited Niagara with the intention of sketching the Falls. Even though he had visited them before – and so believed that he knew the representational magnitude of his undertaking – he was rendered speechless by the sight that confronted him and, realising his inadequacy, abandoned the project. Later, having returned to the inn where he was staying, he saw on the walls 'several views of the Falls, by which I was so disgusted, that I suddenly came to my better senses. "What!" thought I, "have I come here to mimic nature in her grandest enterprise, and add *my* caricature of one of the wonders of the world to those which I here see? No; I give up the vain attempt. I shall look on these mighty cataracts and imprint them where they alone can be represented – on my mind!"'.[2]

This sorry tale of a thwarted ambition to represent the magnificent enormity of nature in two dimensions serves to highlight the fact that Audubon realised that he was trying to present and actualise in paint the idea of something; a struggle to make and communicate meaning. Confronted by the Falls, Audubon was reduced to a feeling of inadequacy and uncertainty, realising that he was not trying to paint something but reveal the idea of something, an intention that he found he was incapable of pursuing.

In front of Niagara Falls, Audubon was faced with the task of making sense. He had to make meaning and the only way that he could was by a recognition of a failure in the figuring of that meaning. In this way the transformative act of representation collapses into an issue of unattainability. It follows that if the sublime is described as 'an object [of nature], the representation of which determines the mind to think of the unattainability of nature as a presentation of [reason's] ideas'[3], then, as it is not something which can be pictured (and, as Kant would suggest, has little to do with art), its transgressive power over the constructions of meaning illuminates and offers a parallel to one of the determining problems of making art which can be sited on that gap between idea and the realisation of idea as image. Audubon could only succeed in presenting the sublime in his mind, and his attempt to realise that idea as image ended in failure. Thought about in this way, the sublime then returns to an issue of making sense and in the failure to make sense communicable, can be identified as a cognitive disturbance within orders of representation. It is this sentiment which is behind Jean-François Lyotard's summing-up of the sublime in a line and a half, where 'an Idea in general has no presentation, and *that is the question of the sublime*'[4].

It is consequently possible to accept a definition of the sublime in terms that see it as, in Thomas Weiskel's words, 'that moment when the relation between the signifier and signified breaks down and is replaced by an indeterminate relation'[5] and so legitimates those discontinuities between sensation and idea as much as between idea and object by which the project of representation ultimately collapses. The sublime, in this sense provides a key to understanding a crisis of represented meaning.

Investigating the issue of unattainability within the workings of the sublime, Jean-François Lyotard suggested that 'the despair of never being able to present something within reality on the scale of the Idea then overrides the joy of being nonetheless called upon to do so. We are more depressed by the abyss that separates heterogeneous genres of discourse than excited by the indication of a possible passage from one to the other'[6]. This abyss defeats framing, and drew Henry Home, Lord Kames, in his 1762 *Elements of Criticism* to contrast the 'sensible pleasure when a work is brought to perfection'[7] with that feeling of uneasiness when something is unfinished or imperfect. In the normal desire to seek out the ends or boundaries of what we perceive, the types of such a textual excess which inform the sublime experience have, of necessity, to be cognitively folded in so that a feeling for closure can be attained. However, the sublime does not so much resist, but is characterised by the very failure to achieve closure.

For Lyotard the idea of the sublime is bound-up with a question of cognitive time and its assertion of a present reality, or place, located by what has been variously translated as the Event, Moment or Occurrence, an irreversible point at which meaning or history is made, and which necessarily has no pretext but which is joined to other events such as history. Furthermore, this is linked in his mind

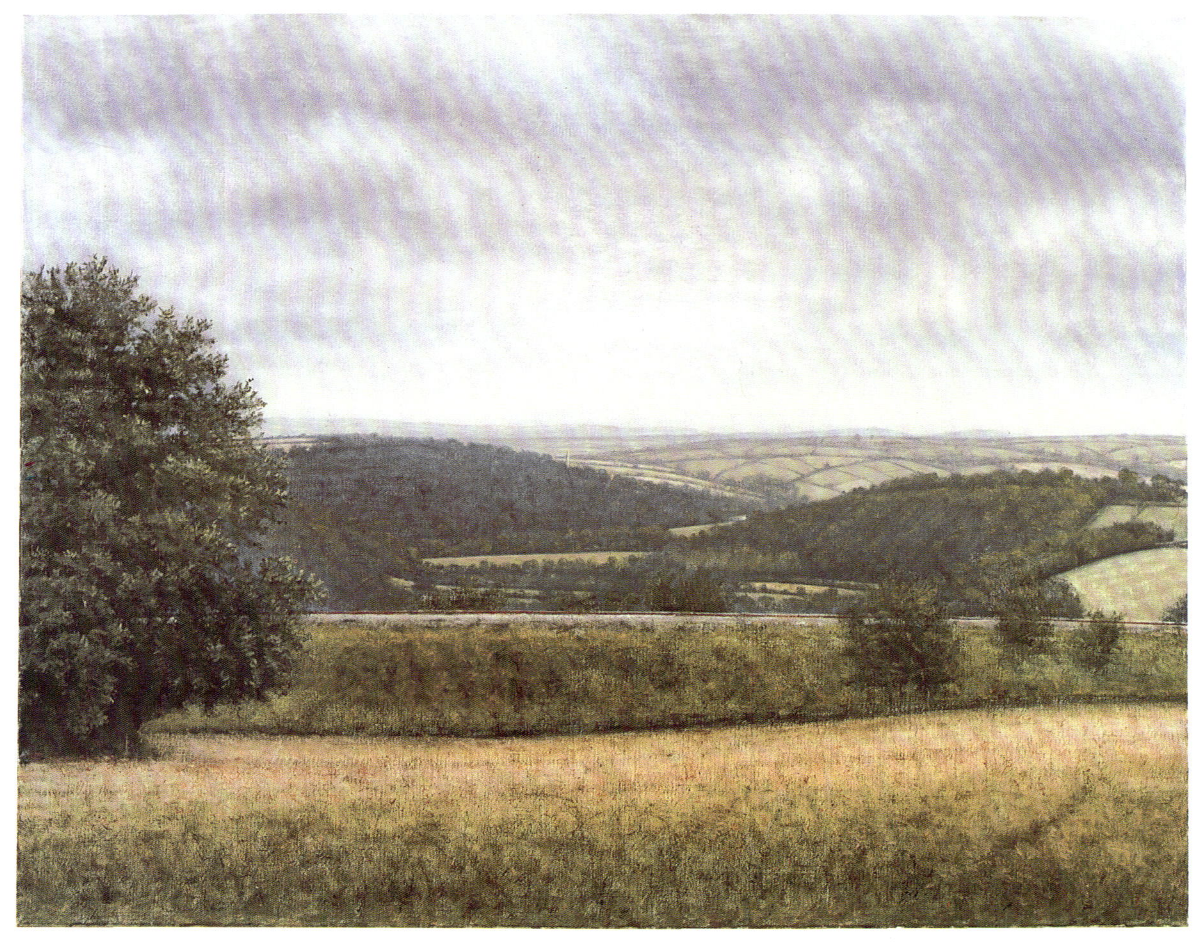

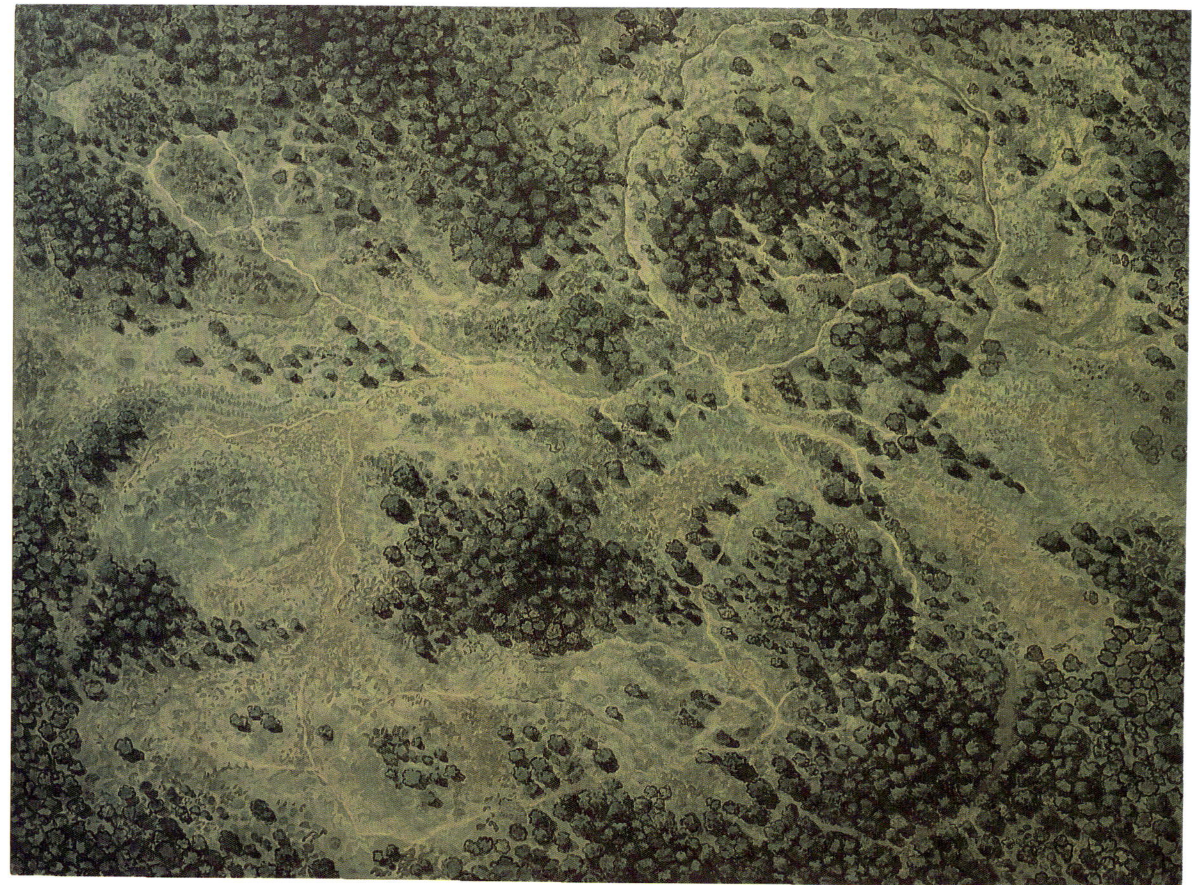

FROM ABOVE: Peter Archer, The Line, 1990-93, 104 x128cm; Peter Duka, Clevischer Rings, 1994, acrylic, alkyd, canvas, wood, 100 x 130cm

with a quality of unpresentability of the idea as a process of derealisation of the object. The context of such an unresolvable tension between the presentable and the unpresentable necessitates analysing works of art, not in terms of style or appearance, but – by putting a priority on idea, on the cognitive event, rather than on image – as an index to creation. In this respect the sublime is tied-down, not to the representation of something, but to a something that happens.

In *Le Différend* Lyotard addresses the problems of linkage that arise between such moments and describes 'a phrase which links and which is to be linked' as being always 'a border zone where genres of discourse enter into conflict over the mode of linking'[8]. It is this conflict that Lyotard recognises as the one figured in Newman's zip; figured as a disturbance within representation in respect of Newman's subject, which Lyotard understands as the realisation of an event and codified in his conclusion to *Le Différend*, such that 'There is not "language" and "Being", but occurrences' which can be phrased in his "Is it happening?"[9]. Lyotard's assessment of the sublime, which has often used Barnett Newman's work as its subject[10], sees it as a description of an event of making meaning which also witnesses the fact of an indeterminacy, where givens are subject to doubt.

In 1949 Newman visited the Indian mounds around Akron in the Ohio countryside. Writing about the effect this had on him, he declared: 'Suddenly one realises that the sensation is not one of space. It has nothing to do with space and its manipulations. The sensation is the sensation of time – and all other multiple feelings vanish like the outside landscape . . . The concern with space bores me. I insist on my experiences of sensations in time – not the *sense* of time but the physical *sensation* of time'[11]. The image in a work of art, such as Newman's, Lyotard tells us, does not refer to an event that is about to happen or that has happened. Similarly, the passage of communication that is conceived in terms of a relationship between transmitter, receiver and referent, is upset. Looking at a painting by Newman, Lyotard suggests that 'the message "speaks" of nothing; it emanates from no one . . . The message (the painting) is the messenger'. There is just the relationship me-you: 'Here I am' – 'I am yours' – 'Be mine'. There is no filter halting the immediacy and instantaneous nature of the event. 'The message is the presentation, but it presents nothing; it is, that is, presence'[12].

Nevertheless, Lyotard's assurance of the unmediated nature of 'presence' is not wholly convincing; a 'this' still has to be made, shown. How can the 'Here I am' be reconciled with an idea of the sublime that cannot be shown or represented? One point of resolution can be found in Lyotard's reaction to Tom Hess' estimation of the subject-matter being concerned with creation and his reference to Newman's statement in *The Plasmic Image*, 'the subject of creation is chaos'[13]. This is rejected by Lyotard because as a beginning, creation does not belong to this world, but begets it. The subject for Lyotard is 'the event which "happens" . . . and once there, takes its place in the network of what has happened'[14]. The event being the 'this' that happens rather than the 'what happens'. By this explanation Lyotard removes Newman from the trap of representation and presents him as articulating the task of showing that there is something that is unpresentable which is not to be found over there but in 'this', as a making of meaning. The event cannot be expressed, presented or represented as it is essentially indeterminate and as a result can only be born witness to as negative representation. Newman, in this way, does not show that there is something as unpresentable, he bears witness to that fact that there is the unpresentable and, in the attempt to show that there is something that is not presentable – in showing the invisibility n the visual – presentation has to suffer as presence.

In Newman's painting the sublime moment opens up as an abyss highlighting a terror of making meaning. His painting broaches a problem of knowledge and language and he is, by his own admission, entering into the chaos of the unknown, an adventure which encourages feelings of both terror and pleasure. When, in his 1946 text, *The Art of the South Seas*, he writes of oceanic and native African sculptures as being constructed as an art of terror that results from a confrontation with endowing nature with meaning, he was also describing his own painting[15]. The search for meaning, the 'this is happening', becomes a question of presence clarified by terror at the inevitable failure to cross the abyss and uncover the hidden object of the search, and also by pleasure at having been called upon to do so. It is not surprising that Newman's sense of place is rooted to a here that cannot actually be delimited or framed except by the event. In a later conversation about that 1949 visit to the Indian mounds around Akron, Newman described 'a sense of place . . . Looking at the site you feel "Here I am", *here* . . . and out beyond there is chaos, nature . . . but here you get a sense of your own presence . . . I became involved with the idea of making the viewer present'[16]. This proposes an idea of painting's existence being perceived as an event of becoming where Lyotard's repeatedly asked question, 'is it happening?'[17] is answered by Newman's '*here*'[18]. Such a state of painting, in which the perceptual distance between it and the beholder is minimised in this way, is not bound-up with questions of process, gesture, or even with apparent translatability of image, but with an occurrence that something is happening.

In his *Peregrinations* Lyotard suggests that he 'would like to call an event the face to face with nothingness'[19], where the event is formed from a crossing of the abyss (notionally of nothingness) to make meaning, framing a process of working – between time and place – where meaning can be found in dead material through the flight of an idea from conception to image; where an attempt is made to reveal a sense of marvellous hiddenness. This artistic motivation to communicate something in the face of an inability to do so leads inevitably to understanding a work as a search for the quality of a thought or idea made tangible, real and concrete despite a sense of creative loss.

The intentions of a Conceptual art can, similarly, be defined in terms of a condition of embodiment through which language might be constructed as object, where the linguistic system of the work is manifested as an embodied presence of making meaning realised as a process of communication. Work by artists such as Robert Barry, Michael Craig-Martin, Victor Burgin, Joseph Kosuth, Art & Language, Sol LeWitt, Lawrence Weiner, Christine Kozlov, Ian Wilson and many others constructs a sense of relationship and boundary in the search to make meaning as the object. Barry, for instance, in 1969, described his concerns as being 'about things that I don't know, about using the unknown . . . Language itself isn't the art. It doesn't even describe or detail the art much. I use the language as a sign . . . to communicate your ideas through language'[20]. What Barry points to here is a disturbance within an attempt to carry out a strategy of realising an idea as image. There is no pretence, no preconception, as language is, as Weiner describes it, 'erratic'[21]. Such a use of language is founded on a notion of indeterminacy and is altogether unprescriptive, it rejects any notion of fixed, imposed or determined meaning. When Weiner defines, he achieves this paradoxically through a lack of definition realised though his recognition of the sense of choice that the viewer should have when confronted by a work ('*Enough Of This Or Enough Of That*'). Weiner recognises the choice the beholder has in making the work's meaning, echoing Lyotard's statement that the beholder, in a situation such as that created by Weiner, can never be secure in their contemplation. The signs that are shown demand more than just idle contemplation, they demand an awareness that the presentable should be surpassed in a search of the unpresentable.

Such work reveals that at the source of an attempt to make meaning is the need to communicate, a need that is essentially and necessarily social in vision, involving both artist and viewer. While the subject of the work might be bound up with systems, structures and means of definition, this is often denied in its immediate figured subject as a result of the very arbitrariness of the subject in the first place. It is this realisation of the arbitrary, the fragmentary, the paradoxical or the discontinuous that allows such a conceptual practice access to an idea of reality or authentic experience by plotting a relationship which is inconclusive, open-ended, and not defined or laid-down.

It is in this approach to a making of meaning that the sublime effect can still be recognised, where the failure 'to present something within reality on the scale of the Idea', is such as to upset order and stress the manner in which Modernity as idea is charged with an abject indeterminacy between the charted and the uncharted, order and disorder. In 1969 Weiner pointed to the heart of this abyss which is figured in his approach to the creative process by the position of a boundary or frame, 'the picture-frame convention was a very real thing. The painting stopped at the edge. When you are dealing with language, there is no edge . . . You are dealing with something completely infinite. Language, because it is the most non-objective thing we have ever developed in this world, never stops'[22]. The determining nature of language is, in Barry's words, an 'unknown' to be found and ratified; to Weiner it is indeterminate, infinite; while Newman encouraged the beholder to go up and be enveloped in his paintings – and in the event of making meaning – so that composition and edge would lose definition.

Such an understanding of language as unknown or infinite points to a state where, because of the failure to create a synthesis of meaning, one arrives at a condition of formlessness. Although this points to Newman's chaos, it also informs work such as Weiner's. With the sublime there can be no judgement of taste, but with the unform, as Lyotard explains, 'it does not mean that the object must be monstrous, only that its form is no longer the point of aesthetic feeling. One result of this is that such a feeling . . . requires the mediation of an Idea of reason . . . The aesthetic of the sublime [is] . . . a progress of the responsibility to the Ideas of reason as they are negatively "presented" in the formlessness of such and such a situation which could occur'[23].

Where there is a loss of definition of form, an unform, there is also a corresponding lack of frame or boundary. Derrida describes that, in as far as the sublime can present anything, it presents itself as 'an indeterminate concept of reason'[24] – what Weiner would term 'erratic' – because of this lack of boundary. So Derrida suggests that 'the sublime is to be found . . . in an "object without form" and the "without-limit" is "represented" in it or on the occasion of it, and yet gives the totality of the without-limit to be *thought*'[25]. The limit can then be registered only at the level of thought as a part of the process of making meaning when the terror of the abyss is confronted. There can be no objected edge or frame to the sublime as its lack of frame, its unbounded infinitude, is part of the process that makes meaning. A form is a limitation, so the without-form is the without-limit, and there can be no presentation without form. The sublime unform, apparent as an event (the 'this happens' rather than the 'that') frames a moment of becoming (as a happening without frame) pointing, as it does, to a constant re-writing as opposed to the defined singularity of the process of creation.

Notes

1 The ideas contained here were first articulated for two lectures I gave to undergraduate and post-graduate Fine Art students in 1994 at Goldsmiths' College, University of London. I am grateful to Lewis Johnson, Chris Want, and Caroline Russell for the opportunity to profit from this valuable discussion. Aspects of these lectures also found their way into a catalogue text written at the invitation of Andrew Cross for the group exhibition *On Painting*, he curated in 1994 at the James Hockey Gallery (West Surrey College of Art & Design, Farnham). As will be apparent, I am indebted to the writings of Jean-François Lyotard on this subject.

2 John James Audubon, 'Niagara' in Maria R. Audubon (ed), *Audubon and Journals with Zoölogical and Other Notes by Elliott Coues*, Dover Publications, New York, 1960 (reprint of first edition published by Charles Scribner's Sons in 1897) Volume 2, pp286-8.

3 This is Thomas Weiskel's own translation from Kant's final 'Remark', see Thomas Weiskel, *The Romantic Sublime: Studies in the Structure and Psychology of Transcendence*, Johns Hopkins University Press, Baltimore, 1976, p22. Immanuel Kant, *Critique of Judgement*, Hackett, Indianapolis, 1987 (translated by Werner S Pluhar) 'General Comment on the Exposition of Aesthetic Reflective Judgements', p127, is translated as 'The sublime can be described thus: it is an object (of nature) the presentation of which determines the mind to think of nature's inability to attain to an exhibition of ideas.'

4 Jean-François Lyotard, 'Complexity and the Sublime' in Lisa Appignanesi (ed), *Postmodernism* (ICA Documents 4 & 5) Free Association Books, London, 1989, p23.

5 Thomas Weiskel, *op cit*, pix.

6 Jean-François Lyotard, *Le Différend, Phrases in Dispute*, Manchester University Press, Manchester, 1988, paragraph 256.

7 Cited in Peter de Bolla, *The Discourse of the Sublime, Readings in History, Aesthetics and the Subject*, Basil Blackwell, Oxford, 1989, p97.

8 Jean-François Lyotard, *Le Différend, op cit*, paragraph 218.

9 *Ibid*, paragraph 263.

10 See especially his texts 'Newman: The Instant' (first published 1985), 'The Sublime and the Avant-Garde' (first published 1984) 'Representation, Presentation, Unpresentable' (first published 1982 as 'Presenting the Unpresentable: The Sublime'), and 'After the Sublime, the State of Aesthetics' which have all been collected in Jean-François Lyotard, *The Inhuman*, Polity Press, Cambridge, 1991, pp78-88, 89-107, 119-128, 135-143 respectively.

11 Barnett Newman, 'Ohio, 1949' collected in *Barnett Newman, Selected Writings and Interviews,* University of California Press, 1992, p175.

12 Jean-François Lyotard, 'Newman: The Instant', *op cit*, p81.

13 Barnett Newman, 'The Plasmic Image' collected in *Barnett Newman, Selected Writings and Interviews, op cit*, p139.

14 Jean-François Lyotard, 'Newman: The Instant', *op cit*, p82.

15 See Barnett Newman, 'Art of the South Seas' collected in *Barnett Newman, Selected Writings and Interviews, op cit*, p100.

16 Conversation with Barnett Newman, cited in Thomas B Hess, *Barnett Newman*, Tate Gallery, London, 1972, pp46-47.

17 Jean-François Lyotard, see 'The Sublime and the Avant-Garde' and 'Newman: The Instant', *op cit*, passim. In the latter essay, *op cit*, p82, Lyotard poses the question in this way: 'For Newman, creation is not an act performed by someone; it is what happens (this) in the midst of the indeterminate. If, then, there is any "subject-matter", it is immediacy. It happens here and now. What [*quid*] happens comes later. The beginning is that there is . . . [*quod*]; the world, what there is.'

18 It is instructive to note that Newman's first three sculptures are entitled *Here I*, 1962; *Here II*, 1965; and *Here III*, 1966. There are also paintings by Newman with the titles *Right Here*, 1954 and *Not There, Here*, 1962.

19 Jean-François Lyotard, *Peregrinations: Law, Form, Event*, Columbia University Press, New York, 1988, p17, see also *ibid*, pp31-32: 'the emptiness, the nothingness in which the universe presented by a phrase is exposed and which explodes at the moment the phrase occurs and then disappears with it. The gap separating one phrase from another is the "condition" of both presentation and occurrences, but such a "condition" remains ungraspable in itself except by a new phrase, which in its turn presupposes the first phrase. This is something like the condition of Being, as t is always escaping determination and arriving both too soon and too late'.

20 From a symposium 'Art Without Space', broadcast on WBAI-FM, New York, November 2, 1969, transcript collected in Lucy Lippard, *Six Years: The Dematerialization of the Art Object*, Studio Vista, London, 1973, p 131.

21 *Ibid*, p132.

22 *Ibid*, pp131-132.

23 Jean-François Lyotard, *Perigrinations, op cit*, p41.

24 Jacques Derrida, *The Truth In Painting*, The University of Chicago Press: Chicago, 1987, p127.

25 *Ibid*.

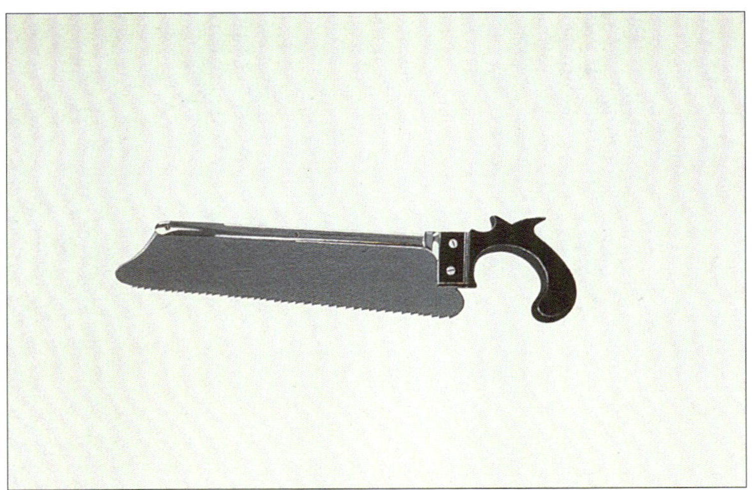

Julie Roberts, Wall Drawing *(detail)*, Wall to Wall Exhibition, Southampton City Art Gallery, 1994

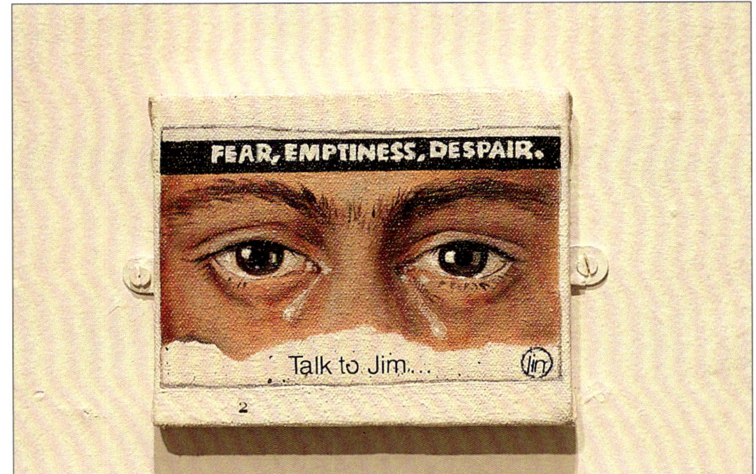

Elizabeth Magill, Talk to Jim, *1994, oil on canvas, 7 x 10cm*

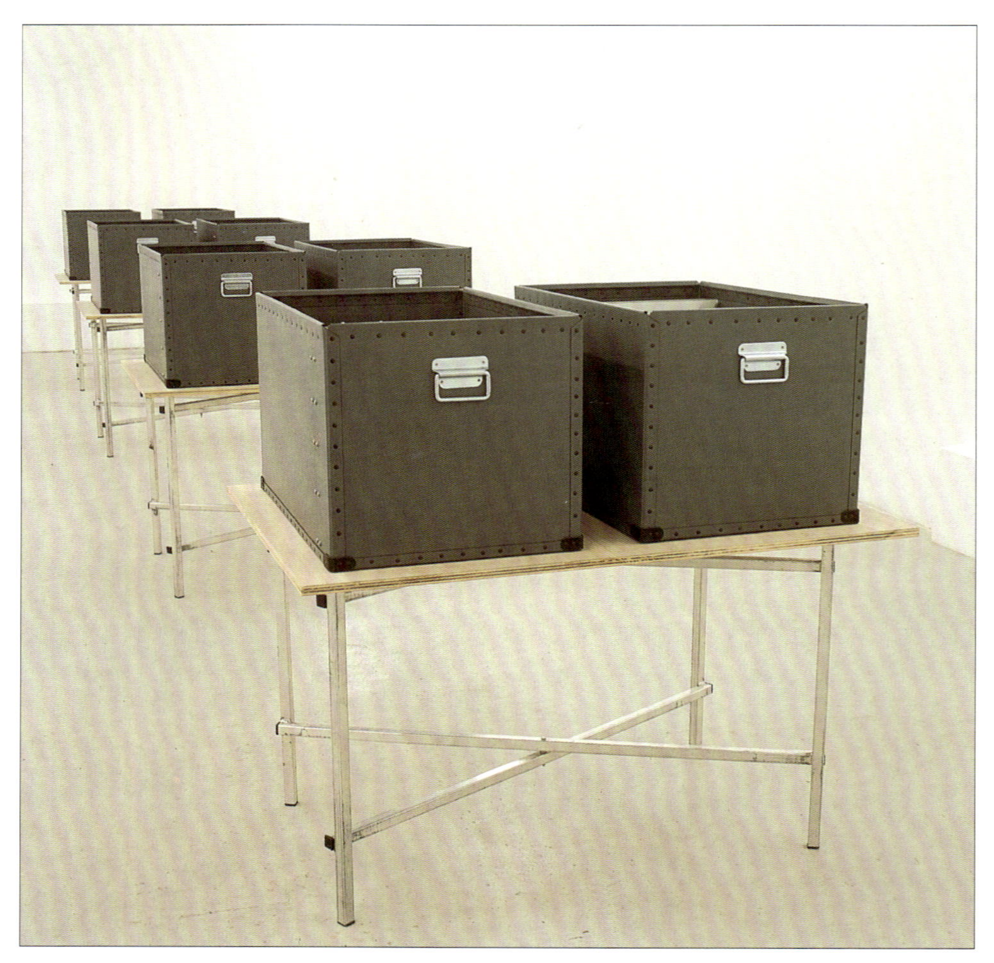

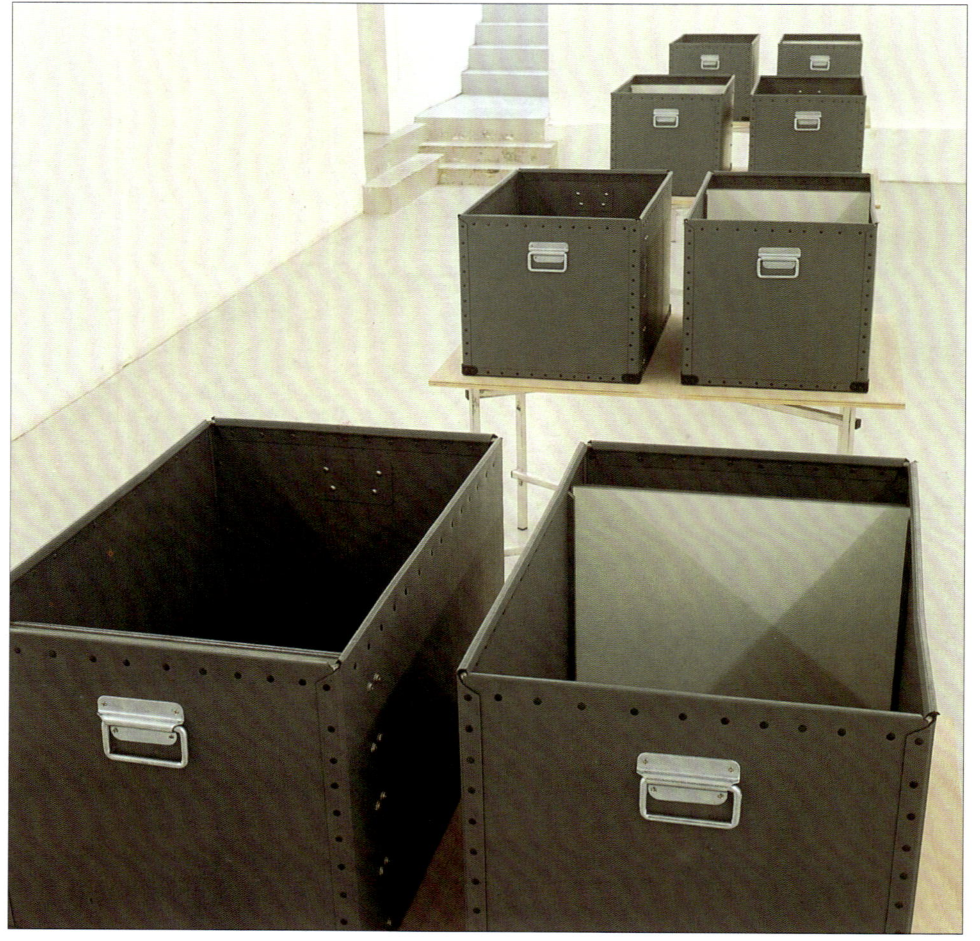

THE IDEAL PLACE: A VANTAGE POINT?
ART & LANGUAGE

In our past work various extremities of various concepts of the site of production and the site of distribution have been thematised – for example, in the Studio paintings and the Museum paintings. It also gave us heart to read in your introductory text some suggestions concerning the possible relations between artist's installations and the curatorial management of art. The artist-manager who is his or her own curator is perhaps exploiting a new place for art where there is no distinction possible between production and distribution. The result is a tyranny of the unproductive. Here there are complex problems. Suffice it to say for the moment that your text 'The Ideal Place: Another Model' gave us encouragement to look even harder at the mechanisms of this dazzling artistic hyperspace.

We also read 'The Ideal Place or The Ideal Place As Destination?' in which you discuss some of the ramifications of 'the ideal', 'ideality', and so on. This has also caused us to reflect upon our response to your project, to its name, to its ethos, etc.

The original memorandum governing the Nobel Prize for Literature requires that it be awarded to literature of an 'ideal' nature. The expression 'ideal' does not quite make sense in this context in English. The best guess is usually that it is something like 'idealistic'. What is clear in practice is that comic writers, and those who stick to 'small' subjects do not get the prize. It is awarded to literature in 'important human themes': no laughing allowed. Indeed, the word 'ideal' is always a little strained in English. 'This is my ideal meal' means 'this is a meal I like very much, the meal of my dreams' – something almost trite. An 'ideal place' is a bit stranger. Certainly it suggests a place that is not 'real' or 'actual' . . . a possible place of words and dreams and attitudes. A model or maquette of 'an ideal place' is, presumably, something which is supposed to suggest what such a place would be like if it existed. The sense of non-actuality of the 'ideal' – the sense of possibility augmented by desire – does not apparently require for ordinary purposes that what is ideal does not exist. What is required, rather, is that it cannot be reached. 'She's my ideal woman' entails that she is somehow out of reach, perhaps to the extent that achieving a liaison with her may be thought of as an unexpected achievement. But the 'She' which designates an actual human being and is the subject of the sentence is not quite what is predicated by the rest of the sentence. A clearer locution might be, 'she somehow seems to fit or match my internal description (or something) of my ideal woman, in respect to the properties p and q'. A claim that x is, in some existentially full blooded sense, my ideal 'friend', 'home', or whatever, is in need of some sort of expansion or explanation, lest it should be thought odd or incomprehensible. (Incidentally, a distinction can easily be made between my 'ideal' destination and my 'actual' one. I was trying to get to London – London was my ideal destination – but I ended up at Birmingham – my actual one. Indeed, the concatenation of 'ideal'

and 'destination' in a sentence of the form 'x is my ideal destination' would almost mean that you are not yet there. A sense that together they constitute a tautology is harder to sustain than to dismiss.)

Very little remains of a sense of the unattainable, or of deferral, when an 'ideal place' is predicated of a purpose. 'It's an ideal place for dancing' or 'playing football' is readily paraphrased as 'it's a very good place for dancing' etc.

There is another slightly different sense of the 'ideal place' which is connected to this one: viz, an 'ideal place' as a vantage point – a place from which to see (something). An extreme attenuation of this ordinary (ie readily paraphrased as 'good') sense is to be found in connection with the viewing of images, paintings and drawings in particular. This sense of 'a place for a purpose' involves (in Wollheim, for example) a high degree of idealisation. The viewer is often 'placed' in thought or imagination at the shoulder of the artist: he or she (the viewer) must view from the 'place' from which the painting was made to be seen. This is a place between the virtuality of the painting or drawing and the real world of the gallery or the studio. It is, of course, a place which is endlessly deferred.

(The name of) your project has enabled us to concentrate on a problem we have faced concerning the status and nature of drawings in relation to the series of paintings, Index: Now They Are, *in which the viewer (including ourselves) encounters an extreme difficulty in finding a 'place' in relation to them. We have constructed 'places' in the form of containers in which images (drawings and textual material) are fixed like the isolated remnants of documents in storage. The 'place' from which they are viewed is far from obviously 'ideal', being acutely angled in relation to the top edge of the graphic and textual material viewed. These materials are in (their) place, a place that might be 'ideal' only for them. The necessarily already deferred 'ideal place' or 'point of view' is displaced to purposes which do not reflect those of the viewer. What is also not entirely clear is whether such a place-ing reflects the purposes of the artists. Is this how these images were made to be seen?*

Michael Baldwin & Mel Ramsden

The following text consists of unauthorised excerpts from a public discussion at HCAK in which Art & Language took part. Although Michael Baldwin and Mel Ramsden, as well as Charles Harrison, are talking here, I have chosen to regard them as representing Art & Language so it is not clear from the text who is saying what. In one sole instance an intervention by another party (Robin Winters) has found its way into the text.

PP

'The work has to do with the problem of situating the spectator in some problematic way. Our interest in that has been exhaustively informed by the work of Richard Wollheim. In his text *Painting as an Art*, he spends a lot of time idealising the spectator's position. He discusses at length a highly privileged position in which the spectator might stand, in the sense that the spectator becomes someone who stands in the place of the artist. This involves a sense that there is an ideal vantage point, an ideal place at which to stand for viewing a work of art. He further suggests that works of art are made to be seen from a particular vantage point. So when the HCAK came along with this suggestion it seemed that there was a decided fit between what we have been concerned with and this project. One of the ideas about an ideal place is the idea of an ideal vantage point, an ideal place to do something or, as in this case, an ideal place to see something.'

'This works consists of boxes which contain drawings. These are parts of a work which we did, a series of paintings called *Index: Now They Are*. These mostly (though not entirely conclusively) consist of an image based on Courbet's *Origine du Monde*, that is to say a marginally indecent image which is then masked by a large slab of pink glass which bears a greeting at its centre, "hello", which is fairly visible. We had a lot of problems finding informative ways to produce drawings and to look at drawings in relation to this painting project. By containing them in a box we had, so to speak, subverted the gaze of the spectator so that the gaze that you are engaged with is not so much the gaze looking at the far horizon or whatever, a thing perpendicular to your line of vision, but something which is rather more like reading at a table. The other sense of the gaze that we had in mind was the sense of a somewhat voyeuristic gaze which most of the women here present will be aware of, of men looking down the front of their clothing. This in turn creates a circumstance in which you are looking at the drawing but there is also a text which obscures part of the drawing and is itself for a large part obscured from view, so that the text which you begin to read falls away. You cease to read it but in ceasing to do so, it transforms itself into a kind of horizon. It ceases to be text and becomes rather more like a landscape horizon or something like that, albeit under somewhat unnatural circumstances. It is like a receding plane. One's gaze is in a certain sense in the realm of reading while in fact one's reading is in some sense dislocated by being turned into a kind of seeing, a way of looking at the world in a non-literary sense.'

'In this installation you can read only three or four lines so it is not terribly important what the text is about. In some of the boxes the text is actually about the series of paintings I referred to earlier, so there is a reference but it is not too tight.'

'The text is there not to be read. There was presumably some point in the history of the construction of those boxes in which the whole text could be read: presumably we constructed it flat on the table, assembled it and put it in the box. The question is also: was it made by us with a view to its not being legible, that is to say, is it a sort of text not to be read or is it a text which has been read and simply finds itself by some misfortune in that circumstance? The text also "goes away", in a sense loses its nature as a text because when it finally becomes a horizon it is as if it were something else other than a text. The experience becomes rather like the experience of looking at a landscape or something like that.'

'There is a circumstance where you can read the text because it is a published text. So the readability is a matter of circumstances.'

'The file boxes look like generic boxes but actually they were designed by us. The file box actually reflects on work which we did in the 60s which is one point of reference. The other reason is that, of course, in that container one has a small space, so to speak, a kind of quasi-museum which itself is a kind of container for looking at things. One has a kind of place in which the thing that is shown is in some sense visible but it is perhaps not accessible from the place that we are in. It conceivably invites the possibility that there is some position in relation to this exhibited work which is appropriate. Does it make your situation standing outside the box inappropriate, involving you in an imaginative leap to think yourself in the box in some sense?'

'At the very least the box constructs a physical context. Presumably it resonates with other kinds of contexts in which you might be looking at pictures.'

'Some paintings which we have done, have text right on their surface so that they are obliterated by texts in which we say that we hide this appalling moment behind our speech. A lot of artwork with a relationship between pictures and text had its origins in an interest in analytical philosophy in the 60s.

In the context of this discussion we are talking about one circumstance suggested by the philosopher Flynt Schier, now alas dead, who starts his book *Deeper into Pictures* by suggesting that Gombrich, Wollheim, Wittgenstein *et al* have never really adequately supplied a workable sense of the structural distinction between pictures and text. He starts his book with the following question: "How come if I take down the picture of my uncle that I have on the wall and replace it with an exhaustive description of him including his blood type etc etc, that somehow I will feel the lack of the picture? What is it? What is the remainder? And it is similar the other way around, if I put the picture back in the place of the description. What will I lack in making those substitutions?" I suppose in offering those kind of little dialectical games, Schier raises a vast number of issues concerning what it is to read and interpret, what it is to even talk about "reading paintings". Analogies are made between reading and seeing. To what degree can we, by making extreme conditions of reading, raise questions concerning the matter of what is and what is not reading in looking at images?'

'There is a difference in experience between a person who knows what is underneath and starts to sort of hallucinate the presence of this image, and the person who does not know. I do not know exactly how to deal with this. That distinction sounds terribly useful but is the judgement of the person that knows, more powerful? What about the other intermediate points inbetween where there is, for instance, a person who does not know but is willing to do a lot of work to attempt to recover what is there? How much detail is necessary in order to recover something? For example, the figure is an extraordinary thing; we found to our great chagrin in trying to mask a figure that the amount of figure that would still resonate as a human figure was minute. So some of those images are not figures at all, they are trees. We can play a game with "politically correct" art history in which a "pc" art historian comes along and tells us that the tree in *Luxe, calme, volupté* is phallic. Well, if that is phallic . . . It is only a poor tree. It is a game to see the tree as a conceivably phallic image. Do you know it is a tree or do you have to start exercising a certain amount of guesswork, use a certain amount of imagination, take a certain number of risks in order to grasp what is involved?'

'In a certain sense it is suppressive of the spectator; a lot of conceptual art was concerned with the matter of the suppression of the spectator as modelled by modernism, as modelled by the manipulative world constructed by Clement Greenberg and abstract painting. There was a specific sort of spectator that we were concerned to suppress in those days: the spectator who claimed to be competent to describe the experience that other people were having, the spokesman for the sensibilities of other people. For example, when Joseph Kosuth presented a real chair, a photograph of a chair and the description of a chair, he killed that spectator through one artwork: there is nothing left for him or her to do, because the art sort of does it for you.'

'This work does that and leaves you with no interpretive work to do: this is its point. When you have got that point, you have got it. You can then go and do it over and over again using other objects as examples as Kosuth did, but there is no more to it. You can also force the terms into some kind of collision in which case the spectator is left with a remainder and with more work to do.'

'What has been said and written quite frequently in the past is that when talking about the suppression of the spectator what is meant is the transformation of that spectator into a participant, that is to say, a person who does work. There is very little for him to contemplate. In a sense this is still true of the work here. You can only look at the outside of the boxes. This is the case with "concealing work". For some strange reason, I do not quite know what it is – quite frequently of late we have a tendency to layer the work. Every time you do this, the work takes on a different kind of visual appearance. So in a way that conceptual art of Joseph Kosuth is totally the opposite of the early kind of conceptual art of Art & Language, certain exceptions notwithstanding.'

'One of the characteristics of what we do is to set traps in one sense or another in the Wollheimian concept. One of the ideas most dear to the heart of grand aestheticians is the idea of the adequately informed, adequately sensitive spectator, the person who is 'up to' the work, all founded on Renaissance ideas of being on your mettle and being in front of the work and so on and so forth. I think one of the things that we can try to do is to make a lot of demands on the spectator in terms of art historical and philosophical information that they have available, but at the same time create a situation in which that grandeur, that competence that they possess in relation to looking at art, is finally of not much use to them because the work creates a snare. Hence, the competence the spectators use to unravel what kind of work they are looking at suddenly becomes an out of control situation. The spectator with this messed up gaze is becoming a potentially ironical spectacle, just as the work is perhaps an ironical spectacle. There is a running out of control of competence here, so that in the end that competence is not quite as potent, not quite as much a privilege as it might conceivably appear to be at the beginning.'

Robin Winters: 'I was thinking of the Jasper Johns piece where he has a mirror on the shoe to be able to look up women's dresses. You use the metaphor of looking down a woman's dress. Would you specifically say that it is a male spectator you are thinking of?'

'It would be hard to turn myself into a female spectator. The point could be answered fairly simply: I would have thought those boxes take upon themselves the conscious fact that when a man looks at a woman's body he is kind of peeking. Now the question is: does the work take that sense of peeking into itself as a form of critical self-consciousness or does it simply use it as a way of enabling the thing to be more succesfully consumed? I take it as a critical question. The question that I would invite anybody to address is: if you find yourself caught in that activity of peeking and you have a sense of what that activity is like, what its comparatives are, is that a critical form of self-consciousness – which leads you to reflect upon the relevant aspects of your experience – or do you simply enjoy looking into the boxes as a man might enjoy looking down a woman's cleavage? That seems to me to be the ethical question. And I would find it very strange if any man said to me: I enjoy looking at this just like I enjoy looking down a woman's cleavage. I would regard him a highly uncritical spectator.'

'We should be aware of the limits of the artist's ability to stipulate the meaning of the work. The meaning is put into a work by the culture you work in. It is beyond your control. I fear that it is a kind of wishful vanity on the part of artists to assume that what they do can have the meaning which they say it has got. It is always open. We cannot count on the fact that our work means what we say it means or what we want it to mean.'

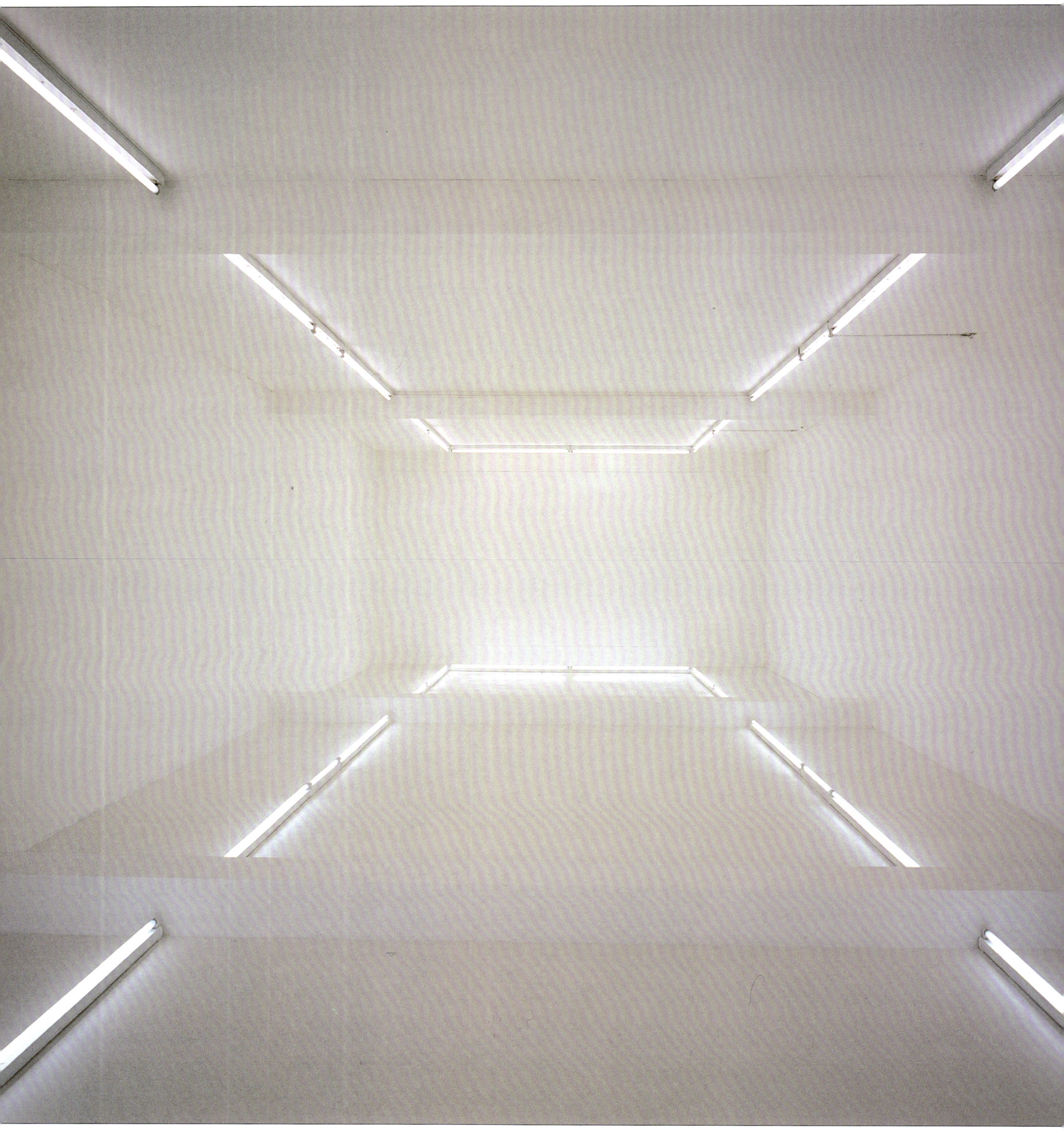

THE IDEAL PLACE: ABSENCE, NEGATION

JOHN BLAKE

'What can you tell me about MA? Yuhei, can you explain?'

'MA?'

'Yes, MA, the concept of . . . here in Japan . . . '

Yuhei frowned, puzzled, reworking the sound out loud several times. I sat opposite my host and friend, Yuhei Yoneya, at his dining table in Sapporo, Hokkaido Province, Japan's large northern-most island, on a very warm and humid summer's evening in 1984. We were sharing warm green tea and cold sake and, like so many previous nights, we spoke in hesitant, truncated blocks of speech, for while Yuhei had a limited but perfectly workable English I was totally ignorant of his native tongue.

'MA?'

'At least I think it's MA, Yuhei . . . ' and I tried to explain further that I only knew this term through a book on Space and Architecture which I had read years previously. (I was still a student at the time – obviously not such a very good one.) I could not recall much of this book, could not even remember the author's name (although both book and author were quite well known as I learned subsequently). However, I had not forgotten part of one chapter (dealing with 'ergonomics' and why should I remember just that?) in which the author had introduced the concept of MA, defining it as an 'interval' or the 'space between', while discussing the famous rock garden at the Rioanji temple in Kyoto. He explained that from any chosen vantage point one of Rioanji's 13 stones – actually large, natural rock formations, many up-turned, representing 'islands' floating in its 'sea' of carefully raked pebbles – remained out of sight: the promise of each and every viewpoint held something back, deliberately so. However imperfectly, however banal ('islands', in the 'sea'?) this idea was still fixed in my memory. By coincidence, I would soon be witnessing Rioanji for myself so I wanted to know more from a true source. My explanation must have been excruciating for him to decode but still, typically, Yuhei fought on.

'MA?'

'MA', I repeated.

'MA, ahh, hei, MU.'

'MU?'

'Hei. MA is MU!'

'Okay, MU, and then . . . ?'

Once again Yuhei frowned, remaining silent for some time. Then he quickly leaned forward grabbing one of our cups, saying, 'In the West you would offer me a cup of coffee.' Saying it he stretched across the table, placed the cup in front of me and added abruptly, 'Please!' He paused, then took the cup back. 'In Japan I would offer you tea.' Now he placed it in the centre of the table, then with the back of his hand gently pushed the cup across the table-top until it rested at my place. After another pause (Yuhei was being an infinitely patient teacher) he repeated his action, but between setting the cup and turning the back of his hand he explained, 'In this is MU.'

Weeks later at Rioanji I overheard an elder American ask her companion – not cynically, not naively but with a little impatience – 'Who's to say they are all perfectly placed?' and I identified with her question easily, fuelled by a similar impatience.

NB This is the first part of a larger text which is to be published later.

John Blake

'Leave them there, sweating and icy, there is better elsewhere. No, life ends and no, there is nothing elsewhere.'

Samuel Beckett, *Imagination Dead Image*, 1965

Normally speaking the upper room at the HCAK can be approached from two opposite sides so that one can walk all the way through the room. This makes it possible to choose different routes through the HCAK, in particular a circular path. For John Blake's work, one of the doorways was eliminated, while the other was blocked by a metal bar – the visitor was hence only able to look into the space. The space was closed into itself as much as possible.

Blake's intervention was done in the most simple manner: the same sorts of beams and neon lights on the ceiling were attached to corresponding places on the floor. Precisely along the middle of the walls Blake had drawn a blue horizontal stripe, which divided the room exactly in two. The obvious point here is to think in terms of mirroring: the ceiling mirrors itself in the floor. However, one cannot speak of a 'real' mirroring because this would imply a spyhole in the mirror where an imaginary mirrored space becomes visible. This can never be synonymous with the 'real' space which is mirrored, the mirror image being no more than a derivative. The principle of the mirror is exactly that: tangible reality and the (reversed) illusion of reality have some sort of relationship with each other (or, rather, several relationships) but that is not the case here, because there is no illusion, only 'tangible' reality; everything is, as it were, 'real'.

At the same time it is also a kind of 'diorama', a glance into a space that is not real for the viewer because he cannot enter it. The space remains 'an image' which suggests a subject/object relationship between the onlooker and a painting, 'into' which he cannot walk. In other words, we apparently find ourselves in a territory of metaphorical meaning and of literal concreteness. This is only the vehicle of attributing meaning. But which meaning?

If we compare this work, as has been done (in my view unjustifiably), with certain works from the 70s there may sometimes be a formal similarity. However, one important difference is the nature of its relation to the public. A good example is given by a work of Michael Asher in the Heiner Friedrich Gallery, in which 'above' and 'below' (ceiling and floor) were 'made equal', but with a completely different meaning. This work aimed to transform the mundane meaning of the different spaces in the gallery (exhibiton spaces and office spaces were made equal so that among other things, the meaning of the work, in terms of art policy and strategy, became apparent). An example of the other extreme is Bruce Nauman's narrow *Corridors*, in which the visitor physically experiences the claustrophobic effect of a space constructed for that purpose. Some similarity with Nauman's work is conceivable here but there is no indication of its immediate physicality – and that is not a difference of a gradual but an essential nature, as we shall see.

There is also a possible misunderstanding in relation to this work (which seems to elicit a lot of this) and that is the obvious interpretation of the empty, brightly lit space as an image of 'the Sublime' or a similar concept of emptiness in the mystical sense. The piece does offers some argument for such a view, but on the other hand, the very complex intervention to reach symmetry by reproducing a whole ceiling on a floor might be regarded as slightly superfluous to the purpose: these associations can be elicited by simpler means. The blue stripe would become incomprehensible, so based on this small probability one must reject this interpretation.

So what is actually happening? In my opinion this installation, however it looks, has absolutely nothing ethereal nor physical, even though both elements are present in a negative sense. I am of the opinion that this work should sooner be viewed as being 'destructive'. To begin with, if we accept the space as it is presented to us as 'the space' and not only as a change in an already existing other space (the 'original' room), then the blue stripe, however minimal and seemingly modest it is, would take on the meaning of an agent which splits the space ruthlessly in two. One should then speak of cleaving instead of mirroring and of aggression instead of serenity. Then the emptiness which is accentuatued or, indeed, created by the doubling (or, rather, through the equality of 'above' and 'below') would become a chilling emptiness, the negation of presence. There would be little left of the modernist idea of emptiness as the symbol of eternity, infinity or whichever term one wishes to use. There would then sooner be the loss of that kind of healing vocabulary or, in more general terms, the sense that something is lacking – there is nothing and that nothing has a frightening emptiness. In a certain way this work therefore says: 'there is nothing'.

This 'nothing' cannot be filled up and cannot be physically experienced by the viewer, because one cannot enter it (justifiably, of course, because in that case the nothingness would immediately be cancelled out by a presence). This does not necessarily imply that one cannot speak of a reference to any sort of physicality. Referral is not a 'literal' occurance but something which occurs in the viewer's mind, triggered by the givens which the work presents.

'Nothing' in itself means nothing, so to speak. However, this work does not concern itself with nothing as nothing, but rather with a specific meaning of nothingness. It produces – at least, I believe – an explanation of (and by) nothingness in relationship to itself. Let us for a moment not view the space in question as nothingness, but as what it is in the physical sense, ie an enclosed space in which, it is true, nothing is to be found, but where one in principle can imagine anything. Connecting this idea with the physicality of the viewer which is not literally involved but referred to, is only a small step to imagining that we are looking at ourselves in a certain sense

(a form of mirroring after all?) or at least looking inwardly. The insides of a human being are composed of cavities, of enclosed spaces and the most obvious cavity from the perspective offered by this work (which, as has been said, occurs 'in the head') is the skull. In other words, perhaps we are looking at a metaphor of our skulls. It is our deepest thoughts and feelings, our existential presence, which are presented here as 'nothing', and therefore as an absence. On top of that, the division in two (by the blue line) makes this an almost unbearable paradox, and, at best, produces a doubling of nothing, which in itself of course, is again nothing. The rhetoric figure is essential, once more clarifying that 'nothing' is the 'subject' here (or, perhaps, not even that). After all, the blue line would otherwise have no more than a superfluous decorative function.

But if one wishes one can imagine, in a somewhat manneristic and, therefore, somewhat less obvious way, that we are looking at the 'complete human cavity', with the understanding that it has been turned a quarter circle. It manifests itself horizontally in opposition to the, in principle, vertical human form. Then the horizontal line becomes a metaphor for the longitudinal axis (the backbone, spinal column) which keeps us upright. Nevertheless, the 'internal cohesion' of the work is not done complete justice in this way, and so perhaps this alternative must be rejected as a less probable sidetrack.

The emptiness of the work is by no means less chilling for all that. It becomes a metaphor for human emptiness, for the emptiness of the human mind, or for an idea referring to its cliché-like, mechanistic construction; we are hardly able to distinguish top from bottom (to maintain the terminology offered by the work). Everything in our minds is preprogrammed and serves no function other than to allow itself to exist aimlessly as the status quo of absence. Nothing makes sense (which is not the same as saying that nothing is something which has a sense which we call 'nothing').

The blinding white of the brightly lit space is hence not the white on which something (a feeling, a fantasy) can be projected in order to be called to life. It is, on the contrary, the white that has absorbed and dissolved these elements like a vampire, and made it into absence. Our shell covers nothing and escape is impossible, for the simple reason that there is 'nothing' to escape from. The circle closes itself. In this manner this work becomes a rather gruesome image of the human condition, expressed in terms of purposeless presence which is maintained as a metaphor for an equally purposeless absence, where presence and absence ultimately come together in a purposeless, motionless dance.

In as far as something real seems to be present in a deceptively literal sense that something functions (organs are a mechanical construction) but to what end? Apparently there is no other purpose than in the case of the neon lights shining in the room which have, in this case, no purpose at all. They shine as long as they shine, after that everything is over and what happens then? Then we have lived and we have died. Then nothingness, by its presence, has at the same time shown its absence and ultimately nothingness also destroys itself. Even a negation of nothing becomes possible (not to be confused with the treacherous formula of minus times minus is plus) which in turn declares itself absent so that nothing remains of nothing and so on, *ad infinitum*. There is no sense, no meaning.

Ergo, the 'ideal place' as negation, the absence, not only of everything, but also of nothing.   PP

THE IDEAL PLACE: IN OR OUT OF THIS WORLD?
RICARDO BREY

This life of ours is a hospital, in which all patients are obsessed with a desire to change beds. One would prefer to suffer near the stove, and another thinks he would soon recover near the window.

I always have the feeling that I would be better anywhere except where I actually am, and the idea of a removal is one which I am constantly discussing with my Soul.

'I say, Soul, poor shivering Soul, how would you like to go and live in Lisbon? It must be pretty warm there, and you would soon be as spry as a lizard. The city is at the seaside, and I have heard that it is built of marble, and that people there have such a horror of vegetation that they pull the trees down. Now that is the kind of landscape to suit your taste, built of sunshine and mineral, with a liquid mirror to reflect them in.'

Not a word from my Soul.

'As you are so fond of stillness and repose, but not without some movement to please the eye, then how would you like living in Holland, the home of bliss? Perhaps you would forget your troubles there, as you have so often admired its image in museums and galleries. Now what would you say to Rotterdam, you who simply adore forests of masts and rigging, and the way ships sleep at anchor alongside the houses?'

My Soul is still speechless.

'Perhaps Batavia would appeal to you more? There we would find the essence of Europe, coupled with the beauty of the tropics.'

Not a word. Has my Soul died?

'Have you become so lost to the feeling that you enjoy nothing but your own wretched state? If so, then let us escape to those regions which are facsimiles of death. I have just the thing for you, dear Soul – we will pack our trunks for Lapland. Or we could even go still farther away, to the farthest end of the Baltic – or even farther away from life, if that is possible, and settle at the Pole. There the sun only obliquely kisses the earth, and the slow alterations of light and dark eliminate all variety, increasing the monotony which is the twin of Nothingness. There we can enjoy long baths of night-ness, while for our amusement the Aurora Borealis will now and then emit great rosy sheaves of light, like reflections of the fireworks of Hades.'

At last my Soul erupted and cried out her words of wisdom: 'Anywhere! Anywhere, so long as it is outside this world!'

Charles Baudelaire, XLVIII, from The Poems in Prose, 1867.
Translated by Francis Scarfe
Ricardo Brey

The work of Ricardo Brey usually consists of a pile of garbage, waste products combined to a 'significant whole'. The installation in the HCAK is no exception. Car tyres, parts of old hospital beds, discarded lamps – they are components of a whole which, supplemented with seemingly casually applied dirty-brown paint on pieces of wall and floor, presents a disconsolate sight which one would not easily associate with the fact that here someone has been working with the theme of 'the ideal place' in mind. At any rate, it requires some goodwill to see this gloomy collection as an ideal place.

Well, it is not. There is something which is referred to as 'negative theology', in which the deity is deliberately called by all the names which do not define him, since the fact that his essence cannot be defined verbally or otherwise is the very characteristic of the deity. Partly this is a process of elimination: when all words have been spent, the deity will show his true shape.

Possibly something similar also applies to a concept like 'the ideal place'. The ideal place can only be made distinguishable by showing what it is not, just as beauty may become visible in (or from) extremes of horror, as perhaps with Sade or Bataille.

The use of 'poor' materials in itself is nothing new in art. Beuys practised it and the name of the Italian 'arte povera' is even based on this. However, this does not mean that we have to deal with the same phenomenon here. Formal (or rather material) similarity does not imply a relation as regards contents. Apart from the fact that they incidentally also demonstrated that art can be made of any material whatsoever, Beuys and the Italians used these kinds of materials to build up often highly personal 'mythological' images, wishing to have a mainly metaphysical meaning. To give an example: an igloo by Mario Merz, no matter what material it is made of, symbolises the nomadic existence of the artist, to put it in a brief, simplified form.

I have the feeling that Ricardo Brey does not view his materials in the same way and that he also wants to uncover other contents. At the risk of using a cliché, I do think it has to do with his personal origin. Brey is from Cuba, a Third World country in a peculiar and highly isolated position (especially right now) and the notion of 'garbage' has a totally different meaning there than in oversupplied consumer societies such as Western Europe or North America. In comparison, it may have no meaning at all there. Anyhow, here we are not dealing with a culture used to throwing away anything that may, momentarily appear to have become superfluous.

In the first instance, with his materials Brey does not want to make a beautiful, metaphysical masterpiece for the museum room. It is probably not too far-fetched to say that his primary need is to show the materials as objects found in the world, and for that reason alone, they have a right to be seen in a different light, not just in their identity of 'garbage'. What is also involved is that once they had a function, played a part and due to this must have experienced some sort of appreciation of whatever kind (be it only as utensils or appliances). The adventures of these objects have not disappeared along with the disappearance of their function or with their becoming unsuitable for that function; on the contrary, the objects continue to

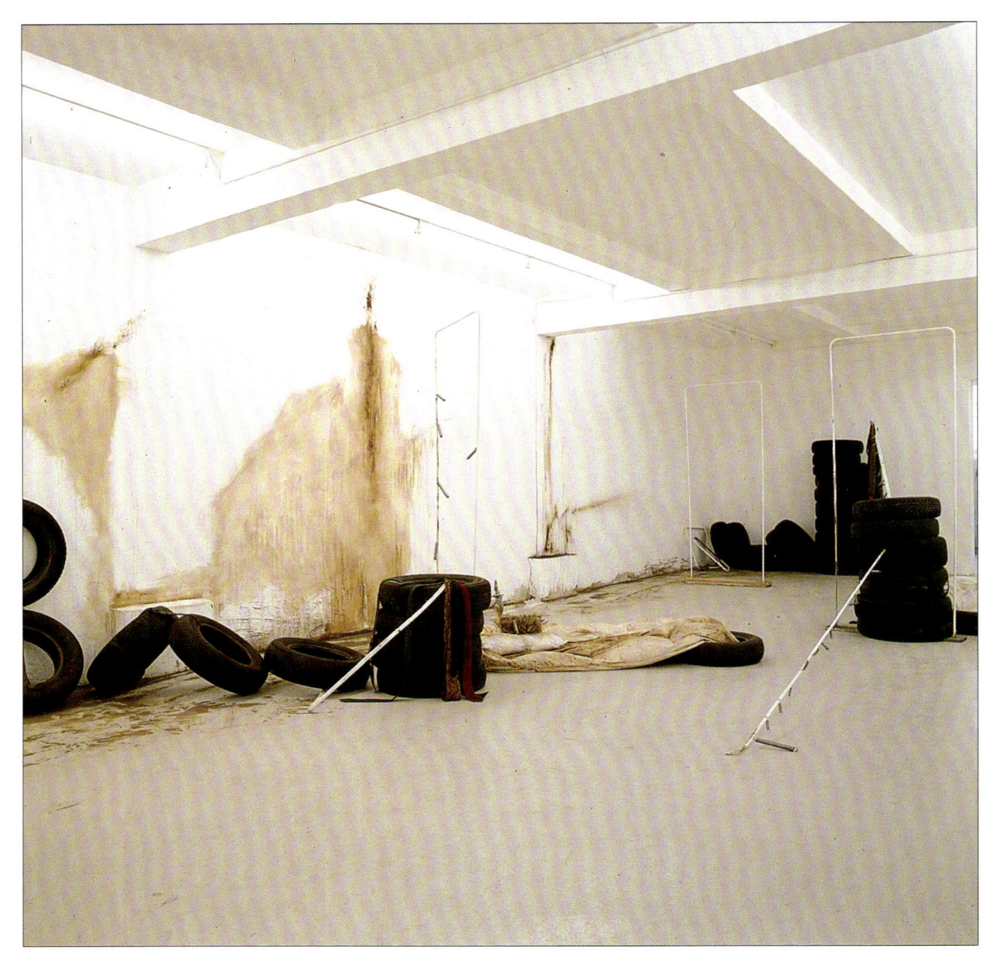

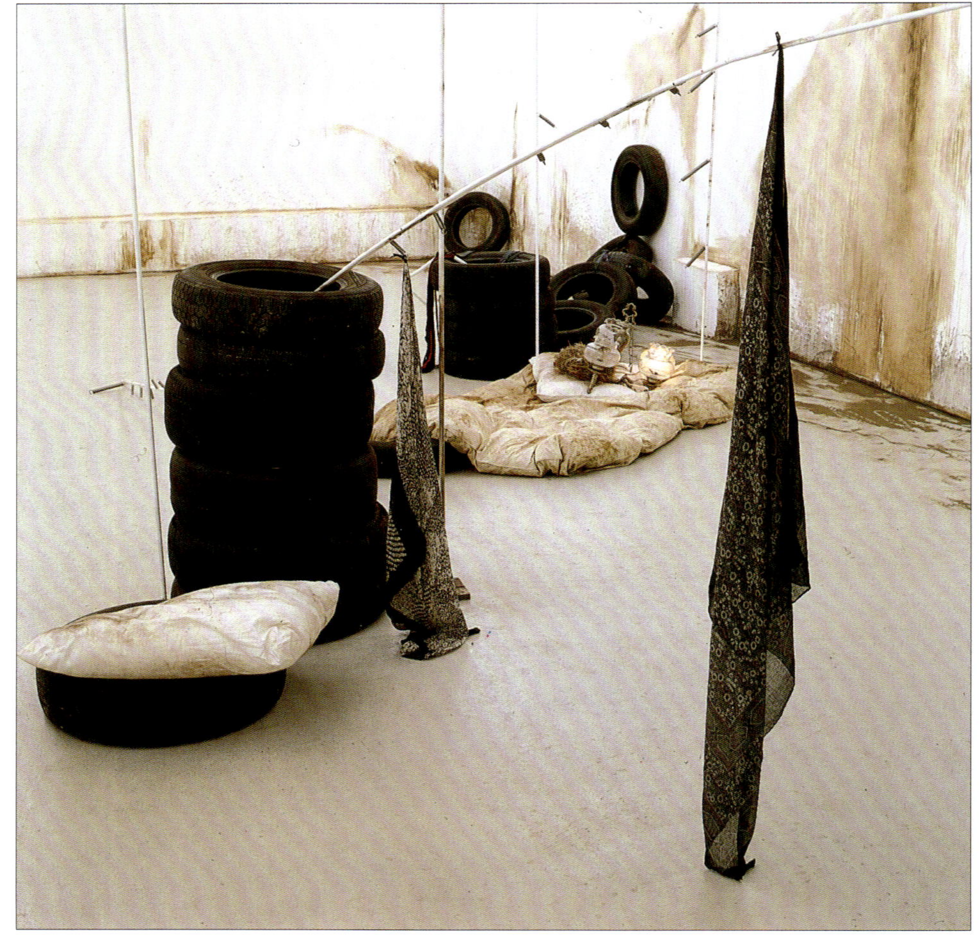

be 'silent witnesses' of a previous existence, which is still incorporated in their physical presence.

Brey re-uses these kinds of objects (they are recycled into art) and of course their meaning changes along with their context – a fact ever since Duchamp. But I do not think that Brey is in search of a purely Duchampian change of meaning in the sense of 'by its installation in the art context, utensil or appliance turns into an art object'. In my opinion the objects used by Brey deliberately remain as close to their 'original' meaning as possible. At the very least they are reminiscent of themselves in their original meaning without immediately substituting a different one in its place. It can be put like this: Duchamp's fountain ceased to be a fountain as soon as it was placed in the museum, but Brey's car tyres are still car tyres, even in their 'art context' – even though there is no car for the tyres to perform their original function. It is debatable whether we have to deal with car tyres here or a kind of signifying mimicry or reminiscence of car tyres, but such a discussion focuses on whether or not the function has been lost. In this case, function is not identical with meaning or identity; it is at most a partial aspect of it and it would be going too far to pursue this matter further.

So it may also be going too far to interpret Brey's work as an 'homage to garbage'. Furthermore, these objects are not garbage but for the sake of convenience let us say, merely objects coming from the world and returned to it – in a context of art – but without having been transformed into splendid art objects in a composition connected with it. On the contrary, in this installation their 'thingness' is indeed emphasised. One could even say that here they are shown in their capacity of 'non-garbage', so that their definition has become: 'things that are not garbage', once again a negative formulation, perhaps comparable to that of negative theology.

Of course it is a fact that more than one sample is present of the greater part of these objects – not in a serial arrangement in the classical sense, but nevertheless connected with other objects (of which again there are several samples) in such a way that referring to them as an 'installation', an 'arrangement' is inevitable. But what is not clear (and I doubt it) is whether this arrangement wishes to indicate anything other than 'itself' – not in the tautological sense which formerly sometimes (and wrongly) used to refer to Minimal Art, but in such a way that the arrangement represents itself in its components, or rather, represents its components. Hence, this is exactly the opposite of what is usually done in a work of art, in which an arrangement wishes to be more than the sum of its components so that an overall meaning is created. Nor is it, to prevent any misunderstandings, a kind of postmodern fragmentation into components that have lost their unity. There is no unity here and there never has been, at least in no other way than as a collection of components, which therefore, strictly speaking, can no longer be called 'components', but 'things' among other 'things'.

Transforming the 'thing' into an art object is a long accepted practice, but I think that here the object found in an art context, exhibited, is therefore probably an art object according to the existing norms – 're-transformed' into a 'thing', into the thing it once was and, *mirabile dictu*, still is.

To put it slightly differently, with his artistic 'intervention' or other activity, the artist does not charge the object with new meaning; it is precisely the other way round. In spite of the art context and in spite of the fact that the artist calculates in and manipulates various (also visual) mechanisms of this context, he changes the supposed art object into an object whose 'thingness' is focused on. Paradoxically enough, he need not change the object for that purpose. Whatever manipulations have been performed with it (taken from the world, arranged and put together with other objects, presented in an art exhibition) the thing simply continues to be a thing, meaning that the objects shown possess extraordinary 'thing' power. Even more paradoxically, it could also mean that it is precisely the artist's artistic intervention that reveals this quality of the things: after all, anyone can put a pile of garbage somewhere without managing to make it become more than just a pile of garbage – that is, without being able to make this pile of garbage evoke any reflection on the objects shown. In such a case nothing has happened. Then there is no moment of transformation taking place in our imagination, incited by the reality shown. And in this respect, Brey's work actually does obey the laws of the art world in the sense that there is transformation, several transformations even, there and back and the other way round, I should say. This implies that Brey's interventions cause various shuttle-like movements in our heads, for which there happens to be a nice Zen parable:

The Zen master says:

'Before I was enlightened, the trees were trees and the mountains mountains. When I was almost enlightened, the trees were no longer trees and the mountains no longer mountains. Now that I am enlightened, the trees are trees and the mountains are mountains.'

When we relate all this to Brey's first verbal formulation of 'the ideal place', a quotation of Baudelaire with the title 'Any Place Out of this World', comes to mind. This concept is to be understood from the disconsolateness of objects regarded as waste. Possibly, the ideal place can only be 'elsewhere' for the man who looks at things in that way, non-existent, away from it all. But for things that have been allowed to keep their value as things, for which the non-denial of their 'thingness' is the essence of their meaning (of their dignity), the ideal place might well be any place where their 'thingness' is accepted as valuable – for instance at an art exhibition concerning 'The Ideal Place'.   PP

THE IDEAL PLACE: SHELTER
PATRICK CORILLON

In January 1952 Oskar Gerti was kidnapped, tied up and locked into the ideal place for over a week. The reason for the kidnapping has never been solved.

During the first days of his confinement, in which he had no contact whatsoever with his kidnappers, he spent his time trying to remove his blindfold, so that he might identify the place where he was being held prisoner. When at the end of the third day he had finally managed to get it off, after having got accustomed to the darkness surrounding him, Gerti was pleased to conclude that the general impression of the ideal place more or less resembled the place he had imagined during his involuntary blindness. The only difference being that with open eyes he no longer felt the presence of another human being beside him, which he had constantly experienced during the preceding days.

On the sixth day he was so overcome by loneliness that he decided to put the blindfold on again.

Patrick Corillon

Patrick Corillon's installation in the HCAK looks extraordinarily simple. At approximately calf-level, there is a partition in the exhibition room made of wood and metal, thus in itself creating new space, a new place. The construction contains one opening through which this space can be entered and a doormat lies in front of it. Those who enter this space by way of the mat evidently come into a kind of house, at any rate a mimicry of a room. At the other end of it a sign has been placed with the following text (in three languages):

> Whenever a stupid publisher rejected one of his manuscripts, Oskar Serti would return home feeling the need to be on his own. Before shutting himself away in his study for hours on end, he would wipe his feet vigorously on the doormat to clean off all the squalor of the outside world. On March 3, 1934, Serti set out to see a small-time publisher in the country. But so reluctant was he to face another rejection that he turned on his tracks without going through with the meeting. Back home, in an attempt to rid himself of the disgust he felt for himself at his own cowardliness, he removed his shoes and wiped his bare feet energetically on the coarse bristles of the doormat. At the sight of dark trails of blood on the mat, Serti decided to wipe his feet again and again, until he was sure they were perfectly clean.

Oskar Serti (in other work also regularly appearing under the name of Oskar Gerti and at times in yet another spelling) is the alter ego of the artist, a fictitious, almost mythological character experiencing all sorts of things, thus giving the at first apparently neutral environment in which the work is situated an unexpected metaphorical tension. Speculating, one might also say that the protagonist's 'fictitious' adventures provide a place which in itself is rather expressionless, a peculiar, realistic value. Those who walk over the doormat on their way in, do not give this any particular thought, at least the doormat does not have another meaning from any other mat, but on his return the visitor has learned that this mat played an important part in the scene of tragedy. The house, or room, is no longer just a place marked out in an exhibition room, it is the house of Oskar Serti, where he licks the wounds he has sustained in the outside world that is forever rejecting him. It is an 'ideal place' in the sense that he finds shelter there in non-compromising solitude against the evil world, so that he can prepare his next attempt at conquering this world from behind his desk for hours on end, evidently each time with the same negative result – a kind of Sisyphus labour. Obviously the two places are incompatible: the house, the shelter, the inner life on the one hand and the hard, un-empathic, judging outside world on the other. One may wonder who eventually is the victim of what (who knows what masterpieces we are missing out on because of these maybe wrongly unpublished manuscripts of Serti's?) What *is* certain is that in the status quo the artist suffers under this dichotomy. Suffering for the sake of art, an idea does not often come across these days.

The conflict between the internal and external world has even become so large that it has to be fought out literally until it bleeds. The wiping of shoes has to be replaced by wiping bare feet until they bleed and as soon as this has become clear, a little extra has to be added. All this to remove the corruption of the world. It will be clear that such a project (which is also to be considered noble and pure, for that matter) is doomed to fail. It is more probable, continuing this line of argument consistently, that the protagonist in this tragedy will in the long run only wipe himself out completely, bleeding until nothing is left of him. And whether the world will have changed remains to be seen, it will probably just go on turning which makes the protagonist's action all the more pathetic.

We are confronted with an image here of individual human impotence in the face of unbearable existence, making demands that cannot be met (for instance in the form of publishers, who might incidentally, well be called Oskar Serti). The only purity is to be found in the inner life, but this world does not care for it, particularly when it does not appear in an accepted and standardised form. It is an ancient conflict, presented here in an apparently neutral, but upon closer consideration, quite extreme form. In essence the issue is the human condition and the ideal place: shelter.

Looking at the entire design of the work once again, its meaning is centred on the doormat, lying there brand-new, looking as if it has just been bought, but in reality the arena of a rather gruesome tragedy. On the border of inside and outside, impurity manifests itself in its harshest form; there the need for 'beauty' in the sense of 'purity', 'innocence' is at its greatest. Thus leaving this house, as well as returning to it has become highly dangerous: man is not pure and knows no ritual for acquiring this purity again. He has been contaminated with what here is called 'the outside world', but it could also be expressed in all kinds of different metaphors not making use of this rather facile opposition – which may be taken as only literal all too soon, with as a result, I think, that the heart of the matter is overlooked. It is true that art always has to do with the world, but I could not escape the impression that it here concerns the artist's obsession with the pure and immaculate and, pursuing this thought, with the impotence, the failings of mankind in general with respect to these kinds of unattainable categories. Translated into art historical terms, it states that whereas the pursuit of purity (of unity) was the highest attainable goal and at the same time a self-evident occupation during Modernism, nowadays the artist will have to bleed for it at the risk of vanishing altogether in doing so.

Without abandoning this interpretation, we might give the doormat even more meaning in its function as border and border-crossing point. One might even say that the work actually deals with the doormat, here so seemingly virginal but at the same time, bearer of residues of all sorts of corruption. In that case it is no longer this special doormat that we are dealing with, but 'the' doormat, 'all' doormats, as symbols of the moment of border-crossing. And are we not living in a culture of constant testing, opening and closing of borders, in a culture of migration whether or not voluntary, of ethnic purges, xenophobia, seekers of asylum? In this light, the work acquires an even wider cultural-critical meaning rising above the intrapsychological conflict and also above the dichotomy between external and internal world. Then the image of human impotence also acquires topical political value and the doormat turns into an emblem of what will have to be fought and abolished: the mat itself gives rise to the bleeding, the image of bleeding, and can no longer be seen as merely an innocent witness and bearer of a residue.

Without such a mat Oskar Serti could perhaps walk in and out undisturbed, so that the whole world would be his ideal place.

PP

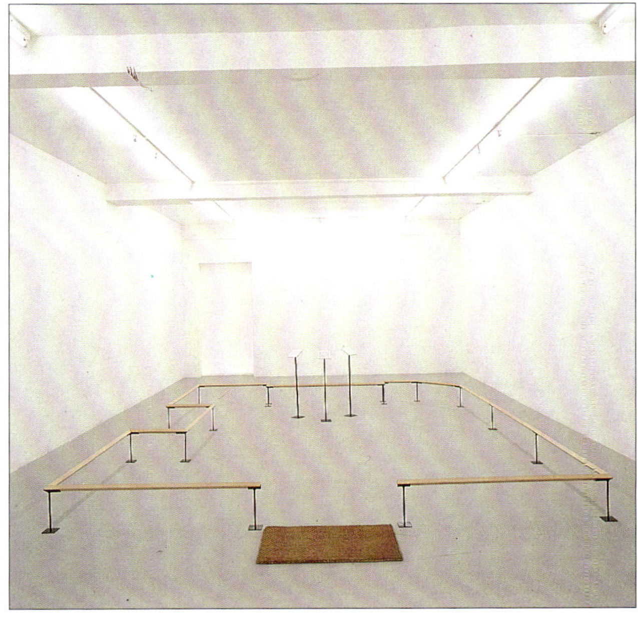

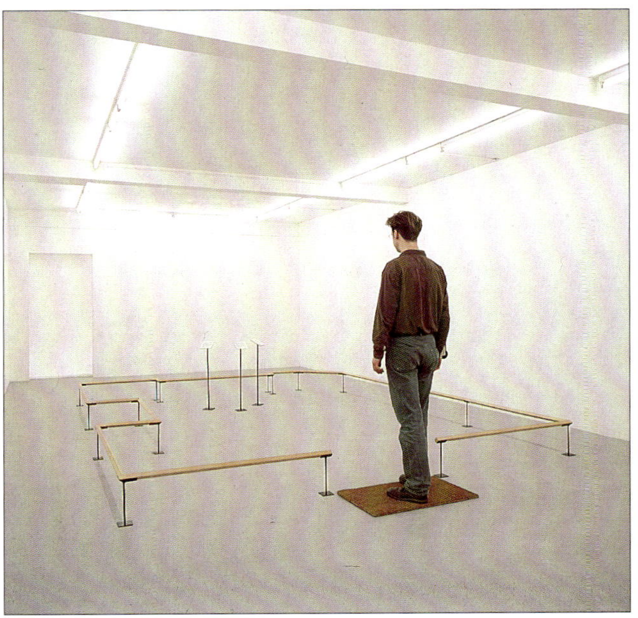

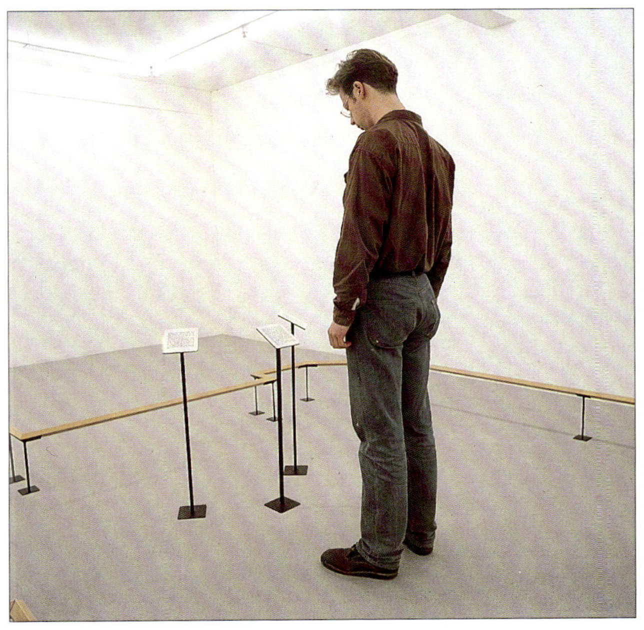

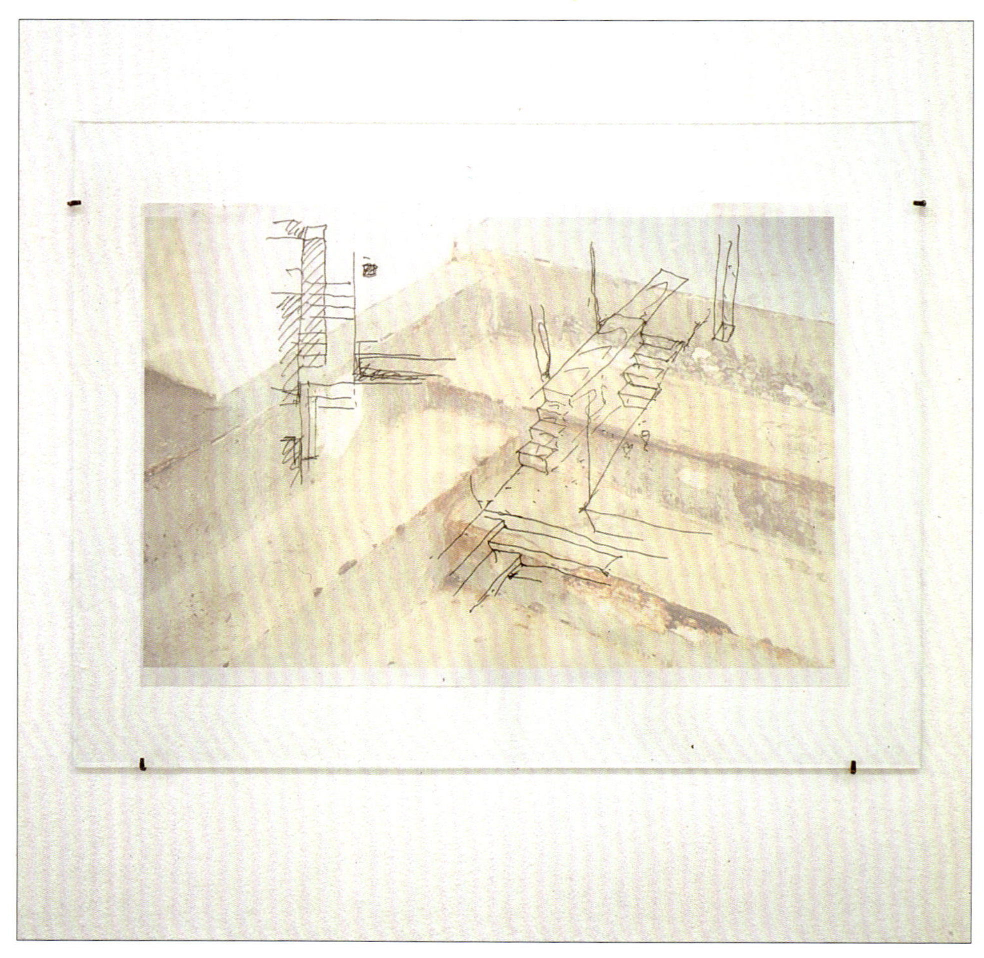

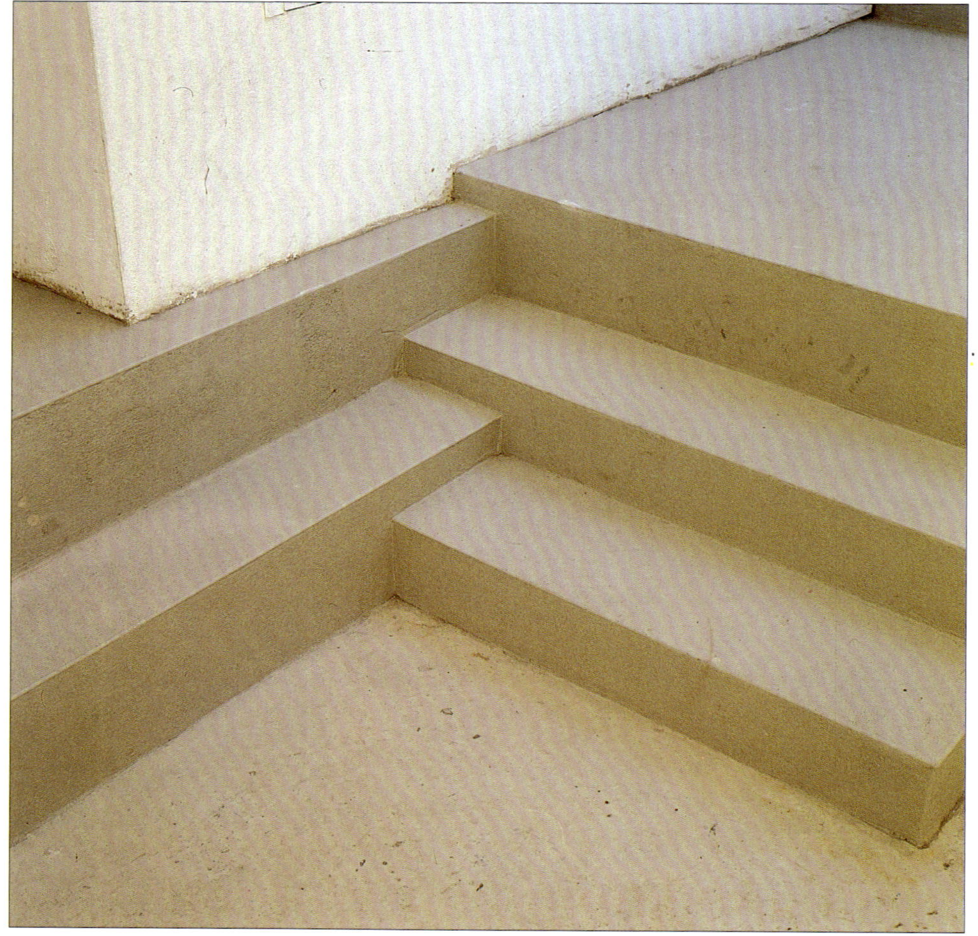

THE IDEAL PLACE: RESTORING TO A NEW STATE
GEORGES DESCOMBES

'Etwas, bis dahin ausständig, trat ein.'
'Something, which had not been forthcoming, set in.' (Peter Handke)
Georges Descombes

Naturally, the ideal place for the ideal place is the HCAK, which for over a year has explicitly opened its doors to receive, show and publish information on this subject. But how ideal is this place?

The physical *accommodation* of the HCAK in itself has nothing to do with the ideal place. For instance, I do not know whether such a thing as an ideal place for art presentation in general is conceivable at all; the presentation of art is always a matter of negotiation between object and space, with the exception perhaps of those cases in which work *in situ* has made this problem its very theme and thus has sometimes 'solved' it in a sense.

The exhibition rooms of the HCAK have been designed as much as possible according to the model of the white box with grey floor, in conformity with the unwritten agreement that such a place should be as close an approximation to a 'neutral' atmosphere as possible. Our exhibition rooms are therefore not 'ideal'; for various reasons (including the one just referred to) this is not possible. Moreover, one of the three exhibition rooms has daylight and the other two cannot be used without artificial light, which one may regret. However, this is a subject in itself. At any rate we have to work with the facts at hand and we may therefore wonder whether the rooms, considering their possibilities and limitations, can function more or less properly. We are not talking about 'ideal' here but about 'optimal', not about the unattainable but about the feasible.

The contribution of Georges Descombes, which is concerned with this subject matter, is remarkably modest. Although an intervention in the building has been effected, with the intendion of making it 'more ideal' – that is to say, 'better suited to its purpose' – this intervention is so minimal that it is hardly noticeable as such. At the 'end' of the ground floor there is a small staircase. These few steps offer two alternatives: either straight ahead to another small staircase leading to the room at the back, or left in the direction of kitchen, toilet and filing cabinet. These concrete steps became the focus of Descombes' interference.

Due to intensive use, the steps have become rather worn down in the course of time. Descombes 'restored' them, a minimal intervention which no one would have noticed – and definitely not as an artwork – if a small photograph had not been hanging in the room as well, showing the steps in their former state, on which Descombes indicated in a few lines what he intended to do.

Consequently, the accommodation was viewed at its own premises and there proved to be aspects which could be 'improved' without effectively *changing* them. The steps were chosen as an example,

but a different choice might well have been made. However, that is not the point, it is in fact, the principle of the gesture that is concerned here: 'the importance of the trivial'.

The artist has disappeared in his work, as it were, and the work is actually 'repair work', restoring something that is of little importance to the best of your ability. The fact whether the steps are slightly worn down or not has almost no effect whatsoever on one's experience of the place, nor on the art presented there. This intervention in the literal space rather indicates that, in spite of all the problems of presentation characteristic of visual art, the space itself should not be seen as the main issue, whereas at the same time it does make sense to treat even the smallest detail *with respect*. One could therefore say that this work in one and the same breath states that the place, the environment, the container is and is not important. It is only because of the given context of 'the ideal place' that Descombes' intervention differs in meaning from comparable interventions carried out by us after each exhibition and referred to as, for instance, 'maintenance'. From now on it will not be easy to change anything on the premises without immediately having this work in mind, and what is more, at some particular moment exactly the same intervention will have to be repeated, but then we cannot attribute the epitheton 'artwork' to it.

Another significant issue was involved in this work: originally Descombes presented a large number of floor plans of the various stages in the construction of this building around the turn of the century. During the discussion among the three then exhibiting artists (Descombes, Rémy Zaugg and Mark Lewis) Zaugg pointed out that the work of Descombes was not likely to benefit from this kind of abundant documentation and that the single documentation already referred to would suffice. After some discussion Descombes decided to take Zaugg's advice: the drawings which did not directly refer to the intervention itself were consequently removed after the opening of the exhibition.

It is moments like these that I consider moments of 'beauty' – in their literal sense and as a reinforcement of Descombes's statement, as well as in the sense of an exemplary sign of the fact that artists *do* participate in conversations with one another and reap the fruits of it. This flexibility of Descombes' mind perhaps also results from the fact that he is the only one of the 24 participants in 'The Ideal Place' who does not in the first place work as an 'autonomous' artist, but as a(n) (landscape) architect, a field in which you have to take the wishes, thoughts and ideas of others into account. If this is so, we had better reconsider the sacrosanct notion of the 'autonomy' of the visual artist. At any rate, in my opinion this incident shows a noble versatility on the part of Georges Descombes, a nearly *ideal* moment in the history of 'The Ideal Place'.

PP

THE IDEAL PLACE: EARTH
ALFRED EIKELENBOOM

The ideal place is a place where there are neither too many nor too few people. In that sense, the works of Nicolas Poussin can be regarded as harmony models, utopian models. In his paintings the people are personages who fill in an Arcadian landscape, with the architecture in the background forming a tasteful coulisse-like complement to the painted composition.

Utopian models are scarce in our time. In the chaotic discussion about how the planet should be saved, utopian models are never mentioned in a concrete way. A prominent intellectual and theoretician such as Thomas More in the 16th century, who without being perturbed by his leading position in society had the courage to formulate his political ideals in the form of a clear work of art, would be inconceivable in our day. All contemporary politicians, all over the world, suffer under the permanent censorship of the electorate so that every intelligent idea, of whichever sort, would be aborted right in the first stage of its development, if it would have come up at all in the first place.

The growing popularity of escapism, as a belief, as a philosophy, as an attitude in life, is disquieting. Escapistic tendencies may be conservative (the Pope advocating unbridled multiplication) as well as 'progressive' (Biosphere II, 'artificial intelligence', the 'colonisation of planets' and other pulp ideas).

It is time to expose the false prophets and fraud-practising innovators.

Our planet rediscovered is the only possible and the only conceivable ideal place.

Down with Biosphere II

Down with the Pope

Down with artificial intelligence

Only our very own planet can be the ideal place, cherished and guarded by 'natural intelligence' (just stay with it).

Alfred Eikelenboom

Essentially the work which Alfred Eikelenboom made for the project 'The Ideal Place' is extraordinarily simple. It consists of three elements brought together in one surface: eight photographs of the Willendorf Venus taken at an angle of 45° from a frontal start, a diagram of the growth of the world population and the following text:

'D'où venons-nous? Que sommes-nous?

Où allons-nous?

These fundamental questions were raised by Gauguin in 1879.

Now the answer is only too obvious:

Our planet: Arcadia, paradise as well as prison.'

Once it was necessary for the survival of the species to engender sufficient descendants. It is therefore not surprising that one of the oldest known sculptures, the Willendorf Venus, is a fertility idol.

Fertility was idolised and there was every reason for it.

This situation remained unchanged for as long as people were hunters and collectors. At a much later stage the world population began to grow rapidly. The period of growth covers a minimal part of the total duration of man's presence on earth so far, as the diagram shows. Meanwhile this growth has become so explosive that the continued existence of man (and of the earth itself) are threatened. The mechanism – fertility – once adored and essential for survival, now threatens the human species.

Thus the earth has changed from a paradise into a prison. But it is still the place we will have to make do with and reshape in order to recreate the 'ideal place' it once was.

The method in this work is that of the 'objet trouvé': all three elements have been withdrawn from reality. The Willendorf Venus is a small statue to be found in the Naturhistorisches Museum in Vienna, the diagram of the growth of the world population can be obtained from every institute occupying itself with this kind of subject, and the original text by Gauguin appeared on one of his paintings. Consequently, the work concerns elements from various fields of meaning: prehistory, demography and classical modern art. By combining the elements, a new whole is created.

It is true that communications from various fields of meaning are made here, but apart from this fact the subjects of those communications are not particularly heterogeneous: in a sense they deal with one and the same issue after all. The theme is fertility and its consequences for our living environment, embedded in a sweeping statement comprising the entire history of mankind. In art historical terms one could say that the relations between the constituent elements in this work are a good example of the, meanwhile, simple Duchampian wisdom that difference in context will result in difference in meaning. The concept of 'fertility' has changed its meaning, its contents. An addition to the Duchampian mechanism is that as regards the concept of 'context', it is not space but time that is concerned here. The change in meaning is not affected by a 'horizontal' difference in contemporary conditions but a 'linear', historical difference.

Although the questions raised by Gauguin derive from 1879, they do in fact date back to a much more distant period; they stand for the basic questions of humanity, which have been raised ever since man has been capable of reflecting on his situation. Except for the first question, they have never been answered adequately (and even the answers to the first question, derived from the theory of evolution, are incomplete). Man is an enigma to himself. This is definitely one of the reasons why art is made: aspects of the 'Seinsfrage' are being raised over and over again. The same thing is done by science. And by philosophy, to which art is related most. Art is to be seen as the less rational, visual counterpart of philosophy.

Consequently, in this work philosophical questions and scientific charts present themselves as auxiliary disciplines. Within the field of visual art all conceivable means can be applied in their transformed shape of visual means.

Whether art can (still) play (and wishes to play) a part in the struggle for 'a better world' in our time, which has witnessed the loss of Utopia, is dubious. On the other hand, one could maintain that particularly in a period of worldwide recession, in this fin-de-siècle of the 20th century, with all its Doomsday connotations, Utopia could be one of the few straws grasped. After all, a characteristic of a Utopia is that it can hardly be overtaken by 'harsh facts', for there is only a rather loose connection between the harsh facts and Utopia.

This connection is by definition an antithesis, in the sense that a Utopia involves the possible realisation of Arcadia from a non-Arcadian situation. If paradise had not been lost, there would not have been any need to regain it. In this sense Utopia itself is 'the ideal place'.

Eikelenboom's work is utopian in character. Although it is not a cheerful communication which is presented here as the state of affairs, the following question is still open: despite the fact that the earth is threatened and mankind is attempting to make its life on earth effectively impossible, a new future may still be dawning. Where are we going? Back to the earth which will have to be transformed into paradise once more. That is what this work confronts us with in all its paradoxicality; it is a pessimistic Utopia.   PP

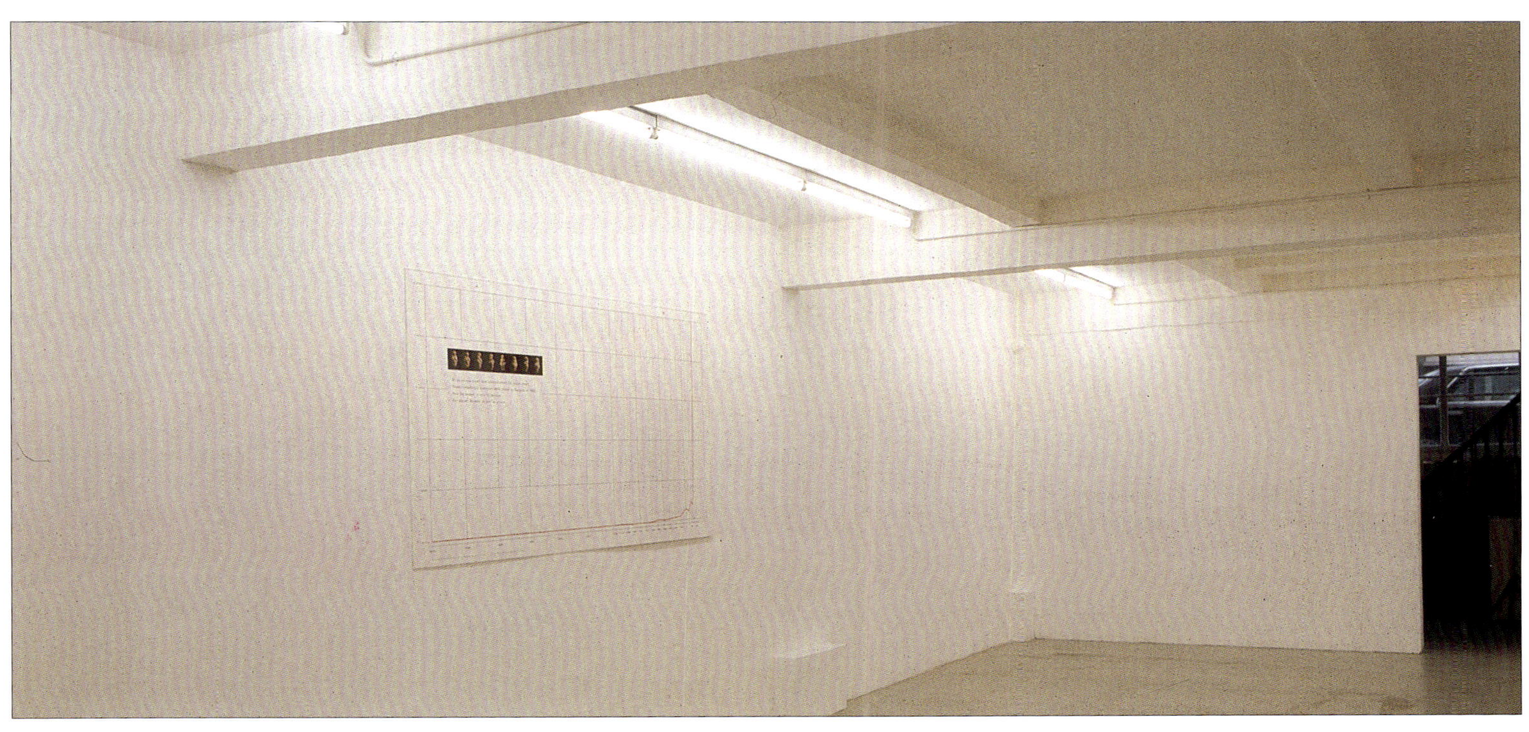

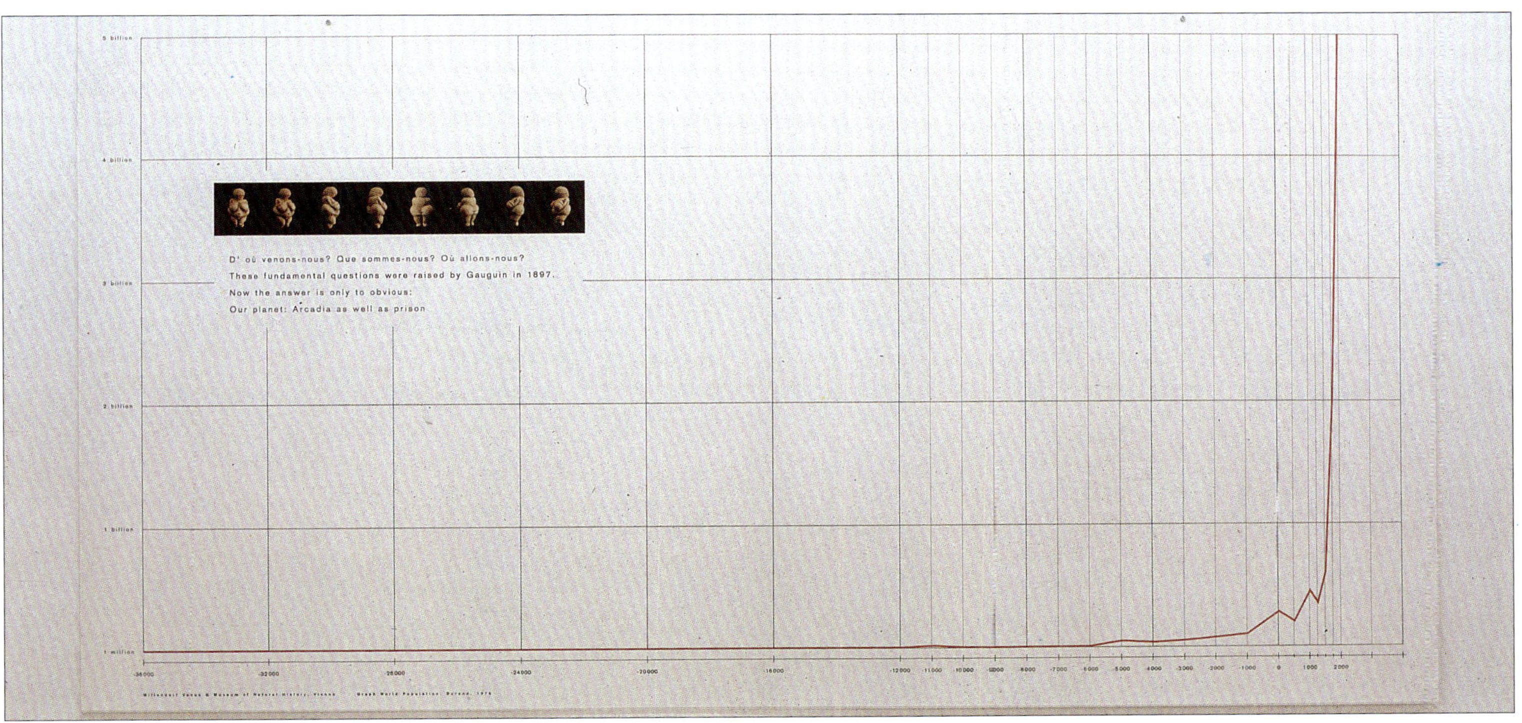

THE IDEAL PLACE: EVERYWHERE
DANIEL FAUST

Monday afternoon, last March, I had the pleasure of meeting this very alive and charming man who just happened to smoke these long cigarettes constantly while speaking at some length about the notion of 'The Ideal Place'. I questioned him to say more but did not get a single good answer. In April I met Lawrence. We conferred – Huh? Place and placement came into conversation. Additionally, discussion of an artwork in a place came up. At the end of April a fax arrived, giving more Ideal examples. Me, I like bad jokes. Richard used to be a terrible procrastinator. Lois and/or Amy tried unsuccesfully to be perfectionists. Plenne L Wingo walked around a good part of the earth backwards – he started in LA and wore sunglasses equipped with rearview mirrors. While going down the street in Pittsburgh PA he received a traffic ticket for . . . walking backwards.

Next to Wingo, at the San Fran Ripley's Believe It Or Not (BION) stood – ever so slightly stooped – 'The Unhappy Clown', 1779-1837. One night, many years ago, a sad-faced man went to see a doctor and said he was sick of life. 'You're working too hard', said the doctor, 'go see Grimaldi the clown at the circus, he'll make you laugh'. 'Doctor', said the sad-faced man, 'I am Grimaldi'.

I needed more ideas and walked to the record store for 12-inch real vinyl albums. The right recording appeared – 'I Hear A Symphony', Motown, 1966. Back liner notes read: 'I sat one night last summer in one of the hallowed halls of the entertainment world. I had come to see three young ladies who have reached the peak. The room was crowded, the atmosphere was alive with excitement, people were busy in conversation, in just plain enjoying themselves. A few moments later a phenomenon that I had never before experienced occurred. A sophisticated urbane audience had suddenly become completely enraptured and had fallen in love with these young ladies. I suddenly had the feeling that this room, which moments before had been crowded with others was now only occupied by myself, Diana, Florence, and Mary. Their hold upon me continued until suddenly I realised they had completed their performance and were leaving the stage. I have seen audiences before unwilling to allow entertainers who have satisfied them get off the stage, but never like this. The crowd that night, I understand, only re-enacted what has occurred many times earlier with The Supremes, and has continued to occur since then.

So much serious stuff – it seemed to me a little relief might be in order, so I gave Josh a phone call. He writes for this TV program. No, not a dumb and antiseptic one, so much as a smart and sardonic funny one. We spoke and spoke. We wrote and wrote. At San Fran Art Institute in 1977 this esteemed Linda instructor looked at a 4 x 6 foot contact sheet consisting of 25 rolls of film placed together on a sheet of black and white paper and said that this is not art. At first I was concerned and then I realised that this was very alright.

A June weekend in Woodstock appeared. We drove up Saturday morning. As usual the conversation revolved around art, awful romance, science and the such. After getting gas and going over this and that, David started to tell a fly-fishing story. A couple of years earlier both Ellen and David decided that this might be the thing to do. While at the tackle shop they looked and looked and were about to choose some basic rods and reels and lures. An older man, who very much appeared to look like what an experienced fly-fisher is supposed to look like, said, 'Don't get those things. Let me you show you the right equipment to get'. 'Follow me'. Well they drove and they drove, mile after long mile. Following him to his cabin as he had proposed meant leaving the comfort of the main road and travelling on this bad, bumpy and dusty road mile after long mile. Up hills. Over valleys. Ideas that the man may be demented and slowly leading them to their death and demise crossed their minds. Who is he? What does he really have in mind? were some of the ideas droping through Ellen's mind. Finally, they arrived. Sure enough his house was completely filled with fishing implements of every variety and description. At great length he told them of his experience and expertise about various kinds of rods, reels and everything else involved with the art and way of true fly-fishing. That next morning David and Ellen returned to that original tackle shop. What did they do, you might ask? They acquired the very rods and reels they had originally considered. Went fishing. Never caught a thing.

In order for me to make art I have to travel. It used to be I would arrive someplace and photograph. More recently, it is often the travelling itself that I try to capture. Planes, trains, automobiles, buses and such. The Niagara Falls Museum 'Home of the Daredevil Hall of Fame', North America's oldest museum. Established 1827. In Canada, the Rainbow Bridge in Ontario reports: 'The First Succesful Trip was made by a plump school teacher on the morning of October 24, 1901'. Her bruised and battered frame emerged from a now-historic barrel some three hours after it had been lossened in the Upper River. The pride of a continent, courageous Annie Taylor was destined to die in poverty after her seemingly magnificent triumph of the moment. Bobby Leach, a diminutive but boastful Cockney went over the Falls in a steel barrel on July 25, 1911. The effect meant a hospital stay that extended over 23 weeks, the result of two broken kneecaps and a badly smashed jaw.

Daniel Faust

Daniel Faust's contribution to the project 'The Ideal Place' consisted of a series of 1,400 small photographs, taken on a large number of locations. They had been fastened to the wall as neutrally as possible, without any internal hierarchy.

Faust is a traveller, he is mostly on the road. While travelling he keeps taking photographs, both of places where he happens to be for a while and of the journeys themselves (the means of transport and so on). Although a personal element of choice is present in the selection of destination, as well as in the places photographed, this does not appear to be the theme of the work. On the contrary, the places photographed have almost lost their individual meaning in the abundance of images. They have become random indications, parts of a further unspecified whole. I think in principle this work is to be infinitely extended, until all places (that is, the entire planet) have been visualised, leaving us a kind of catalogue of the world, a non-systematic encyclopedia in pictures.

The nomad does not have a home, at least no 'fixed abode'. He is at home everywhere and nowhere – potentially the whole world is his home. He is in that place where the bare necessities of life are to be satisfied, but for the rest it does not matter so much *where* he is: more important is the fact *that* he is. According to some, this is the spiritual core of nomadic existence – the nomad is said to live in a continuous awareness of the 'here and now' to a greater extent than the resident of a fixed abode.

Time and again nomadic existence has been compared to being an artist, never 'at home', always on the road. This causes a considerable distance from the 'fixed abode'. The artist puts up his tents in a work and after its completion moves on to the next work. Each work is a camp, a 'home', but 'coming home' is out of the question: each time the temporary home has to be put up all over again at a different site. The artist lives everywhere, at least everywhere his work takes him.

Daniel Faust literally makes his work on, and in response to, all sorts of existing locations. The metaphor has been made literal here, as it were. Not only, as in all art, is reality used as a metaphor. Later (or rather, at the same time) the stylistic figure is turned around – the metaphor, as we might put it, is taken literally, 'applied' to concretely existing places. In the end 'place' and 'metaphor' coincide.

Thus in principle, each place in this work has become 'the ideal place': the ideal place is the place *where one is*. Walking is just as much lifting one's foot as putting it down. Each moment is a 'here and now'. The ideal place can be everywhere and always, and is in effect everywhere and always.

PP

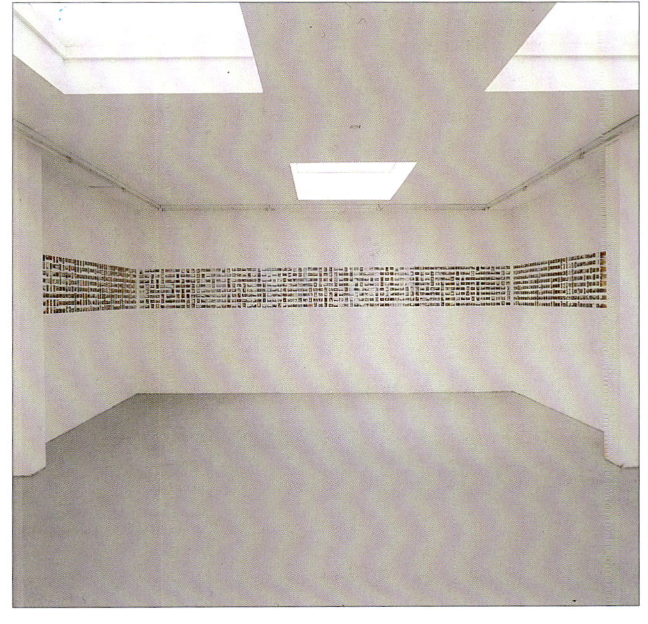

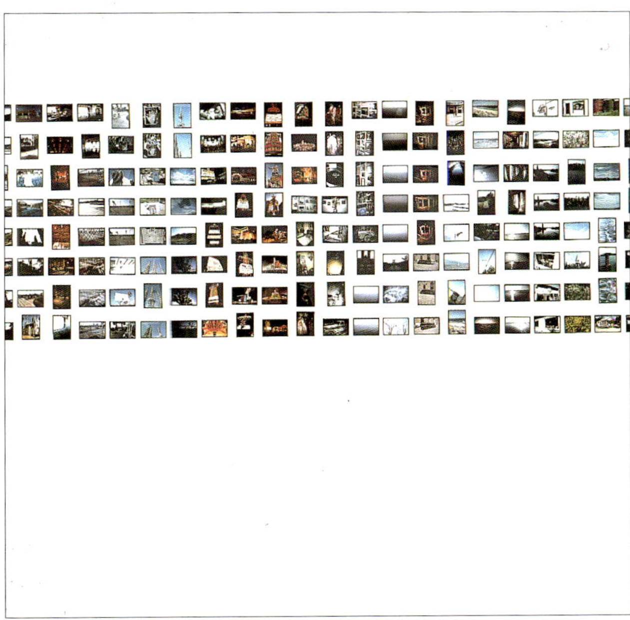

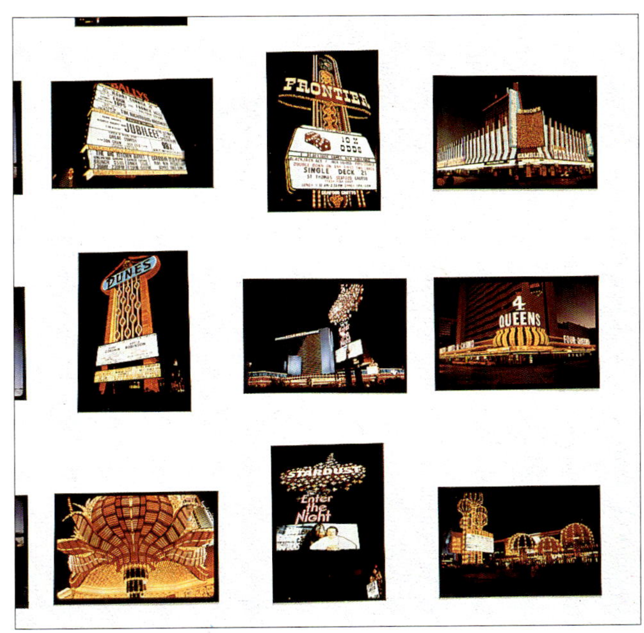

THE IDEAL PLACE: A SUBVERSIVE POSITIONING

RENÉE GREEN

Renée Green
Mommsenstr. 9
10629 Berlin
July 19, 1994

Dear Sowon,
I'm writing to invite you to participate in a show which has been an ongoing project for the past year in The Hague at the Haags Centrum voor Aktuele Kunst (HCAK). The year-long project is called 'The Ideal Place'. There are three separate spaces there and for approximately one month different artists are invited to use the space as they choose.

I was invited there last October and I've been tkinking about it since then. It was around that time that Nils and Merlin were working on tha Gallery Z brochure. That endeavor seemed to relate in some way to something which could be referred to within the context of 'The Ideal Place', which is a totally general idea. I continued to think about that. Gallery Z seemed to be referring to some ideal location which it was not necessarily possible to ever reach. Yet whether it could be found was still a question.

Time passed. Merlin did his show, I did my show and there were photos which intersected, at least with bits of Potsdam. I liked the way the photos formed a strange mixture of places, and made everything into a fiction.

Between then and now. You, who appear in one of Merlin's photos, gave a presentation for the 'Contact Zone' symposium which I enjoyed very much, and for which I am still anxiously awaiting the text for publication. (But that's another letter). Your presentation and the work you've been doing in relationship to these thoughts interested me and I thought of inviting you to do something related to the talk and the idea of the Peacock Room.

Many conversations and walks with Nils revolve around different ideas of space. When he made the 'egg room' (an organic and obsessive cavernous structure to which he has transformed the former guest room) it seemed as if it might be possible to think about each of your works: yours, Merlin's and Nils' in relationship to the notion of an 'Ideal Place'. The idea didn't go away and I thought I'd like to write about why I was interested in your different works, or ways of perceiving, and I wanted to propose as my contribution an essay and a proposal that to me an ideal place would be one of communion of some kind, and that I would like to invite the three of you to share it.

Renée Green
Mommsenstr. 9
10629 Berlin
July 19, 1994

Dear Nils,
I'm writing to invite you to participate in a show which has been an ongoing project for the past year in The Hague at the Haags Centrum voor Aktuele Kunst (HCAK). The year-long project is called 'The Ideal Place'. There are three separate spaces there and for approximately one month different artists are invited to use the space as they choose.

I was invited there last October and I've been thinking about it since then. It was around that time that you and Merlin were working on the Gallery Z brochure. That endeavor seemed to relate in some way to something with could be referred to within the context of 'The Ideal Place', which is a totally general idea. I continued to think about that. Gallery Z seemed to be referring to some ideal location which it was not necessarily possible to ever reach. Yet whether it could be found was still a question.

Time passed. Merlin did his show, I did my show and there were photos which intersected, at least with bits of Potsdam. Your photos were a part of these. I liked the way the photos formed a strange mixture of places and made everything into a fiction.

Between then and now. Sowon who appears in one of Merlin's photos gave a presentation for the 'Contact Zone' symposium in which she referred to a room in the Freer Art Gallery in Washington, DC called the Peacock Room. The painter Whistler had been commissioned to do a painting. When it was hung, the collector who'd requested it wanted the entire room redone to work with the painting. That's a truncated version of the story. Anyway, her presentation and the work she's been doing in relationship to these thoughts interested me and I thought of inviting her to do something.*

Many conversations and walks with you have revolved around different ideas of space. When you made the 'egg room' it seemed as if it might be possible to think about each of your works: yours, Merlin's and Sowon's in relationship to the notion of an 'Ideal Place'. The idea didn't go away and I thought I'd like to write about why I was interested in your different works, or ways of perceiving, and I wanted to propose as my contribution an essay and a proposal stating that to me an ideal place would be one of communion of some kind, and that I would like to invite the three of you to share it.

Renée Green
Mommsenstr. 9
10629 Berlin
July 19, 1994

Dear Merlin,

I'm writing to invite you to participate in a show which has been an ongoing project for the past year in The Hague at the Haags Centrum voor Aktuele Kunst (HCAK). The year-long project is called 'The Ideal Place'. There are three separate spaces there and for approximately one month different artists are invited to use the space as they choose.

I was invited there last October and I've been thinking about it since then. It was around that time that you and Nils were working on the Gallery Z brochure. That endeavor seemed to relate in some way to something which could be referred to within the context of 'The Ideal Place', which is a totally general idea. I continued to think about that. Gallery Z seemed to be referring to some ideal location which it was not necessarily possible to ever reach. Yet whether it could be found was still a question.

Time passed. You did your show in New York, I did my show in New York and there were photos which intersected, at least with bits of Potsdam. I liked the way the photos formed a strange mixture of places and made them into a fiction.

Between then and now. Sowon who appears in one of your photos gave a presentation for the 'Contact Zone' symposium in which she referred to a room in the Freer Art Gallery in Washington, DC called the Peacock Room. The painter Whistler had been commissioned to do a painting. When it was hung, the collector who'd requested it wanted the entire room redone to work with the painting. That's a truncated version of the story. Anyway, her presentation and the work she's been doing in relationship to these thoughts interested me and I thought of inviting her to do something.*

Many conversations and walks with Nils revolve around different ideas of space. When he made the 'egg room' it seemed as if it might be possible to think about each of your works, yours, Nils' and Sowon's in relationship to the notion of an 'Ideal Place'. The idea didn't go away and I thought I'd like to write about why I was interested in your different works, or ways of perceiving, and I wanted to propose as my contribution an essay and a proposal stating that to me an ideal place would be one of communion of some kind, and that I would like to invite the three of you to share it.

** CORRECTION.*
Actually, part of what Sowon describes in her talk is how James McNeil Whistler, after having completing a painting he was commissioned to paint by shipping magnate Fredrick R Leyland, realised that the red in the painting clashed with the red in the room in which it was to reside. With Leyland's permission Whistler wanted to alter the painting to work better with the room's decor. Leyland left on business and in the interim Whistler's project took on greater and greater proportions which involved changing the colour scheme of the room to turquoise and gold. A scandal ensued.

Thinking about my own work it seems as if a fascination with finding an 'ideal place' – in terms of my interest in observing this desire on the part of others as well of myself – runs through different works. The definition of such a place is very relative and the space in which it may be found is variable. Even the titles of different projects suggest this recurring, or maybe compulsive, desire on my part to address the topic: 'Anatomies of Escape', 'VistaVision: Landscape of Desire', 'Sites of Genealogy: Loophole of Retreat', 'Idyll Pursuits', 'World Tour', 'Secret', 'Taste Venue', 'Negotiations in the 'Contact Zone', 'Quest'. These works combine public discussions, performances by others and myself and film series in addition to discrete objects, videos, audioworks and installations, all part of the work

Sowon Kwon, Nils Norman and Merlin Carpenter are each artists whose perspectives, each for different reasons, interest me and with whom I've been in dialogue for a few years. The possibility of dialogue is rare enough these days, akin in its scarcity to a precious addictive drug or a spiritually induced state of euphoria. The notion of a place of communion, which I am proposing, is no doubt a utopian one, yet it continues to be necessary to make repeated attempts to engage in this possibility. The process of thinking and of exchange is what is intended to occur in this 'ideal place'.

Attaining this sort of place was also one of my objectives in organising the symposium 'Negotiations in the Contact Zone', held in New York at The Drawing Center in April 1994. Sowon delivered a paper at that event, as well as Lynne Tillman, James Clifford, Manthia Diawara, Karim Ainouz, Joe Wood, Diedrich Diedrichsen, Miwon Kwon, Judith Barry and Simon Leung, and from which there will be the documentary tapes at the HCAK. The participants formed an international combination of writers, academics, cultural critics, film makers and artists. The symposium was initiated as a plea for a voicing of increased critical thought in the cultural realm and each of the participants were urged to take up this challenge by relating this intention to their own production. It was also an invitation for a discussion across disciplines which have already been contested

Somehow the work of both Merlin Carpenter and of Nils Norman in its diversity can also be seen as addressing related concerns, albeit from different angles. Gallery Z is described as a 'cement-link-broken -network-pulverizer machine of identical cells, well only two actually' in Göttingen, which is now a gallery, amidst other galleries, or rather that is how it appears at certain times of day because it is a trompe-l'oeil stage set, among other things. Gallery Z seems to be a mysterious place. Here is an excerpt from their joint Gallery Z brochure in which they pose many questions:

' Is Gallery Z really so very sophisticated?'*
** It has been used as a museum of project rooms, an independent HQ, a media fanzine, a community art fair, restaurant, pirate hang-out, animal sanctuary, and as a venue for all other academic activity. We re-arrange the walls before each meal. It becomes an inverted mystery train: Public Art as something to enthuse. Yet does the public want to be helped? Questions lie rotting.'*

The following is an initial list of associations, which could develop into questions regarding a notion of an 'ideal place' and where such a space might reside: a place of communion, one which is sought because of a primal urge for a womb, a safe place, a bond, yet a place which contains frightful aspects which excessive contact can generate:
a body

a cyborg (Donna Haraway)
cyberspace
dream
movies
the imaginary
a book (Walter Benjamin)
memory
a song
a space on paper (Corbusier and Piranesi)
a concrete form in space (a portable location)
a photo (trace transformed)
a video (an edited place)

Is it so important to find this place or does its importance lie rather in its potential to dangle above us like a carrot and goad us on?
Renée Green

The ideal place, no matter how it is interpreted, is in the first place a human construct, at the least a thought that may occur to us. But if an ideal place existed, what would be the use of it? And what is it that determines its ideality? In principle I think each place in itself is neutral, or indifferent, and as long as there is no one to observe this neutrality or indifference, even this may not hold – the existence of this place can be argued about (or, worse, even that is impossible then, for observation and hence awareness of the place are required for this, and awareness automatically entails the attributing of meaning. Consequently, this place does not 'exist' at all, not even as a fictive construct).

'Neutrality' and 'indifference', just as much as 'ideality', are mental constructs, meanings that can be attributed to something (a place, for instance) in almost all cases essentially examples of anthropomorphisms, of the 'pathetic fallacy'. We have a strong inclination to attribute human qualities to things and constructs. Consequently, places are subject to interpretations and meanings given to them by people, and only then have they become places capable of being defined. In themselves they possess no qualities, and should this be so after all, we cannot know about it until we know these places or at least can imagine them. In other words, we ourselves create these (all) places. This implies that the place to which we attribute the epithet 'ideal' has evidently not just been 'invented by people', but is also 'meant for people'; this place is not ideal 'as such', for that does not mean anything – it is ideal for people. In other words (but at the same time formulated differently) it is people that make a place ideal, for if there were no people there would not be a place, there would not be any (perception of) ideality either and no 'ideal place' of any kind would then exist.

I think that Renée Green, in her conception of the 'ideal place' wanted to stress this aspect – she refers to the ideal place as 'a place of communion' and invited three other artists to share it with her (thus turning it into an 'actual' ideal place). Without meeting terribly often, these artists (Merlin Carpenter, Renée Green, Sowon Kwon and Nils Norman) have been in regular debate for several years. I think their cooperation in the HCAK is to be regarded as a stage in this debate.

For the visitor all this resulted in a presentation on the upper floor of the HCAK of photo works by four obviously different hands, which do not immediately strike you as related. They did not clearly deal with a common theme, either in narrative or iconography or other symbolism, at least not to such an extent that the observer could easily define it. Finally, a video monitor had been placed in the exhibition room playing a one-and-a-half-hour tape with texts spoken during the symposium 'Negotiations in the Contact Zone', organised by Green in New York (in which some of the present exhibitors had also participated, who were, among others, to be seen on the screen). The term 'Contact Zone' in an even more general sense appears to have a meaning related to a place in the sense of 'communion'; at least, 'communion' is a specific circumstance which can only exist when there is a 'contact zone'.

One may wonder in what respect this presentation is different from any other group exhibition compiled by an artist who invites other artists on the basis of not further specified empathy and affection. I do not think that the idea will soon occur to the visitor that he is in 'a place of communion' here, but rather that this is a room with very diverse work by four different artists, which in some not immediately visible way seems to be related to 'The Ideal Place', since that has been agreed upon as the coordinating theme at the HCAK at the time.

In my opinion, the 'ideal place' here should not be regarded as being the room in which the work can be seen, nor looked for in the direct meaning of the various works, nor in their demonstrable (lack of?) coherence, but in the process of which it is a reflection not immediately visible to the outsider. The process is the continuing conversation among the four artists involved. The question could be asked here whether an un-understandable reflection of a process in which it did not take part would be of any use to the public (after all, art is a communicative discipline). Moreover, this implies that the public is explicitly excluded from this 'ideal place'. At best, it may be pointed out to the public, also by means of the textual explanation in the form of Green's formulation of the ideal place as 'a place of communion', that something like the 'ideal place' might be present in an otherwise unnoticeable interaction among four people, a kind of meta-ideal place therefore, not possessing any general relevance, but reserved to the members of a kind of 'secret society'.

This leads us to the problem of the relation between process and product, between intention and effect. On the one hand it is rather obvious that the process produces a product and that this product is shown to the public. On the other hand one could also opt for showing the process in various ways, though this may never result in a completed art object. In the late 60s and early 70s this was thoroughly tried out. But these are the 90s and there is a whole period inbetween, in which the object was of central importance again, in art production and even more so in presentation. Could it be possible that in a period of extreme fragmentation some artists are seeking for new contact, a new 'contact zone' and that somehow presenting this fact as such contributes to this continuing process, just as much as being a reflection of it, so that the presentation includes a stimulation and testing of the process? The fact that intention and effect do not always keep pace with each other can be seen as a drawback or not, but in this case it may not have been the intention at all to produce a universally understandable and accessible 'unity in diversity' that could, for instance, be described as 'an he) ideal place' or 'a place of communion'. Possibly, the value of Green's contribution is rather to be found in incorporating the place offered in order to create an ideal place ('of communion') there, in the sense of a good opportunity to carry on the continuing process the conversation among artists, the 'communion') temporarily at the HCAK. In that case this work is to be regarded as an act of almost subversive confirmation of identity, like 'taking power in one's own hands' by 'abusing' the art institution, as it were. If this is so, the work has a clear and possibly significant value in the positioning of the artist in the infrastructure of the art circuit.

PP

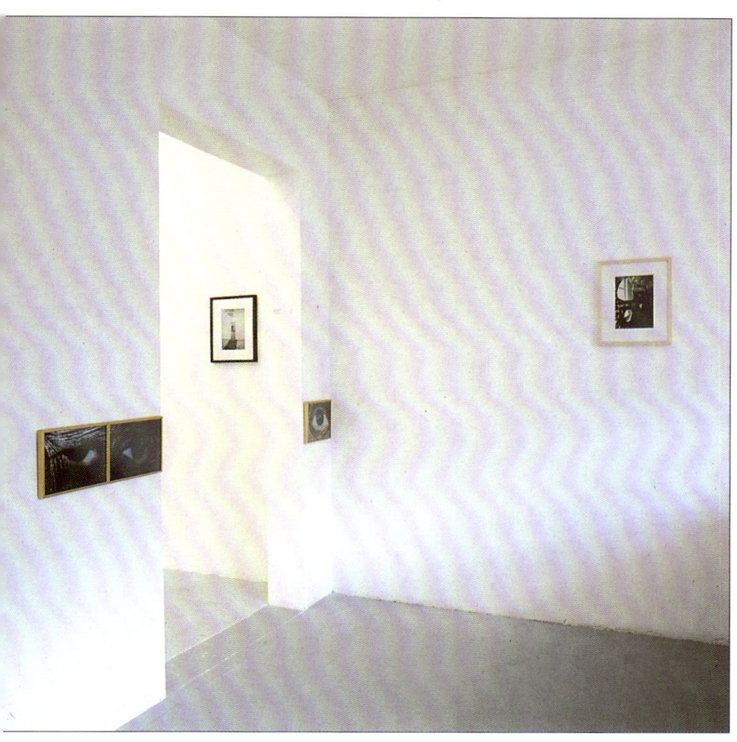

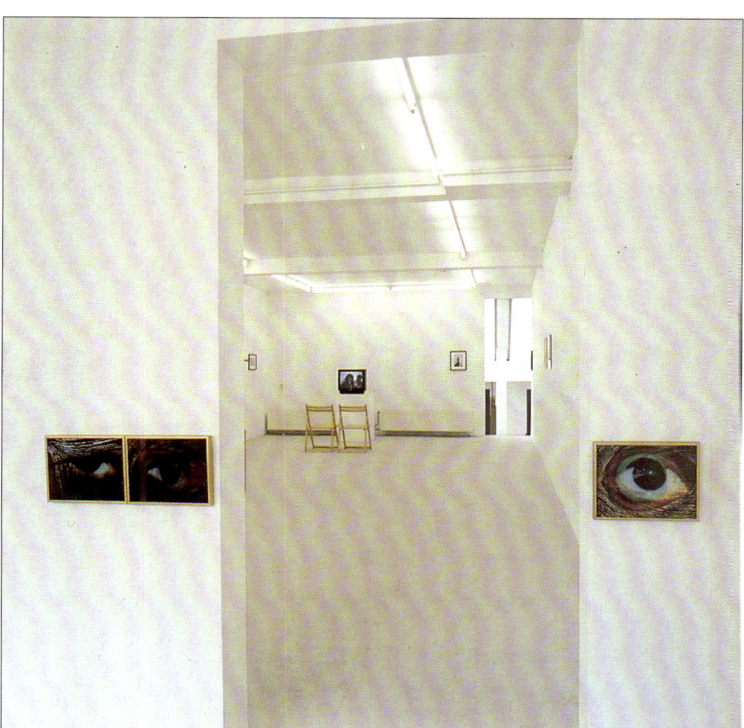

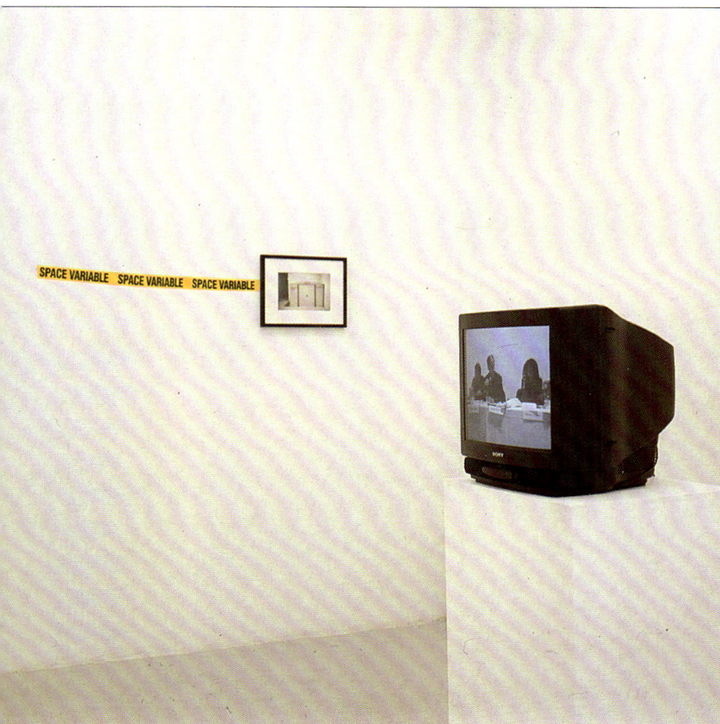

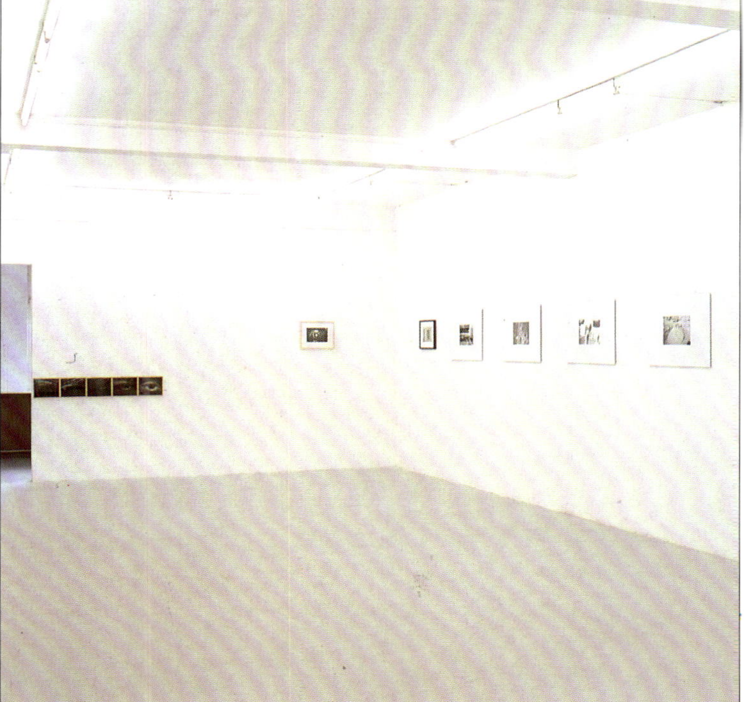

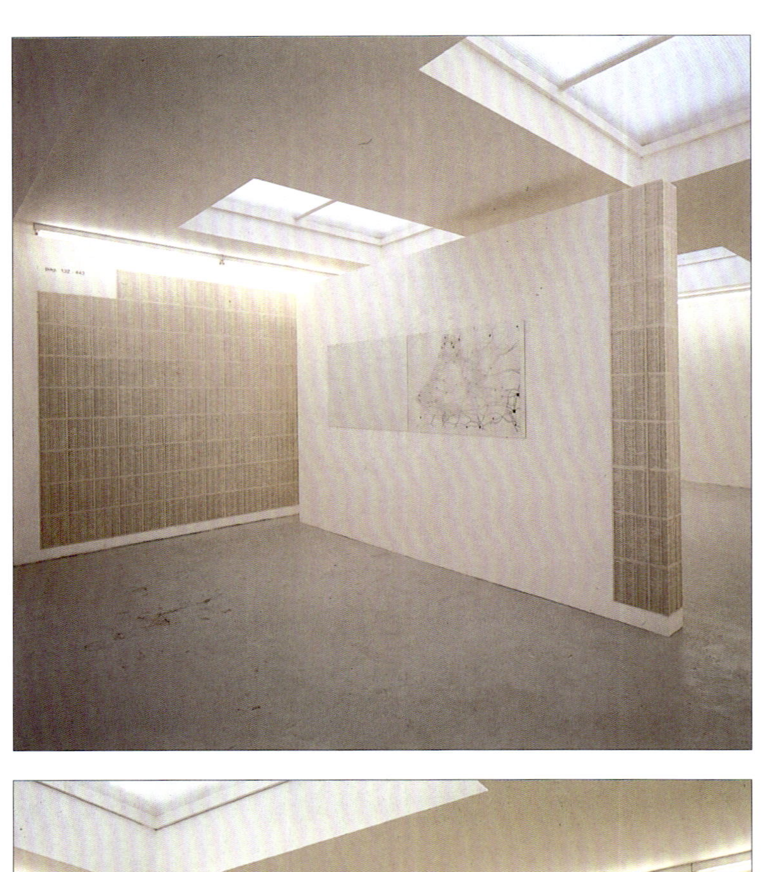
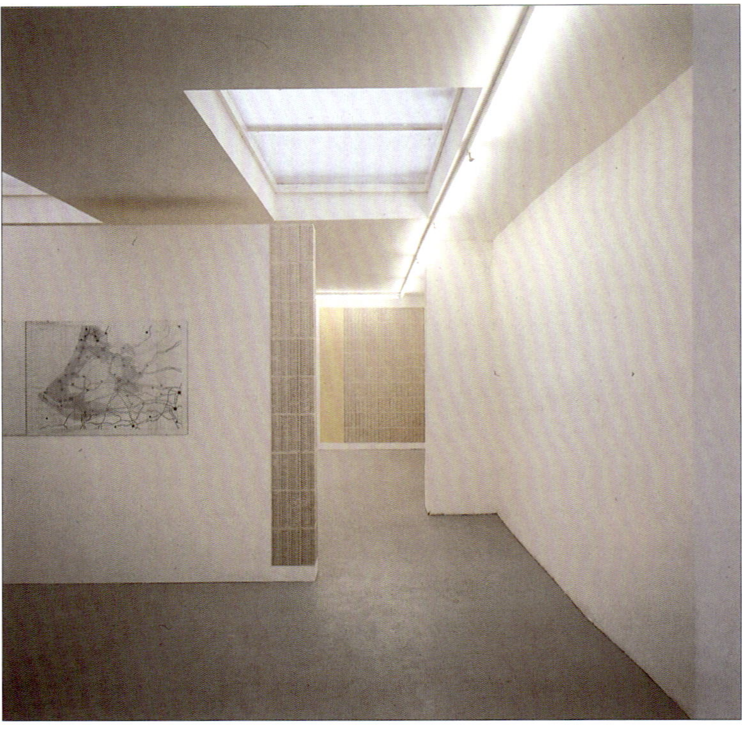
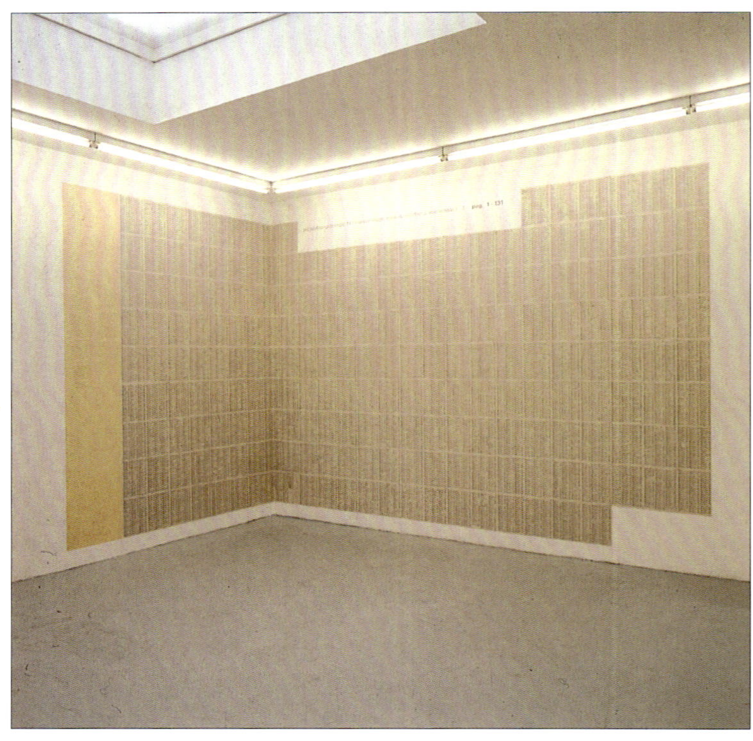
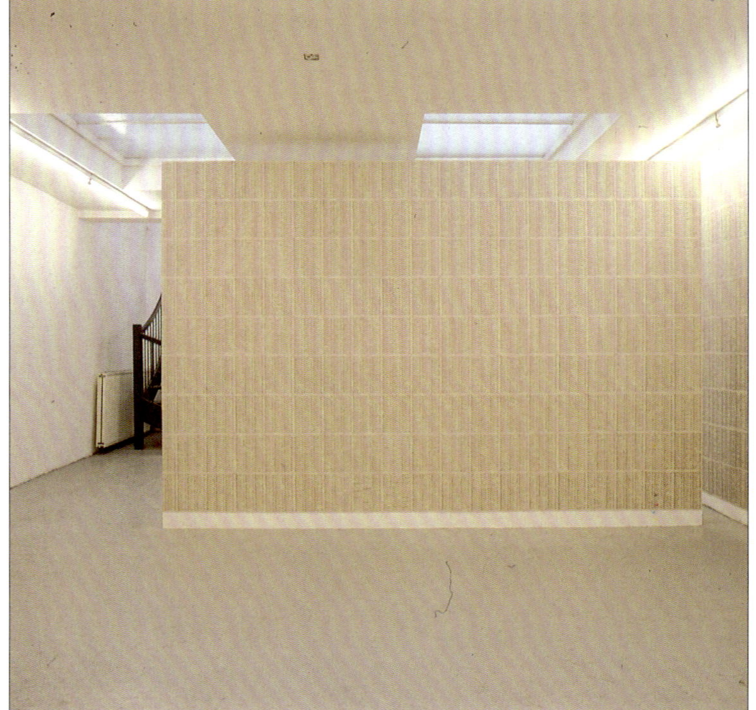

THE IDEAL PLACE: CHANGE IS THE ESSENCE OF CULTURE

JAN VAN GRUNSVEN

ideal

I adj   expressing possible perfection which is unlikely to exist
in the real world; perfect

II n   1 idea looked upon as perfect
2 perfect example

(Longman Dictionary of Contemporary English)

'It is obvious, the third world and the first world no longer exist. The third world is working hard at establishing itself in the first world and Los Angeles is a forerunner of what the fourth world will look like; a city without a centre, where population groups from all over the world will have to try and live together and where violence will only increase, as long as the white community aims at retaining its privileges.'

Peter Sellars, I Het Parool, 18/05/93

If Los Angeles can be called the forerunner of what is already relatively noticeable in Europe, that is, of the irrepressible development towards a genuinely multicultural society or the so-called 'fourth world' Sellars refers to, with respect to a formulation of 'the ideal place' this raises the question of what will be meant by 'ideal' in such a social structure. To what extent can such a concept be applied to a circumstance characterised by the parallel existence of various and divergent cultural identities? And if so, who makes what the ideal and for whom? From what motives and on the strength of what right?

'Since Khomeini sentenced Salman Rushdie to death in February 1989, because he was said to have offended the prophet in his book The Satanic Verses, Rushdie's life has been at stake in a holy war. More precisely: in a war on sacred matters. The fatwah which Khomeini pronounced on Rushdie is a breach in our views on cultures. The fatwah has made it clear that the geographical distance between the West and the rest of the world indeed has become smaller and smaller, but that the cultural distance, on the contrary, seems to become greater and greater. A few hours flight takes us to Teheran. But in order to grasp Islam from the West we need a few centuries.'

Anil Ramdas I 'In my Father's House' I Mets, Amsterdam, 1993

In connection with the cultural breach, it is clear that a formulation of 'the ideal place', whether or not utopian or universal in nature, can only be understood in a very limited sense. And does Western culture, which as the embodiment of modernisation increasingly serves as an example or spectre for the rest of the world, possess sufficient credit to venture making a pronouncement on 'the ideal place' at all?

Or, put differently and closer to home: how desirable or practical is making such a pronouncement in the eyes of a migrant, a fugitive or a homeless person?

Jan Van Grunsven

A temporary transit position in a network under conditions formulated in advance and assumed to be ideal, as opposed to this definition of the ideal place which concentrates on a fixed point (no matter how temporary and changeable) another and more dynamic concept of space can be formulated; the concept of implementation or annexation. In doing so, the epi-phenomena of a specific region are related to the region itself; the region is infected, as it were, with its own peripheral phenomena. This is already taking place.

The classic relation between geography and infrastructural topology – the physical and logistic circumstances of the landscape, which are a decisive factor for what can be realised in the field of urban development and architecture – appear to lose significance due to an increasing number of artificial interventions. Through the extension of the networks too far beyond one's own region and supported by the development of new media technologies, information is distributed all over the world in real time. The West hardly seems to realise that the far-reaching consequences do not just concern the (outside) world, but in reverse also influence its own culture. The increasing flow of migrants, partly due to the above developments, is not accepted as a result of its own strategy.

Under the influence of the above-mentioned processes it has become impossible to define a scale within which these processes are taking place on a social and cultural level. It can only be concluded that they do indeed take place and cannot be stopped.

Thus, the essence of our cultural self-image appears to be determined by the extent of flexibility of the response to changing circumstances. In this view there is no room for models derived from historical preoccupations: they are simply no longer applicable.

JvG

THE IDEAL PLACE: RIGHT INSIDE THE IMAGES
THOMAS HUBER

The ideal place is in the painting.

Thomas Huber

Thomas Huber's contribution to the project 'The Ideal Place' consisted of a series of four paintings placed on easels in a square formation. They were 'looking at each other', giving the visitor the opportunity to enter the square and either look at the paintings separately or as a whole.

Apart from all its other layers of meaning, this work is to be read as a kind of comic strip, in itself nothing new in art – instead of the story of Christ's birth or suffering, these paintings describe their own vicissitudes.

In spite of the neutral and closed square formation, it is not so hard to find the most obvious sequence (although in principle it is not inconceivable that other 'routes' could make sense too, there is no time or room enough now to further investigate that possibility). On the 'first' painting we see the back of the four paintings stored in the studio, possibly waiting to leave it and go out into the world. That it concerns 'these' particular paintings is something we can only deduce from what follows, ie the other paintings, on which they also (partly) show their fronts and thus become recognisable. A rostrum is also present in the studio: evidently words count as well.

The 'second' painting shows the four paintings on easels in an exhibition room of a museum, essentially in the same sort of arrangement as at the HCAK itself. Children without eyes appear on all the paintings, but on one of the four– which is only partly visible – large eyes can be seen (parts of one of the paintings at the HCAK).

The 'third' painting shows one of the paintings (also present at the HCAK) in the exhibition room of the museum – a kind of mimicry therefore of the actual situation or the other way around – the only difference being that a vase of flowers has been left out. Meanwhile it is no longer clear which is the original and which the reproduction, and whether these categories apply at all here. Fact and fiction start to mingle. The paintings are 'here' at the HCAK as tangible, concrete objects on which the artist has depicted those very same objects in different situations, and at the same time they are present in those depicted situations themselves, where, naturally, they must be just as concrete and tangible. Depiction and 'reality' continuously alternate: the 'concrete' reality of the HCAK presentation is no 'more real' than the imaginary presentation in the studio or exhibition room looked at from the HCAK. From the point of view of the depicted place, the situation at the HCAK will be experienced as imaginary.

The situation is therefore tantalising and unsolvably ambiguous, more or less in the same way as there is no chance of finding out whether a pupa dreaming that it is a butterfly is a pupa dreaming that it is a butterfly, or a butterfly dreaming that it is a pupa dreaming that it is a butterfly. In the same way we are never quite sure whether at a particular moment we are dreaming or awake – it could be that we are dreaming that we are awake. This implies that the intrinsic reality of (on) the painting increasingly presents itself as at least just as plausible as the reality at the HCAK. Meanwhile the rostrum also returns in this 'third' painting, which we had come across earlier in the studio. There is a row of benches in front of it and behind them an open passage leading out of the building. Evidently someone is expected to give a lecture on these four paintings (perhaps the artist himself, who frequently does so) but for the time being we are kept in the dark. We could stipulate, though, that word and image are not necessarily separated in Huber's view, but the absence of a speaker and an audience may also point to the contrary.

The 'fourth' painting shows us what the 'third' had already promised: the world outside the exhibition room. Or rather, it is painted from a position somewhere outside the museum, which is visible as a peculiar building with one exhibition room (the room in which the paintings are arranged which are also presented at the HCAK), decorated with little faces and bones and taut outlines. We see the 'entrance' of the museum, which was the 'exit' on the 'third' painting, as well as a second entrance at the 'side' of the building (front and back are not specified). In view of the earlier images of the museum arrangement, it is not very likely that there are any more passages from inside to outside (although one could also maintain that it might be desirable if each painting had the disposal of its own 'view'). Anyone who happens to know it, may recognise the artist's house behind the museum. His studio is also there and thus the circle (or the square) has eventually been closed in a sense: the work 'started' and 'ends' in the studio. Thus art is created in the studio, tours around the world and finally returns home (whether this always takes place in a material sense or not does not really matter, as the work of the artist will always remain his spiritual property).

I think this painting makes a strong plea for the reality of the painting. not in the sense of 'a window towards the world' nor purely in its aspect of object, but to such an extent that the 'depicted' reality can claim this term just as much as the reality in which the observer finds himself while looking at it. There is no difference in value and meaning, it is not sure which is which, the current categories lose their reliability.

But there is a difference of course, for the painting confronts us with a reality made by the painter – a devised, construed reality (insofar as this does not apply to any form of reality in any more or less conscious sense); a directed, not coincidental reality, having the right to exist in itself and moreover, by the use of tautologies and paradoxes, entering into a special, even radical relationship with the 'obvious' or 'coincidental' reality in which the observer in the art institution finds himself (insofar as this does indeed imply a contrast, which could be different for every case and on which subject entire books have been and will be written – but we cannot pursue it further here). These paintings literally interfere with the reality of the observer: they show him another variant of exactly the same situation as the one he is confronted with and which he himself is automatically surrounded by (hence the square) which is at the same time completely different. In this respect, the pull of 'reality' is very strong. It is as if these paintings force us to step through the looking-glass, like Alice, into a dimension where everything is the same and yet quite different. And eventually we never know, of course, on which side of the looking-glass we actually are.

Consequently, it is not without importance, and definitely not a superfluous presentation mannerism, that Huber presents these paintings, as he has done before, on easels. This makes them independent of the place in which they are present and together they construe their own significant place. In terms of place, that is what the 'ideal place' is: in the painting, or perhaps also, in the place where the observer stands, right in the middle of the work, right in the middle of confusion. Besides, the easel produces the association with 'work in progress': the painting is created on the easel (whether this is really the case or not, is not to the point here) and as long as it is on the easel, one cannot be faulted for thinking it is not 'finished'. The reality presented by these paintings is indeed in no way 'finished', nor was the reality of the observer before his reality and the one of the paintings started to mingle to make matters even more complex: reality (for lack of a more convenient concept) is never 'finished'; that is not at issue here, nor is it the responsibility of the artist to create this 'finishing', it is rather his natural task to question this supposed 'finishing'.

That is what Huber has done here, I think: question our conditioning with respect to reality by confronting it with a just as plausible (or just as nonsensical, if you like) proposal and making the two interweave, possibly resulting in clashes and confusion, but chiefly providing an opportunity to question accepted truths once again. In this respect Huber's 'ideal place' is a rather didactic place and this is not meant as a term of abuse, but as an epithet which has a long tradition in the visual arts, only occasionally cropping up again here and there in our day. And sometimes we can indeed learn something from a work of art.

PP

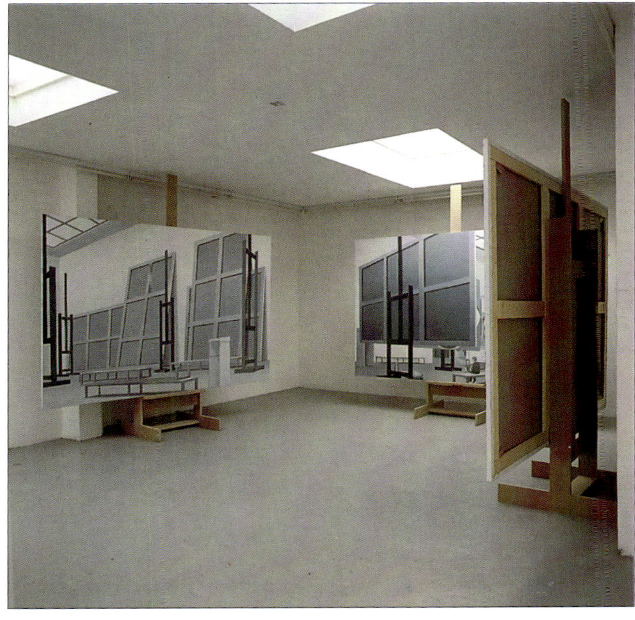

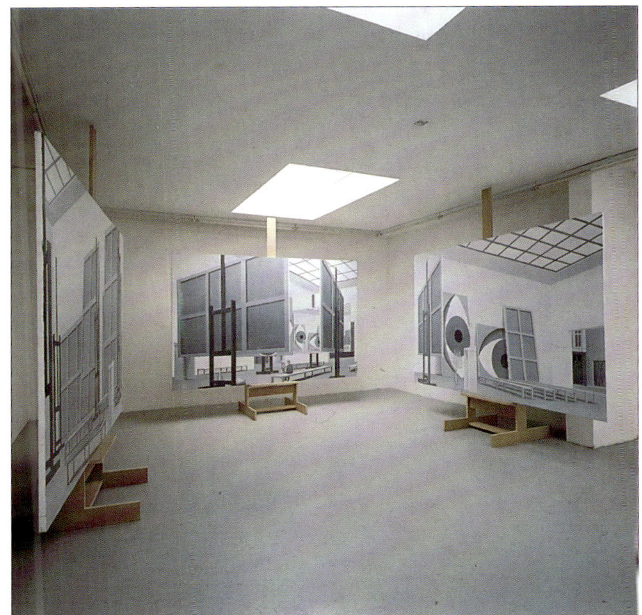

THE IDEAL PLACE: A STATE OF ALERTNESS

MARK LEWIS

The unruly crowd swarmed towards the stark expanse of ceremonial concrete that sprawled slovenly in front of the Ministry of Culture. The Ministry building is imposing in the calculated way that all the Stalinist architectural monuments of the period are: cascades of broadening platforms, each supported by doric style columns, sweeping down from a neo-gothic tower towards the base; one so magnificently large that it spoke for more than half of the giant square that it occupied. Standing in front, erect, arm outstretched, somewhat patinated, but nevertheless in much the same state as he was when it was first installed, [Lenin] the Father of the Revolution. Being located slightly off the central axis of power, he may have missed out on all the activity that had gripped the nation these last few days. The crowd, however, was there to put him right. By deftly toppling him from his granite perch, they hoped to defile him, to teach him a lasting lesson, and perhaps without even realising it, to establish an iconoclastic emblem for the passing of the ancient regime.

Unruly crowds had gathered before other statues in times such as this. Sometimes their unruliness had been meticulously organised, and sometimes the gatherings were so spontaneous that they had proved to be treacherous to the very participants. Crowds had hurried and run, bolted and fallen over in their enthusiasm to join in or witness the demise of some hated figure cast in bronze or carved from expensive stone. Some had even died as tons of metal and stone plunged precariously to the ground; a kind of revolutionary repetition, a choreographic moment that after a monumental explosion, leaves in its wake a stunning silence. This silence, like a vacuum, is the instant when those who have participated in, or simply watched the felling of the giant, are forced to take stock: the silence is as much terrifying as orgiastic, it registers both the demise of the ancient regime and the immanent emergence of something new, often the old dressed as new. Crowds are dazed and in their own silence they wait, often without really knowing why; they wait to see what form of order will materialise out of the silence. Just as Napoleon, in full Roman regalia, had been pulled down from his perch on top of the Vendôme column, so too, in an earlier age, had Louis XIV descended ignominiously to the ground in the very same location. If Lenin was to fall, then he would have to join these illustrious precursors and perhaps, like them, would have his removal dignified and immortalised by the Courbet of this age.

Except the crowd was confused. Confused perhaps, because unaware that what they were about to embark upon was ritualistic in form, and without instruction, their spontaneous roles had still to be defined. Confusion gave way to some sort of order when a few of the more vocal members of the crowd managed to persuade others to help them in their quickly thought-out plan. Someone had brought a rope and those gathered near the front of the crowd enthusiastically

grabbed one end of it as two large individuals, taking turns, repeatedly tried to lasso the large statue of Lenin with the other. That these two individuals in their revolutionary joy had consumed a liberal amount of alcohol probably contributed to their patently rueful aim. The rope was thrown up seven times and seven times it fell to the ground. With each failed attempt the roar of encouragement from the crowd diminished and threatened to turn into howls of vilification. Order now, as always, perched precipitously on the edge of anarchy. Eventually a young boy, tired of all this unproductive bravado, took the rope from the men and tying it to his waist managed to scramble to the top of Lenin's shoulders. Turning to the crowd for a moment, as if to underline the magnitude of the achievement and the gravitas of what was soon to follow, the boy looked around and shared for a second Lenin's majestic vista. Ceremonial expectations below, however, trumped his own more modest reflection and to the burlesque cat-calls of others, he threw the rope over Lenin's neck. The crowd exhaled with mad satisfaction and began to pull and pull and pull.

And the statue moved not a bit. At the very moment when everyone beneath wished for nothing more than to see it tumble like so much rubble to the ground, the statue had never looked more dignified and invincible. Indeed, one was struck with the idea that this very moment, characteristically theatrical and quotational with its litany of historical precedents, might just have been the epiphany of the statue's heretofore silent existence. Except for its official inauguration some 50 years earlier, could anyone really confess to having paid much attention to it? Having disappeared like so much useless furniture into the city landscape, it re-surfaced only occasionally as a directional prop – take a left or right turn at the statue – for those unfamiliar with the city. Looking at it now, completely surrounded, commanding voluminous celebration (albeit one dependent on the anticipation of its demise) one could not help but think that the statue had finally achieved its real power of inscribing the very mortality of its detractors: while it stood triumphantly still, the crowd below was literally tripping and falling as the torque of the rope threw people back each time the syncopation of the pull collapsed. Even the white paint that dripped down its front, which foolishly someone in the crowd had hurled at the statue just as the boy began his dizzy ascent (and thus guaranteeing that he would return marked by oil), even this minor blemish could not detract from the feeling of rigid transcendence that the statue seemed to be almost deliberately acquiring minute by minute.

Perhaps this rigidity gave life and movement to the statue, in much the same way as Pushkin had animated the Bronze Horseman more than 150 years earlier. For without moving, in refusing to move as a sea of antagonism swarmed beneath it, the statue seemed to be saying that its own life force was more other-worldly, more transcen-

dental than the prosaic arrangement of bodies and ropes below it. Any moment now, the statue threatened to leave its perch, step nimbly between bodies already exhausted from fruitless toiling and make its way to a more exalted place: crowds would be transfixed by the medusa-like movements and for a moment realise that it was they, and not the statue, who were frozen in time. They were frozen, perhaps, in the necessary repetition of this event, an event that in all respects seemed to add further strength to the possibility that the statue might be alive, each time it was repeated.

Certainly, the boy's movements across the statue's surface might have seemed to be the necessary foreplay to awaken such a movement. Not a movement that might be detected by the eye, rather a stirring from within, like the frenzy of a forgotten desire, one that swells up, at first without notice and then suddenly exploding, so that the surface, its cold metal literally perspiring, registers delirious riot. And then again, in the boy's calculated antics (pretending to slip, grabbing onto the statue's hand as if to shake it, throwing his arms around the neck in mimicry of a passionate embrace) there was an uncanny recall to another wholly cinematic moment. Without the clothes, of course, but the boy nevertheless seemed to recall the funny but tragic Chaplin who in the opening moments of City Lights, found himself increasingly caught up in a monument that, without actually moving, managed to choreograph a characteristically clumsy Chaplin through an animating dance.

A car drove up. Out jumped a rather mysterious figure. He was dressed in the robes of the orthodox church, so the crowd had every reason to believe that he was a religious man, but these days one could never be sure. Indeed, casting some doubt on his authenticity in this regard, were the giant sandwich boards that hung around his neck (and which at that moment gave the cleric something in common with the statue). On each board, front and back, were scrawled slogans of various forms and in various degrees of intelligibility. The theme of these twin graphic displays was nevertheless identifiable and, given the circumstances, not at all surprising: the Antichrist and Lenin were even depicted in rudimentary form holding hands and sharing a glass of wine, and beneath their meeting, the words 'the devil's deadly companion'. 'The cleric' was the closest thing to a leader that the crowd had so far been able to muster and, taking advantage of all visible lack in that respect, he took to his self-appointed role with great élan. What they needed, he told them, was a powerful truck with which to attach the end of the rope (which, he added, needed to be doubled up so that it would not snap). Someone in the crowd who volunteered the possession of just such a truck, was immediately dispatched to go and get it. The impatient crowd roared with approval. The cleric, seeking to take advantage of the dead time that had now emerged, urged the crowd to join him in prayer for the immanent demise of the antichrist who stood there before them, 12 tons of bronze and – including the four meter high marble plinth – a full 11 meters high.

If Lenin had a camera in his head, he was not showing it, but the scene as viewed from up there must have surely been spectacular. He might have even thought that the assembled masses below, now being led in worship by some mad cleric, had been brought there to perform a collective act of genuflection. And only he knew that for the time being, at least, he was going nowhere. For 50 years he had watched them as they moved through his shadow, seemingly oblivious to his presence. And now he had captured their attention: spontaneous, excited and growing, the crowd billowed beneath him, each of its members never failing to look up or wave a hand. Glory. Of course, the events below could be seen from above; but from a slightly different angle and from slightly higher up. The video cameras at the top of the Ministry of Culture building had been training their numerous lenses in the direction of all this activity for some time. So many cameras were there, in fact, that the view from behind had been broken down into more than seventeen different angles. All of these images, shifting slowly according to the pan of each individual camera, were relayed back to a darkened and serious room in the basement of the Presidential Palace. Huddled around the bank of monitors were three youngish men, members of the party, growing, not unexpectedly, more frenzied by the second. It was clear that the spectacle represented a moment of crisis, and panic was palpable in the room as the anticipated tumble of Lenin became increasingly more likely. But Lenin was not tumbling, and the ceremony of prayer was providing valuable time to re-organise – or even organise – the matter in question.

When the party officials arrived, prayer was over and the crowd was once more becoming agitated. After all, some of them had been there for nearly two hours and Lenin, far from shifting, looked even more dominant, with his outstretched arm, forceful and intimidating, pointing forever towards the glorious socialist future. Except now the arm's sight line delivered into view and identified the approaching truck that the cleric had ordered to be brought to the site. Lenin was the first one to see it, and even though he was pointing right at it, no one seemed to notice. And the crowd had to wait a further three minutes before they greeted the truck's arrival. This was the moment when the party officials took control and the cleric watched angrily as authority slipped from his hands and he found himself reduced to an iconic extra, clearly visible in all the images that would be produced of the event, but his voice now mute, or at best reduced to a kind of mocking and irrelevant off-stage heckler. He was right, but of course did not know it, when he muttered to himself that the party had yet again conspired to rob him of his moment. Indeed God, in any of his forms, peculiar or otherwise, was not to preside over Lenin's removal. Loyal members of the party would see to it that in a moderately bureaucratic and orderly fashion, Lenin would be lifted from his pedestal and laid to rest gently on the back of the flat bed truck that had by now pulled up alongside the statue.

For reasons of safety, they told the crowd through the megaphone they had not forgotten to bring, that the statue would have to be removed with cranes and professional help. And they did not have to argue with the crowd too long (not a single dissenter had the support of amplified sound, so whatever disagreement there was, was simply not heard) before, as per instructions, it began, like an amorphous mass, to move its way back to allow the cranes to enter the inner circle.

Three hours later Lenin was down, lying on the back of the flat bed truck. A single perfunctory circle of the centre of the city was organised so that people could sing and dance at the spectacle of a fallen leader lying with bathos on his back. People threw garbage at it, while others let loose vituperative volleys of saliva. The cleric, not to be denied some form of histrionic display, managed to scramble on to the moving truck (thus guaranteeing that his body would share

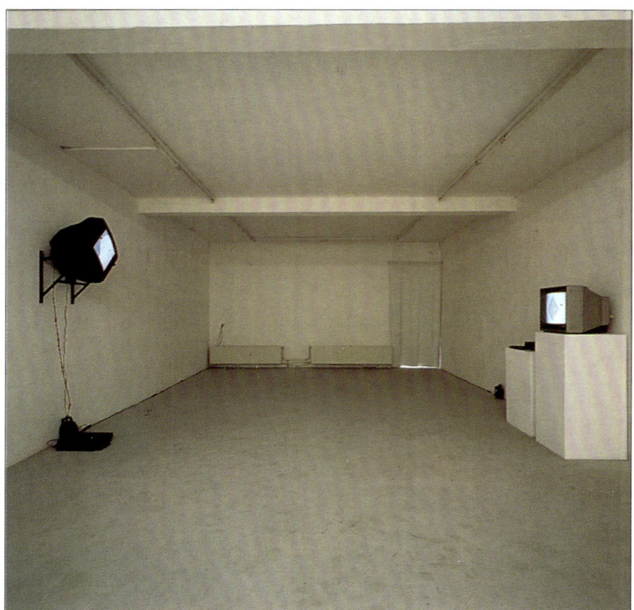

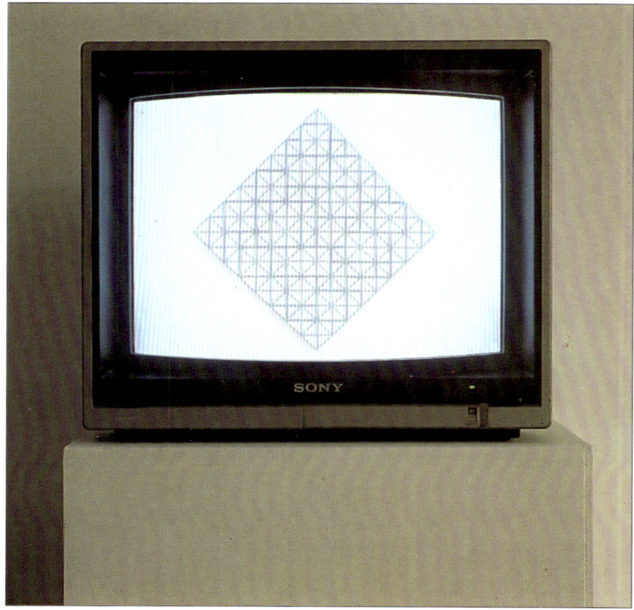

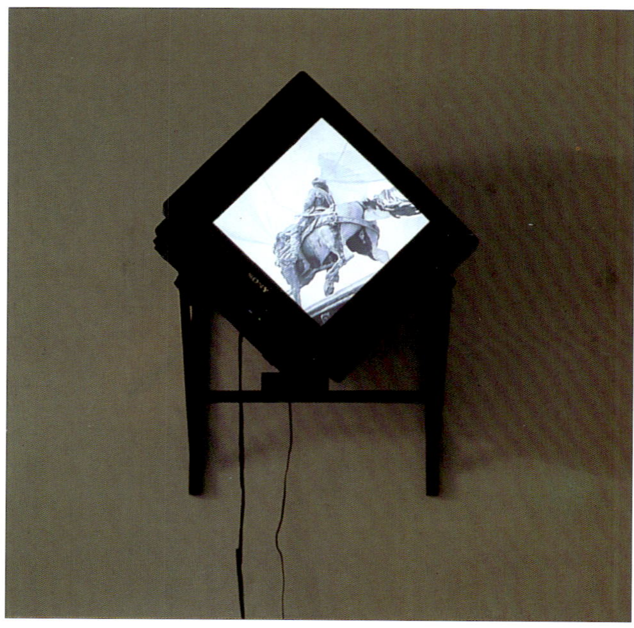

in the very unholy shower), his sandwich boards almost precipitating his own upending in the process. As he stood upon Lenin's breast, it looked, for a moment as if he was going to administer the last rites; except he was not Catholic and instead raised up a cross that he took from around his neck and moved his arms across the expanse of the giant statue. It was as if he was throwing holy water onto the Antichrist, burning him for all his usurpation of iconic power, except again, he was still not Catholic. It was a fantastic spectacle, a clash of great cults that was indeed idolmachiac itself in its very respectful acknowledgement of the power of that image, of Lenin's image, of the image of all idols. And if he was burning, Lenin was still not saying and his mettle served him well as he continued to bear the brunt of projectiles and abuse for the hour-and-a-half that it took the truck to circle the downtown streets.

Finishing its ceremonial turn, the truck with its bronze cargo (the cleric having fallen off earlier on a particular jerky bend) headed up the main airport road and once clear of the assembled crowds, picked up speed and disappeared from sight. A mere 500 meters from where he had once proudly stood, Lenin came to his final resting place. The truck circled behind the Ministry of Culture and out of view from anybody who might have cared to investigate the oddness of the trips's denouement, backed into the waiting open door. Inside, men in overalls worked to remove Lenin from the truck and lowered him to the floor. He would stay there for a while, until the party men could decide on what to do next. Relieved, however, that a situation that had at one moment threatened to undermine their most carefully prepared plans, had now been successfully contained, they adjourned to eat and drink.

A strange symmetry haunted this entire manoeuvre, for where Lenin lay now was indeed the very place he had lain some 50 years earlier while he had waited to be installed with pomp and ceremony on the pedestal in front of the building. Indeed, if Lenin had a memory, then the whole day's events could have been replayed as a precise mirror image of the day half a century earlier when he had left this very room and moved, via flatbed truck, to be installed where he had once stood. On one of the shelves in front of where Lenin now lay, was a striking photograph of the statue as it was unveiled, and apart from the splashes of paint that ran down one side of his coat, Lenin today looked exactly as he had on the day that he once received the highest honours of the land.

(Excerpted from Justice, A Novel about Alchemy and Revolution*)*
Mark Lewis

The 'installation' of Mark Lewis consisted of two monitors placed opposite each other across the width of the exhibition room, one of which showed works by Mondrian from the collection of the Haags Gemeentemuseum in The Hague and the other, the unveiling of a number of statues and monuments – that is to say, a white cloth was removed from existing statues, situated in The Hague.

Monuments of such a more or less heroic nature are erected in commemoration of someone, the commissioner and the person represented often being one and the same. A well-known classical example also present in this collection is the equestrian statue.

The marvellous series of Mondrians constituting the heart of the museum collection has a similar function in a sense: apart from being paintings, they are also trophies of an almost mythical quality, traces of the 'Classical Modernists' in The Hague. They are just as sacrosanct and inviolable as the equestrian statue.

Consequently, what these two kinds of images have in common is the fact that (among other things) they function as symbols of power, power presenting itself in disguise but capable of being revealed, something that ought to take place again and again so as to prevent us from becoming insensitive to the meaning of the images. In this way these power emblems from former times refer to circumstances of hierarchy and repression still prevalent today. In this respect, they are no different from, for instance, the Auschwitz commemoration: rethinking the past must be a sign for the future.

It is obvious that this presentation does not do justice to Mondrian or the Haags Gemeentemuseum. Nevertheless, it will always be meaningful to analyse how the icons which have somehow gained power – that is to say, which exercise power, but also (and therefore prior to it) to which power is attributed, which are invested with power by people, relate to what they (appear to) refer to. In practice the image and what it represents are frequently mixed up, whereas in a different context a different meaning emerges. In this world it is seldom a question of either/or, but almost invariably a question of and/and (sometimes even of both at the same time). This is why 'pure choice', 'clean hands', is difficult, if not impossible, in our time.

With respect to images from an earlier period which are neverthe-less our daily fare (for instance, because they are situated in the city or hang in a museum) one may wonder what they mean *now* – are they 'old images' which did have a topical meaning *then* but are now only functioning as references to a past situation (and as embellish-ment of the city or something similar, the notorious aestheticising of politics 'revealed' by Benjamin)?

It goes without saying that they are signs of past power, but power has always existed in a society based on inequality and hierarchic differences. Besides, these kinds of signs are taken for granted on the basis of their – whether or not supposed – aesthetic qualities rather than examined for their 'actual' significance as emblems (and are thus simultaneously made both harmless and highly dangerous). Our time frequently makes use of other means than painting or sculpture to manifest a similar power (notably the mass media) and hence it was quite natural for Lewis to opt for the actual unveiling of old statues in 'real time' – that is to say, by means of the contemporary medium of video. In that way both formulations of power coincide and it is clear that what seem to be startling differences at first sight are indeed no more than just differences in means of expression. One could say that in a sense the old statues once again appear 'for the first time', for they are once again unveiled, this time in the light of their current significance, a refresher not unlike a slap in the face.

Both categories of images, the statues and the Mondrians, could of course also be interpreted as different from each other: the statues, right in the middle of daily life, are icons of power, whereas the Mondrians witness the pursuit of 'pure representation', of a harmonious balance that is untainted and impossible to be tainted, in the safe chapel of culture which the museum can also be. In that case, we have to make do with the familiar dialectics of the museum as a sanctuary and as a powerful (powerless?) moment of 'defence-lessness' ('Everything valuable is defenceless' as the Dutch poet Lucebert put it) versus the 'real' world beyond it, the world of power and the icons belonging to it. Then the two kinds of images have become two sides of the same coin (and so on and so forth – there is no end to the preludes to be made from a dialectic point of view).

In both interpretations (which are not essentially different) the main issue is that the artist using this older art as his material, has a typically moralistic message: be alert to the signs of power, to put it cautiously. In the era of irony, morality is often spoken of slightingly. We cannot do without it though – each step, each act has a moral significance and moral consequences. Even in a time without meanings, man is a moral, and therefore moralistic creature, al-though it is often a matter of shades of grey rather than of simple black-and-white polarity. Without (a relation to) any kind of morality the world will come to an end, literally and metaphorically. If the cap fits, wear it.   PP

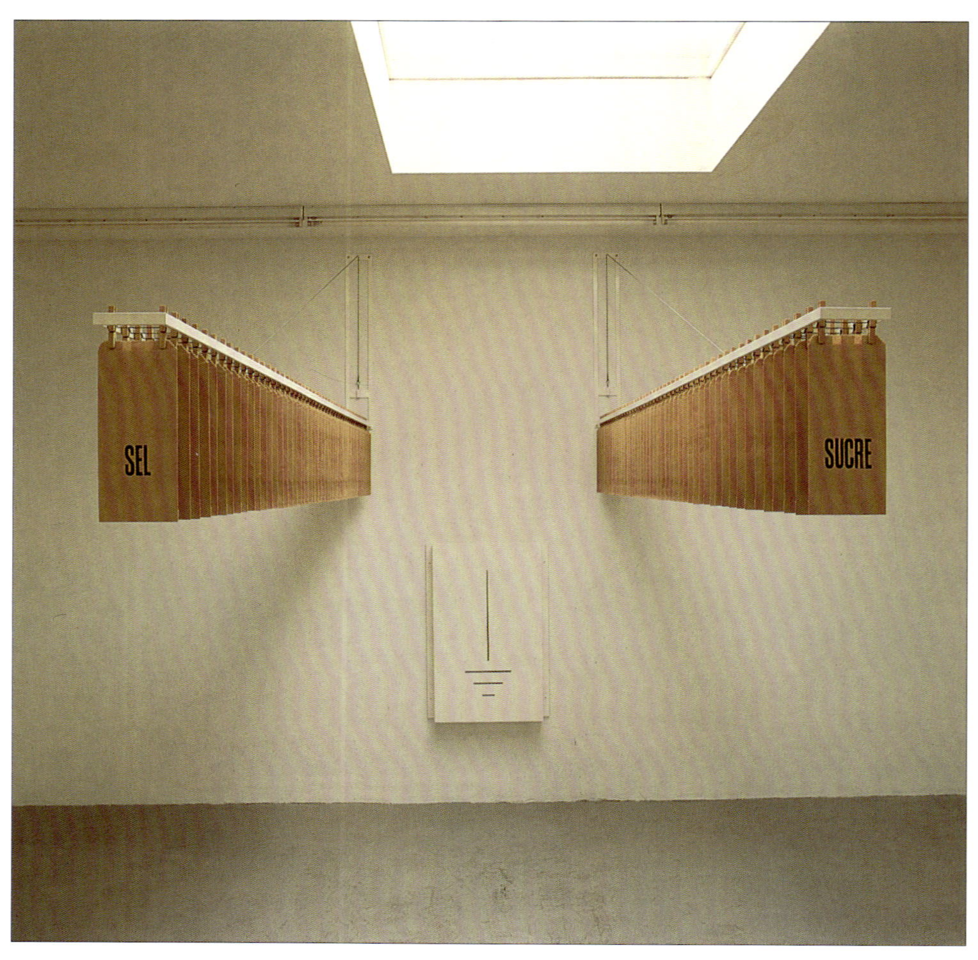

SEL
SUCRE

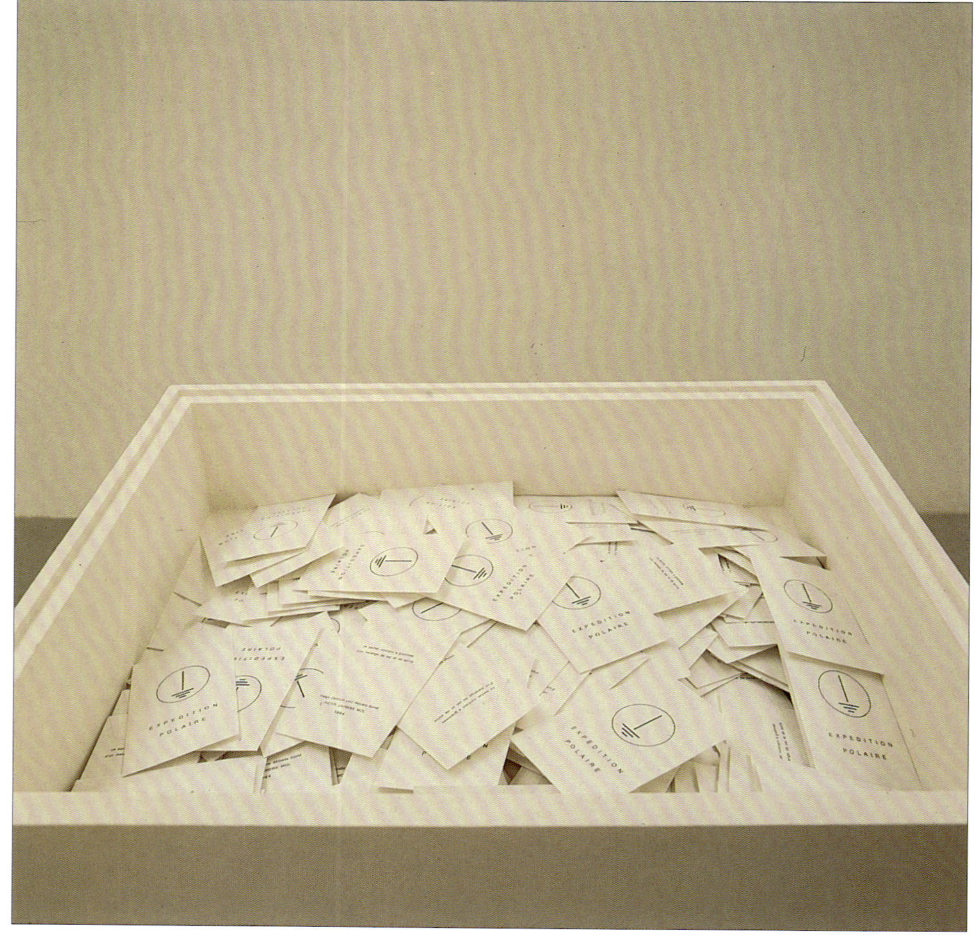

EXPEDITION
POLAIRE

THE IDEAL PLACE: THE FOCUS OF EXTREMES
PIETER LAURENS MOL

In one ear, out the other

Dayclear my course
and I can gaze at a dry, powdery
and chilly white
cover my blind spot with lilies
be transported by the rays of providence

But let me sit down quietly
with precious inclinations on my lap
and silently set my compass free from heroism
wafting lightly on the tariff of a northern light
and there is room
and there is time
for the supposed surplus
to present itself

Pieter Laurens Mol

Extremes are always to be found on either side. Together they create balance. It is generally advised to try and be 'in between' two extremes, that is, in the place where there is maximum equilibrium. That is where it is safe.

But safety is no concern of (contemporary) art. On the contrary, in art it is only the most extreme formulation of an extreme point of view that counts. Of course, it is also conceivable to have such a thing as extreme equilibrium and this may be what we are dealing with in the case of the work *Expedition Polaire* by Pieter Laurens Mol.

Expedition Polaire (in its second meaning of 'expedition to the Pole' also a rather extreme proposition) consists of two stakes projecting from the wall – on one side hangs a series of brown paper bags with the word 'SEL' on them, on the other side a similar series with 'SUCRE'. Roughly, this construction is at eye level. The observer can walk into the work, as it were, and in fact, has to in order to fully experience it. At a lower level, against the wall in the middle of the components just referred to, there is a plate in which the 'earth' sign has been left open, as is practised in electrotechnology. Evidently, there is powerful energy here.

It is therefore obvious that with and in this work we are on dangerous territory. One could say that salt and sugar in themselves do not involve much risk. Maybe, but they are still contrasted tastes, sweet and salt. They are extremes, extreme formulations.

When one has to deal with a work in which two extremes are to be found on either side and, consequently, there is a 'centre', it is quite tempting to think of simple dialectics: the extremes are reconciled in the centre. That is where there is synthesis, equilibrium. Here it is 'safe', here is peace and quiet.

It will be clear that this is out of the question in this work. In between the extremes, in the place where the observer is, potential danger is lurking. Nor do the extremes touch one another: there is only a 'passage' inbetween and this comes to a dead end at the earth sign where energy bores its way into the earth. This implies that the extremes are not 'reconciled', but continue to exist as extremes at full power.

The observer is therefore exposed to two contrasted influences and the contrast is not dissolved where he is standing, but on the contrary, in this very place it is formulated most acutely. Consequently, the 'ideal place' indicated by this work (or which the work is) is not a peaceful place, but a place where daggers are drawn, where there is maximum tension. Whoever strikes two stones together will experience fire.

During the presentation of this work a limited edition of 'sugar bags' was issued, containing both sugar and salt, a portable variant of the actual work. The tastes do not mix, but can still be tasted in their extremity. It is not the dissolution of the poles (the neutralisation, the disappearance of energy) but the focus of the convergence without compromise of extreme, polar points of view that supply the 'ideal place'.

PP

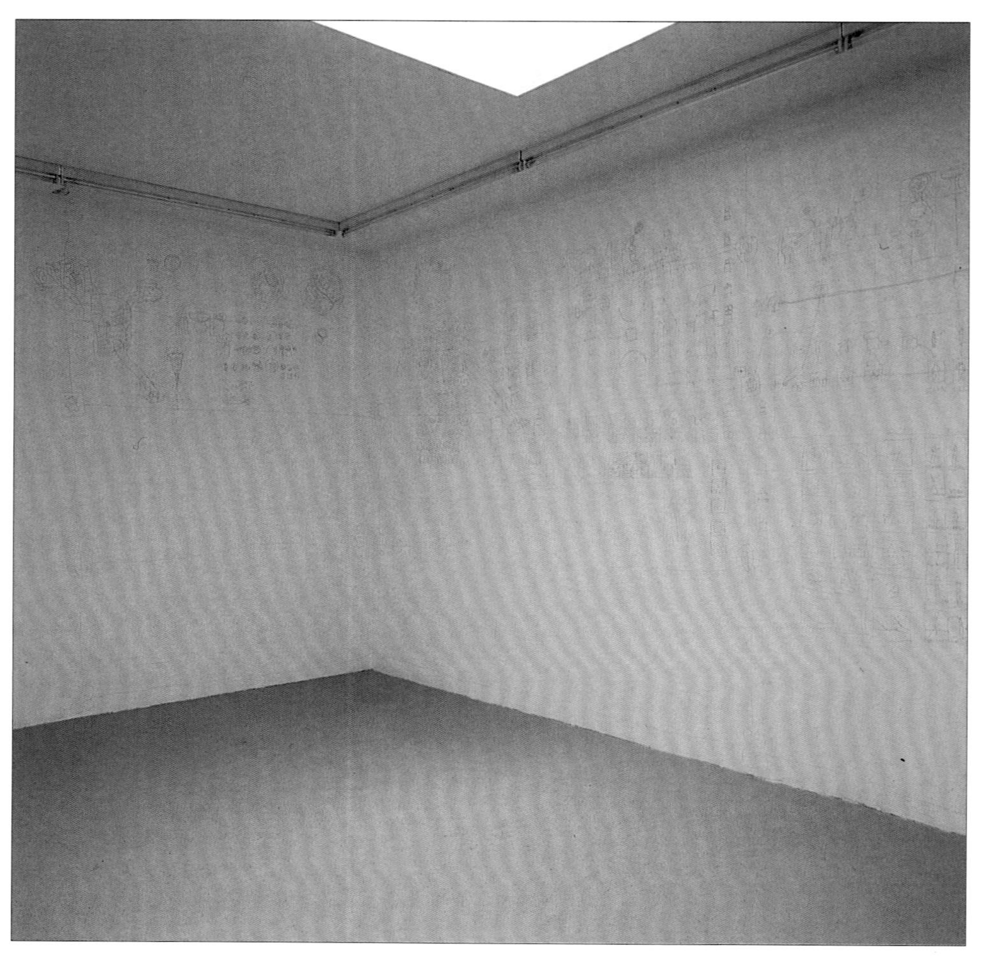

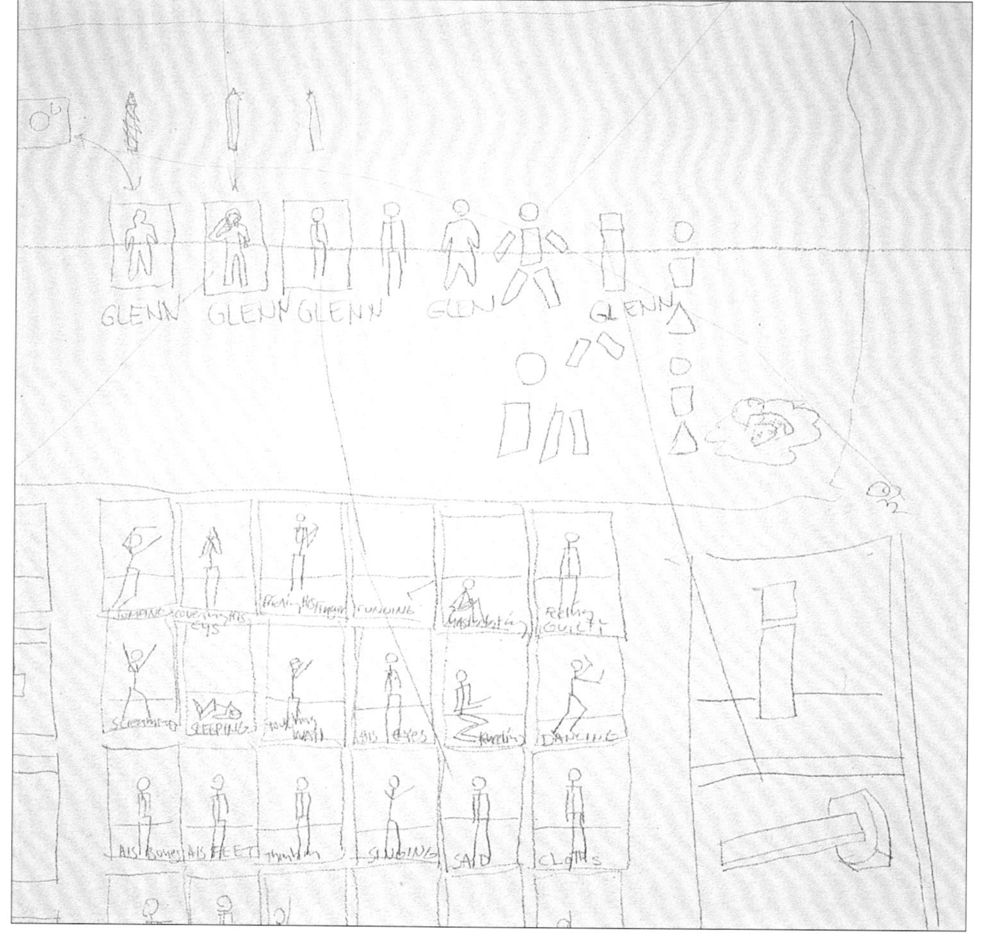

GLENN GLENN GLENN GLENN GLENN

THE IDEAL PLACE: THE LABYRINTH
MATT MULLICAN

THE HEAT FROM THE
KITCHEN STOVE
THE STREET NOISES COMING
IN THE WINDOW
** THE DOOR BETWEEN HER*
AND HER ELDER SISTER'S ROOM
TASTING THAT
THERE'S TOO MUCH SALT
IN THE SALAD

Matt Mullican

All art is a reflection in images of a world transformed to opinion (which does not mean that such an opinion is *per se* a clear, rationally definable idea).

The work of Matt Mullican is often spoken about in terms of 'cosmology' because its subject matter is so all-encompassing and because he has consciously made the (place of people in the) universe its theme. What human beings are and the kind of universe we are discussing here, is a different matter.

Although in this work, in a manner of speaking, all thinkable phenomena can (and, who knows, perhaps one day will) appear, there is no question of a sort of encyclopaedic construction in the traditional sense, but of a sort of labyrinth, perhaps the current variant of the encyclopaedia. Mullican does not pretend to know – just as anyone in our time does not – what all the phenomena in the world could be (let alone all thinkable phenomena, which by the way calls up the question of all unthinkable phenomena and their possible place in this cosmology) and in no circumstances can his work be seen as a systematic classification of what he, Mullican, should then 'know'.

There is, moreover, practically no distance between the artist and his work; at least there is no preconceived idea which is then transformed into an image and presented to the observer in a clear way. The work develops, so to speak, just as life develops – a piece keeps being added which, however, is not necessarily a direct effect (or continuation) of that which had occurred in the immediately preceding moment. This means that the universe of Mullican is a very personal, mythical universe. It makes no appeal to general acceptance, other than in the sense that any other work of art may under certain conditions (if that is true and whatever that may precisely mean).

Mullican's contribution to 'The Ideal Place' is a drawing which was done directly on the wall with pencil (and is, therefore, of a temporary nature) in the back space of the HCAK, beginning more or less at random somewhere in the middle of the last part of the left wall, continuing over the back wall and ending at the last part of the right wall. The drawing is divided by a horizontal line over the complete length which divides 'subject' and 'object' above and under it, and at another level, perhaps also 'heaven' and 'hell', not a wild assumption in connect on to Mullican's way of thinking in which these elements are explicitly referred to several times over.

Practically all the elements in the drawing refer to earlier work, beginning with a very early period in which Mullican did performance-like experiments with hypnosis and drawings of stick-figures, but also including a rather comprehensive work which was finished only a few days earlier in Hamburg. Furthermore, we encounter several 'charts' and 'cities' and more of the themes that, in the course of time, have become recognised as Mullican's. All references were made spontaneously from memory and will most definitely not correspond exactly with the original.

Of course the question arises whether we are dealing here with reproductions of earlier works, and in the literal sense of 'producing anew' this is certainly the case (this being different to what traditional reproduction aims at – namely to depict the original as close y as possible). On the other hand, earlier works have been new y produced, but in another medium, in the context of other earlier works transformed in the same manner and, therefore, in another context of meaning. One work, quite definitely, is something different from that same work (if need be even in its original form) in combination with other elements as a part of a new work; certainly when that work is composed of a combination of other works plus additions which occurred at that moment, sometimes as a consequence of the conversation being carried on at the time of the composition of the work.

The earlier work is, therefore, not really reproduced, but quoted, and (re)presented as a part of a greater whole – in this instance as part of the large wall drawing in the HCAK. This is again a reference to the fact that all Mullican's work (including this piece) are parts of a greater whole, namely the labyrinth-like encyclopaedia.

It is for this reason difficult to talk about the 'proper direction' to read the work, although I lean towards maintaining the usual western standards and read from left to right, especially because then the oldest work is located at the 'beginning'. On the other hand, one can just as well choose (and that must, of course, be done as well) to rest one's eye upon many points in the work. This applies to any work, especially if it is too large to be taken in in one glance. One more argument for the conventional direction of reading may be that the work then 'ends' with a gigantic explosion, a kind of natural disaster maybe, in which everything which is known and accepted is torn apart and disappears, dissolves in a boiling mass: an apocalyptic vision. But whoever so desires, can just as well maintain that we should consider this scene to be the Big Bang, the beginning of the universe, which after all is what this work concerns itself with. This would be rather difficult to argue against. It can even be defended that this part of the work carries both meanings in it at once: after all, all dualities in Mullican's work appear in many cases more or less simultaneously. In this way the entrance and the exit of the labyrinth merge (and perhaps the centre as well, although it is doubtful if there is a centre at all; a golden fleece seems not to be found here).

I am inclined (and maybe this is valid for all of Mullican's work) to view this piece as a series of annotations, by itself. However hermetical it may be, it still expresses a strong urge to 'explain', and again to explain the explanation and so on. What is being explained is primarily the position of humankind in a mythical universe. This is at the same time a derivative (or perhaps also the origin) of the 'mundane truth' and whatever may happen and be reflected on in everyday life. The explanation is then further explained in almost the same terms as those used in the first explanation and, in this manner, calls into existence an accumulation of explanations and annotations. However, these, like everything coming from the world, in the first place 'point to themselves' as if in a closed system. But this is not, however, a closed system in the proper sense, because new elements are admitted all the time, which having become part of the whole are subject to the same treatment. This work in the HCAK could then, with all its additions and its completely different appearance, be understood as an 'explanation' or 'annotation' of the large work that Mullican made for the last Documenta: it speaks about the same subject(s) in terms which have become 'more serene' through the use of the material. The Documenta work, incidentally, was in itself again a summary of an (also physically) labyrinthine connection of previous explanations and annotations.

The apparent form of the work at the HCAK was unique. It was mostly made at night under artificial lighting, but in daylight it appeared extremely ethereal, hardly visible, almost retreating into the wall itself as if it had always been there. This, for me, called up an association I had never before experienced in connection to Mullican's work which may be surprising since it is rather obvious: it reminded me of prehistorical rock drawings. The similiarity of depiction for the sake of explanation seems clear. On the other hand, depiction for the sake of explanation is here, again, internalised and replaced by explanation for the sake of explanation (for which some sort of depiction or image is maintained as medium). No argument has been created; only a complication of the relation between depiction itself and the aim of depiction which lies in the intention of the depictor and which in the course of many centuries has not remained exactly the same, but nevertheless recognisable enough not to differ in essence. Obsessive explaining, however complex the construction is made, in the end still remains a way of confirming life, of establishing identity – the more obsessive the stronger, one could maintain. The more obsessive the urge to explain, the more chance one has of achieving identity in a labyrinth which is, as such, insensitive or indifferent to identity.

Mullican's drawing in the HCAK contains many of his attempts to attribute meaning to the cosmos, to determine a kind of identity in a labyrinth, in a design which in itself, again, shows labyrinthine aspects. Maybe that is why it is so beautiful. Because the work is barely concrete, hardly visible, it is a minimal but also very meaningful note in the margin of the physical space in which it appears. It is also a bit like a Fremdkörper, a sort of 'crop circle', something which ultimately seems to have been 'put there' by a mysterious power, left for interpretation for those who feel the urge to interpret it. One must also mention – and this might even be seen as part of the work – that it has (after the exhibition) again disappeared behind the white wall paint. But underneath the paint it is, of course, present for all time, even though less visible – in actual fact not visible at all. In this way every presence has, again, disappeared and every explanation has been deprived of its explanation and this is, in itself, a kind of ultimate explanation. For those who appreciate these kinds of theories, the wall painted white again for practical purposes, could be viewed as a monochrome which encompasses all explanations within (or, in this case, underneath) itself. For me, in any case, my trusted back wall in the HCAK will never be quite the same.   PP

THE IDEAL PLACE: A PLACE WHICH COULD BECOME IDEAL

JAN VAN DE PAVERT

The ideal place is the cinema seat you forget as soon as the film has started.

In one of the bulletins accompanying this project, Philip Peters tells us why the original title of the project, 'The Ideal Destination', was changed. Among other things, he makes the following remark on the combination of the words ideal and destination: 'It is almost as if a decree is formulated: this is how it ought to be, in this direction, and not otherwise. Artists of all countries, unite, on the way to the Ideal Destination! And of course this is about the last thing we wish to achieve.'

Nevertheless, it would not have seemed such a bad idea to me. There is hardly any artist who is likely to overindulge himself in an appeal to formulate the possibilities of an ideal with his art. But if collectors, critics and organisers of exhibitions were to wake up one particular morning and happen to look upon art as such, this might lead to another kind of art within a decade. Another consciousness and another language concerning art would then arise.

In some texts in the bulletins with this project, the word 'Utopia' sometimes suddenly crops up right after the concept of ideal place. The connection with the utopia is striking, since in general people no longer think in terms of utopias.

The realisation of the utopia frequently meant the end of art. If class distinctions were solved, philosophical problems would also have been solved and art would have lost its role. Or, as in the case of Mondrian and Malevich, the balance in the work of art was a forerunner of a new society. And if this would have penetrated to all utensils and appliances and all buildings, the role of art would again have disappeared.

We no longer use the utopia as a starting point. Nor do we see the ideal place as a large-scale and long-term phenomenon.

Since the 60s there has been a lot of art which, from a critical point of view, discusses the material conditions of art: its commercial value, the role played by the gallery (the white cube), the artist's handwriting as an economic value, etc. The argument of art concerning the functioning of art initially had clearly social, political or ideological implications.

A theme which has recently become more important is the relationship between art and the observer. The fact that in the avant-gardes of the beginning of this century the observer was not often discussed, whereas nowadays it is a dominant subject, is significant. Among the avant-gardes the idea lived that active participation in social change was possible

In the 60s the attitude taken was mostly critical and participation in society did indeed exist (arte povera), but the idea of presenting a model for future society was less dominant. The recent reflections on the relationship between art and observer need no longer concern such participation. Art exists which only concerns the functioning of art, without any of the social, political or ideological implications which prevailed in the 60s. It is a new form of formal art. Eventually this art implies a confirmation of the present notions legitimising art. One of the most boring works in this style is the work Ohne Titel by Zobernig for Documenta in 1992: a long, whitewashed wall closing off for visitors the exhibition rooms lying behind it. The form of the work shown by Art & Language in this project, 'The Ideal Place', is also based on such formal reflections.

Formal art no longer concerns the relations between colour surfaces on the canvas so much. It concerns a questioning of the appearance and reception of art itself. Frequently it has become the justification of the work of art, without any further implications. The wish for social interventions is no longer presented as Utopia. It is known that gestures may exist which do not work as decrees, but as arguments or possibilities. For decades philosophers have taken the nonsense of closed systems, the ambiguity of language, the limitations of models for the future, the impossibility of talking about The Origin and of explaining our objective from there, as their starting points. I would agree with such notions if for a period of about five years collectors, critics and organisers would come to terms with the idea that art implicitly contains a notion of the ideal place and destination within itself. From there we will see what happens next

Jan Van de Pavert

By means of projection, a black-and-white computer simulation is made visible on the wall, showing the exterior of a kind of building. We are being let in and are subsequently walking through it, and the sound of (our?) footsteps can be heard. At a certain moment the route is completed and we are walking back along the same route. The work 'ends' with a picture of the exterior, just as it had 'started'.

The function of this building is obscure; it is definitely bare (concrete?) consisting of various spaces that are hard to define; no windows are visible on the screen, but stairs are. Somewhere, a large concrete chair-like construction appears to be almost part of the structural elements, and somewhere else three constructions have been placed, the purpose of which are not immediately clear, but which resemble 'screens'. The overall impression is inhospitable, gloomy and, in a way, it also looks as if it is 'under construction', waiting completion (although it is also conceivable that the building is to be seen as discarded).

New media, such as computer simulations of this type, or one step further, 'virtual reality', have just as little meaning in themselves as, for instance oil paint or marble – they are materials which can be used in order to create meaning. Of course, each material does have specific qualities and possibilities: in principle, it is hard to create a sculpture with oils or a painting from marble.

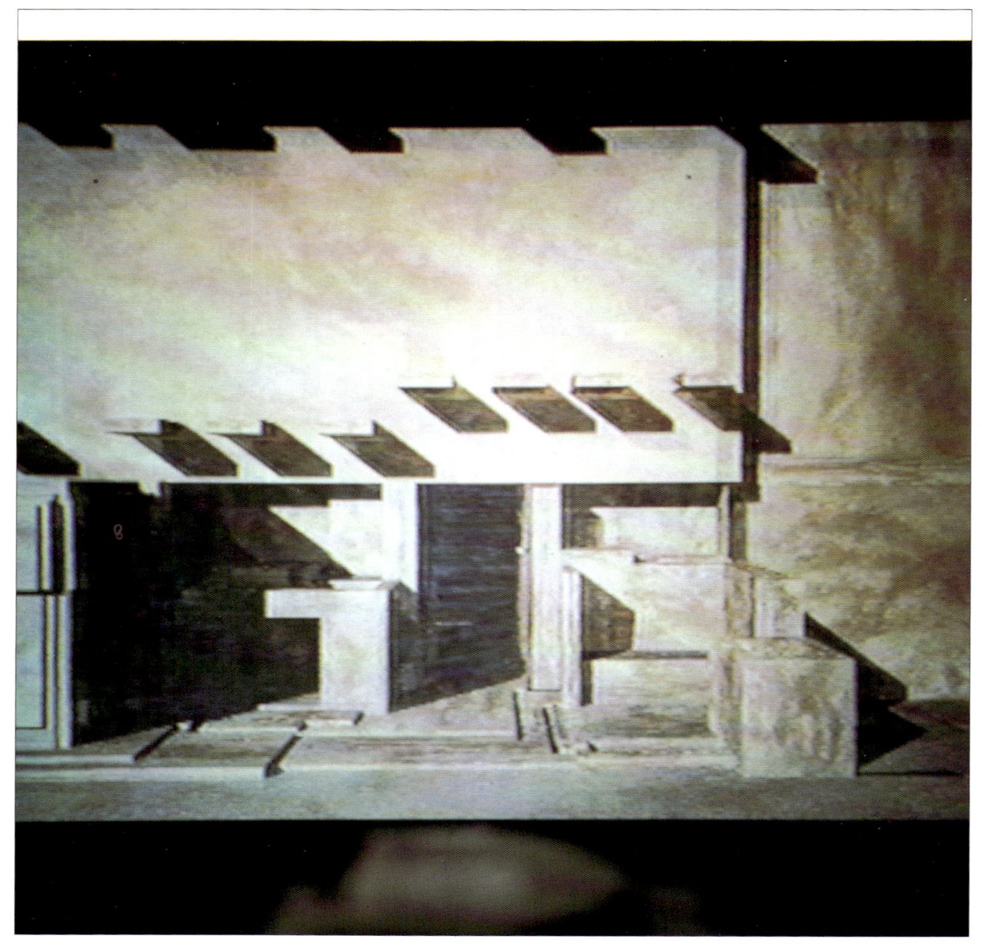

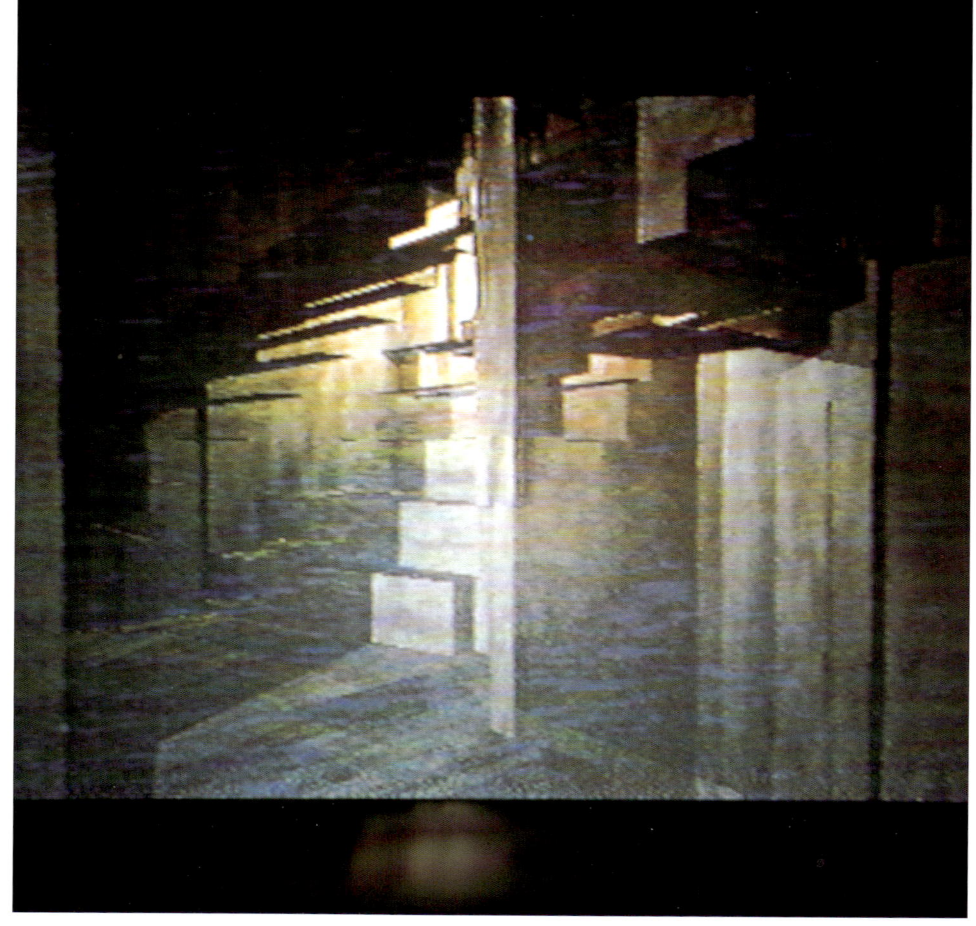

One of the possibilities computer simulation entails, for instance (but in a sense, this also applies to photography and already centuries ago to illusionist painting), is to make something seem 'real' or at least make it refer to something 'real', although this 'real thing' does not exist at all. The building shown here does not exist in tangible reality, it only exists as simulation, as the construction of an image. This implies that at any rate we are dealing with the relation between imaginary and concrete reality here, insofar as terms, a vocabulary, are borrowed from concrete reality in order to make a statement on 'a place' (as concept, as mental construct) by way of an imaginary, visual construction.

In the first instance, when the exterior is shown, this place, this building seems to be a scale-model and this also applies to the last image, which after all is identical to the first. It is 'nowhere', as it were, it lacks context – all that can be said of its immediate surroundings, insofar as is visible, is that it is totally black. Meanwhile, however, it turns out to be possible to enter this scale-model and to walk around inside it. Such a paradox seems to indicate that the shown (simulated) 'reality' must and can indeed exclusively be judged on a metaphorical or even downright symbolic level. This means that this building, although provided with an exterior, should not so much be looked at in its primary function of 'shelter', but one's attention should rather focus on the meaning of the interior with its undefined spaces, labyrinth-like structure and bare walls and floors without a view of any kind of 'outside'. One could even say that the only function of the exterior, and its lack of context, could be the fact that in this way it is made clear that actually there is 'nothing', nothing beyond the interior. Although the interior is evidently contained by a structure briefly shown to us at the beginning and end, the interior is our only frame of reference, our only 'living space'.

We might as well leave the word 'interior' for what it is and simply refer to 'place' or sequence of places with at least one walking direction (there could be more, for it is not sure if we are told all there is about this place, in a literal sense: whether we are shown 'everything' or only a kind of *pars pro toto*. Calling to mind the apparent size of the 'exterior' once again, one would be inclined to consider the latter possibility).

Then this place has turned into an inwardly directed, 'introverted' place which does not appear to be functional in any way whatsoever. In principle, a space, a place like this, could contain anything, but at the moment of presentation this is not the case and in this respect the images do not point to any unequivocal objective. This leaves us the choice between two possibilities: either we accept the place as it is presented to us as 'the place', or we want to decorate it with intentions and meanings not concretely offered, so that it is our own activity (or rather, our awareness of the fact that this is possible) that turns it into 'the place'. In both cases the question remains of exactly what sort of place we are dealing with here.

What is empty has a natural inclination to (wish to) be filled, the house has a natural inclination to (wish to) be decorated and furnished. So essentially, there is no antagonism between the acceptance of the bare space and the desire to fill it: one proceeds logically from the other and in a sense one could even say that filling the empty space is therefore at the same time its fulfilment, its destiny, its completion.

This does not alter the fact that we must still decide upon what is the appropriate, or most obvious filling for this place, effectively making the space a 'place' with a specific meaning. We may of course think that everyone should decide this for themselves (and in a sense this is true) and any fantasy in this respect is just as valid as any other. However, we could also try to come to an argued metaphor, having more general validity, without wishing to claim that this is the gospel-truth.

Taking the closedness of the space as a starting point and the fact that some non-constructive elements have been indicated (the 'screens', the 'chair') I myself would feel like 'looking in'. 'Screens' and 'chair' will then be examples of what else could be found in the interior; denotations of kind. The words themselves which I now use to denote them ('chair', 'screen') could acquire a function in the explanation of meaning, they could produce associations of a metaphorical nature: just as the 'building' is not a 'real' building, the 'screen' is not a 'real' screen either or the 'chair' a 'real' chair, they are visual means (which in this case can also be verbalised). Without much difficulty I could interpret 'screen' – a principle of partition; and 'chair' – a place to rest the body – as kinds of psychological contents: thoughts, feelings. I could even imagine myself thinking about the 'screen' while sitting on the 'chair', so that 'internally' all kinds of interactions arise and all possible and conceivable 'chairs', 'screens' and a great many other metaphorical 'objects' are getting interwoven. 'I' could imagine that, is what I wrote. And I think that it is this very 'I' that is the actual subject, the actual meaning, the actual identity of this space, that this identification turns the space into a real and factual 'place', namely my skull, a three-dimensional representation of my awareness of an 'I' (quite different again from the work of John Blake discussed earlier). In this view of the work, the scale-model-like aspect of the 'exterior' also acquires meaning. The 'I' seems minuscule and that is what it is with respect to the outside world (just as the brains take up a minimal place within the totality of the body) but once 'inside', anything is possible and it can be seen as an autonomous whole on a 'human scale', in which emptiness has been filled and is aspiring for fulfilment. Thus semantic and visual meanings here bounce up and down in various ways.

In the work, the space remains empty and dependent of interaction with the observer for becoming a 'real place', because, if there had been a further filling of any kind, we would have seen a self-portrait of Jan Van de Pavert which was evidently not the artist's intention. Naturally, the self-portrait is an exemplary genre in the sense that the person portrayed does not choose himself as a model out of vanity, but as *pars pro toto* for 'man' in general and in another sense any work, including this one, is inevitably also a self-portrait in a way. This cannot be avoided when someone makes something, but this does not concern us now.

I think that Van de Pavert has given us a special present with this work, namely ourselves, or at least the possibility to reflect on the 'fulfilment of ourselves'. But of course we could also continue to walk up and down between entrance and exit forever – that is up to us. The place only becomes the 'ideal place' by our own completion, by the completion of ourselves.

PP

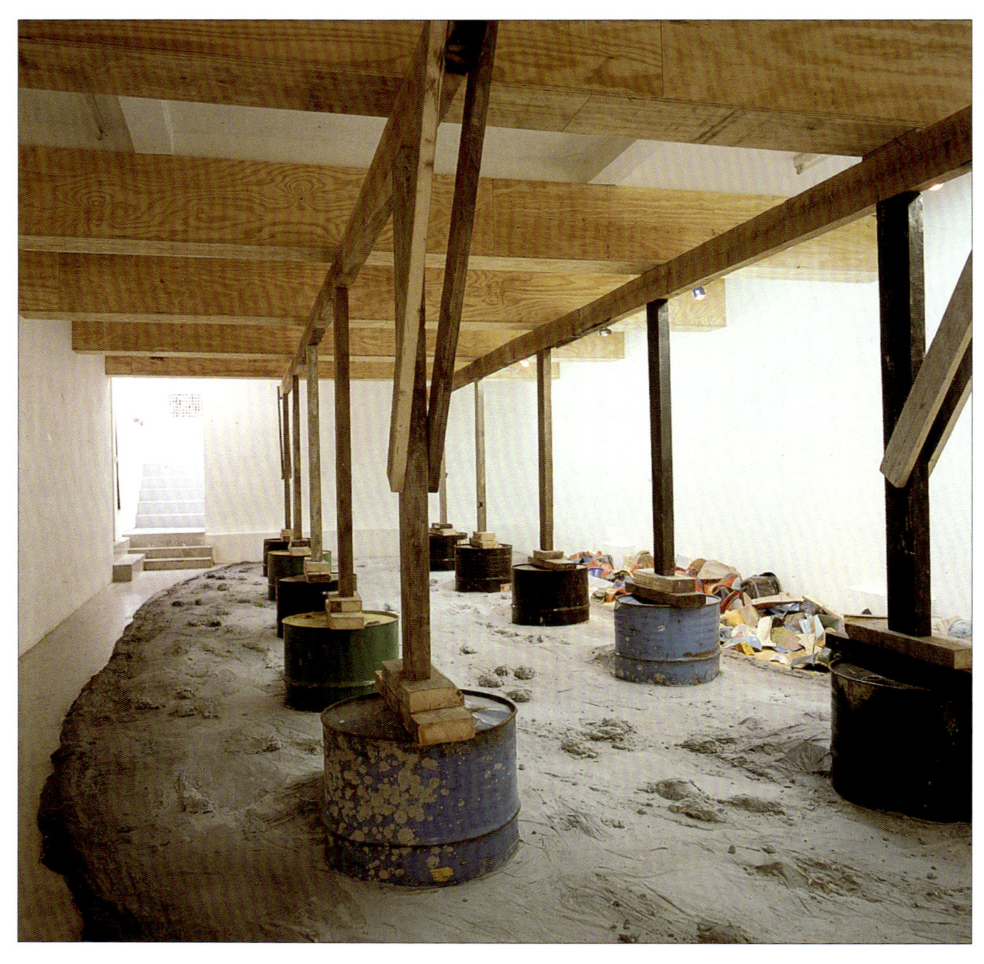

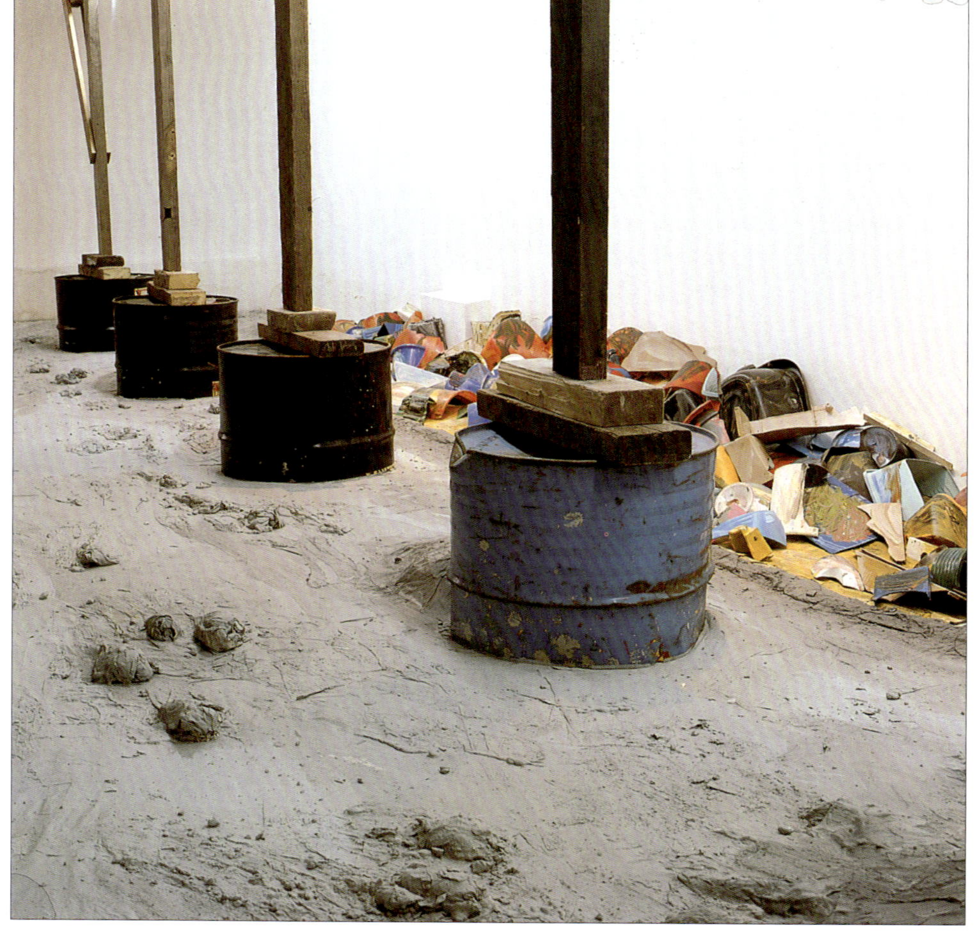

THE IDEAL PLACE: THE UNDERWORLD
URS PFANNENMÜLLER

Perhaps one doesn't quite understand the word in this country or maybe one does know the feeling but has no word for it. 'Sehnsucht'. The ideal place as destination for me is always there where I can make this idea visible: in a painting, in a space, in a landscape. Shouldn't people everywhere know this feeling? In the city where I live, you are very close to it anyway, you almost sit on it with the city at your back and your eyes on the sea.

Urs Pfannenmüller

The lower floor of the HCAK is a basement, it is a good deal below street level. Urs Pfannenmüller built an installation here, which really appears to be 'underground': a palisade of wood on a foundation of oil drums seems to support the ceiling (the 'real' cellar space evidently coinciding with the illusory one of the work). The palisade is surrounded by a grey 'mud stream' made of papier-mâché. All along the length of the stream lie obscure kinds of waste matter (made of painted plastic). At the other side a narrow strip has been left free, so that the visitor can only just pass by (and which makes this place a fictional construct within a 'literal' space).

The ideal place? I had not expected any of the participating artists to present what I might call 'the underworld' as 'the ideal place'. On the other hand, this combination induces a further investigation of the meaning of this underworld. There must be more to it than its relative gloom at first sight.

It is true that this underworld in the first instance consists of a mud stream with rubbish. But at the same time a support construction has been erected which is apparently capable of propping up the entire building. Although we do not really know what exactly is propped up, it is a fact that this is so: if there is a support construction, there is bound to be something that has to be supported, since this is characteristic of such a construction, otherwise it does not make sense.

From this point of view it is tempting to give the work a somewhat psycho-analytic interpretation: 'the underworld' as the world of the unconscious where all sorts of 'rubbish' can be found, but which at the same time is the foundation of spiritual man, consequently the 'creative subconscious', in Jung's terminology. *De profundis lux*: light emerges from darkness. Life emerges from death.

Then this 'underworld' is a warehouse of creativity, then the stream is no longer a mud stream, but a source. Then the rubbish is not useless waste matter, but on the contrary, material for construction (as it actually is in Pfannenmüller's other two- and three-dimensional work). Things are not always what they appear to be.

There is more: Pfannenmüller himself describes 'the ideal place' as a place of 'Sehnsucht' (nostalgic longing). 'The ideal place' is invariably the place where he can evoke this 'Sehnsucht'. Moreover, he refers to his place of residence, The Hague, situated by the North Sea. Here he finds th s 'Sehnsucht': 'with the city at your back and your eyes on the sea'. Extending into the sea near The Hague there is a long pier supported by concrete posts, commonly known as 'The Pier'. Everyone who is familiar with this pier (or with any other similar pier) will inevitably associate this work by Pfannenmüller with it. From the sea (the mud stream, the underworld) a construction rises on which one can walk a considerable distance into the sea (or rather, across the sea). But not further than the length of the pier; where the pier ends, the visitor is left peering at the infinite sea, at the forever moving horizon, in silent, melancholy longing: 'Sehnsucht'.

From this point of view one could say that eventually the work has not been conceived from the underworld (the unconscious) but on the contrary, from the 'pier'. The direction is mainly downwards in an insatiable longing for unfathomable depth and distance, for the depth and distance man was once an integral part of, for this 'ideal place', of which we may have felt an echo when we were children playing in deserted places by the sea, in bunkers, under piers.

PP

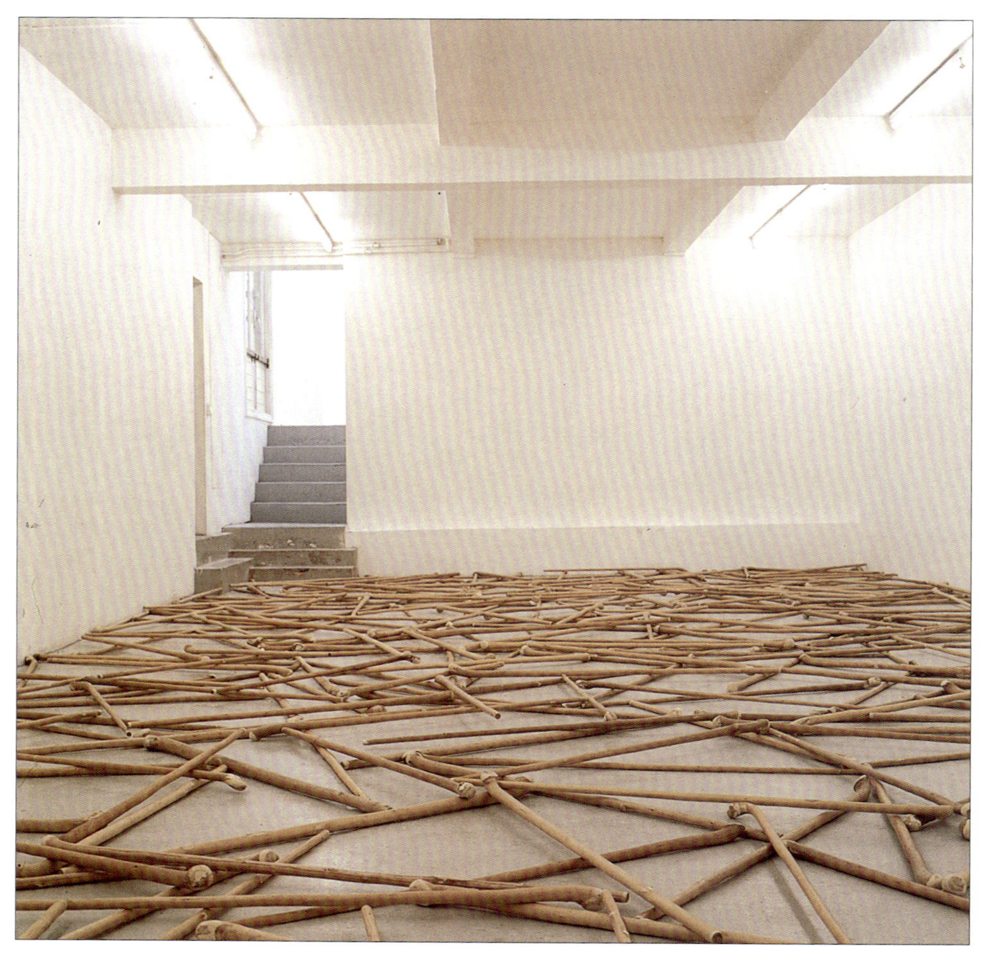

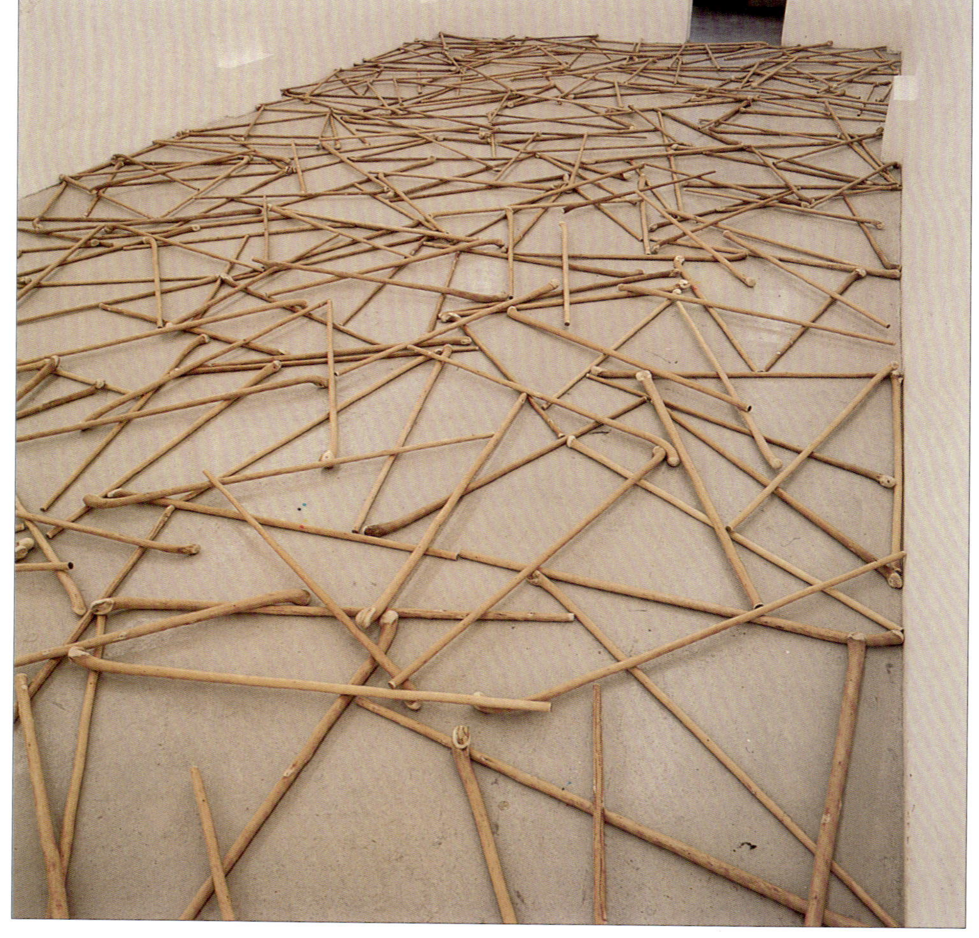

THE IDEAL PLACE: EN ROUTE
NORBERT RADERMACHER

One can go and search for the ideal place.
When it is found,
one will establish that it cannot be taken along.
The quest goes on.

Norbert Radermacher

The word 'place' in the sense of 'the ideal place' seems to suggest that it concerns a static entity, something that actually can or cannot be found (like a concrete place or a mental concept) but which at any rate – once found – is where it is and continues to be there. If the ideal place exists, you are fortunate to have arrived there.

On the other hand, the ideal place could also be something eluding you again and again, or something that may lose its 'ideal' quality once it has been found and will have to be regained and rediscovered over and over again.

Norbert Radermacher covered the ground floor in the HCAK with a construction composed of a few hundred sticks – resembling walking sticks – from the Czech woods, which were then produced in a factory in Thüringen in former East Germany. The origin of the sticks as parts of trees is still clearly visible. They have been arranged in a rather loose manner according to a more or less geometrical pattern, covering the entire floor area. Although at first sight it might look a bit like an atypical work by Richard Long (but actually is the exact opposite as we shall see) this does not imply that it is an aesthetic construction to be admired from a respectful distance; one can (must) walk over and across it. This does not mean that you are free to go where you please: each step must be made with some caution so as not to affect the construction unnecessarily. After all, that is what art has taught us – even if you are allowed to walk right across a work, it should not be disturbed. In this work, however, a disturbance definitely takes place, but in reverse as the visitor's natural step is disturbed by the sticks. In this sense the sticks are obstacles, like trees lying right across a path. But then the visitor is also allowed to take a stick with him. So on second thoughts, the visitor is definitely meant to disturb the construction of sticks after all: by removing a stick the image in the gallery room changes. It does not wish to be unapproachable; on the contrary, from a static starting position it wishes to create an awareness of the dynamic possibilities, which subsequently will have to be effected if the work is to function in the way it is meant to. After a while, the exhibition room of the HCAK had undergone a radical change compared to the situation at the start of the exhibition. In theory the room will be totally empty at the end of the exhibition (which was actually very nearly the case) and the work will

have moved, put itself into motion, on its way to just as many different places whether ideal or not. No one can tell exactly where the work *is*, except in 'different places', taken there by people who visited the show for purposes unknown.

The construction of sticks on the floor is therefore not the actual work. In a sense, the sticks on the floor are no more than a cause for the actual work, for the visitor is invited to take a stick from the gallery and to use it for whatever purpose he or she thinks fit. So after having been installed in the gallery by the artist, each stick is to lead a different life, a life over which the artist no longer has any control. Possibly, from its initial position as part of a static gallery installation, each stick is setting out with its new owner in search of the ideal place. The role of the artist is utterly modest in this: he cannot determine this ideal place, at most he can suggest the means to look for it and in this case the means is a journey, metaphorically indicated by the attribute of the journey, the walking-stick.

On further consideration the stick used has a special, ambiguous character. In the first place it evokes certain associations with something like 19th century Romantic *Wandervögel* and suggests an almost Schubertean meaning as a symbolic companion in, for instance, the *Wanderlust* of the miller or the doomed wanderings of the protagonist in *Die Winterreise*, where *Das Wandern* may be in good spirits, *des Müllers Lust*, at the start of the journey, as well as end in a meeting with Death in *Der Leiermann* (two extremes of the ideal place, I would say).

On further consideration, the stick may have more functions, varying from a crutch to lean on to a weapon to hunt with and all sorts of functions inbetween. That is why this is the right stick for the purpose: its adventures have not been codified in its formal construction in advance.

What is an ideal place? Radermacher puts it like this: you cannot take an ideal place with you. A good example is the wanderer who during the daytime does not know yet where he will sleep that night. Once the moment is there, it does not take him much trouble to find the ideal place to pitch his tent for the night. But as soon as it is daytime again, this place stops being the ideal place and what could be the ideal place for the next night is again an open question.

The artist – and possibly to an increasing extent, the world's population – is a nomad in temperament. He travels from one place to another, installs a work and leaves it again on his way to the next place for the next work. Each place briefly is the ideal place. In this special case the artist has gone one step further: the work itself has become a nomad and thus perhaps a metaphor of human life; always on the move, possibly from one ideal place to another.

PP

THE IDEAL PLACE: WHERE THERE IS NO PLACE FOR IDEALS

ULF ROLLOF

Certain images keep coming back in my head. Most often they are not interesting but sometimes there are different combinations of scattered images made up out of beliefs or accidents, experiences often achieved through mistakes, love and failed love, beautiful memories and brutality, and so on. On a second level the simple polarity of positive and negative is lost and things rather exist in a comparative relationship: childhood and your own wife and family, physical experience and intellectual experience, domestic animals and wild animals . . . All these experiences and images (not to forget dreams) function together on a third level where action is taken, and maybe it is the combination of the day that decides the outcome. Maybe it is all a question of creating a few seconds of frozen time to reflect on your own history and the history you are a part of, that in my perspective is possible. To me the concept of this exhibition 'The Ideal Place' implies singularity. In my vision it is the polarity that is life (or death).

Ulf Rollof, Stockholm, April 1994

In a considerable part of the Western world the fir is not regarded as just another tree, but chiefly as a symbol referring to Christmas – the birth of Jesus, the solar turn, the return of light. In that sense it is a sign of hope and the centre of the house, around which the family gather in an atmosphere of peace on earth and goodwill to mankind.

Unfortunately, that is not how the world operates – neither the 'real' world nor the world of art (after all, Christmas tree decorations are not art, but harmless adornment, and therefore precisely the opposite). The world, our present-day world, is dominated by catastrophe, or at least it is in the transitional phase in which catastrophe is either a predominant or threatening presence, already broken out in one place, in another still hanging over everyone's heads as the sword of Damocles.

In spite of the fact that Ulf Rollof's installation consists of a large number of Christmas trees, it is not a cheerful image of the world that we are faced with here.

The installation can be divided into two groups: trees with (wrapped up) lumps of earth applied to the wall in a row, hanging upside down from simple metal constructions; and a number of metal racks placed freely in the exhibition room and looking somewhat like weighing mechanisms, at the upper part of each rack there is a Christmas tree separated from its lump of earth, which has been placed at the other, lower side of the rack.

The row of metal constructions clearly reminds you of gallows. The trees still have their lumps of earth (because they have been turned upside down, the lumps look like heads) so they are still alive, but barely so and certainly not for long. The other trees are already dead and are even bleeding (resin is actually oozing from the wood).

In this installation war is being waged and lynchings have been staged in such a way that – almost literally – you are not able to move around it. The setting forces the visitor to zigzag his way through the objects until he finds himself right in the middle of the scene where he is clearly a participant, rather than an observer.

This also applies to the artist: this is not a 'politically correct' moralistic installation, in which the artist, wagging his finger at us, keeps out of range himself. He draws our attention to the mass murder he himself is committing, by acting as the perpetrator. No one can escape being an accessory to the catastrophe.

Of course the trees can be looked at in all possible metaphorical or symbolical functions, this is a matter of the observer's personal interpretation. What is most likely is that we are actually dealing with nature here, with the nourishing part of the world supplying us with oxygen so that we can breathe. An additional factor is that it is particularly the corruption of the Christmas tree, this symbol of peace, that makes the statement even more penetrating, and one might also question peace symbols themselves, which, after all, can only originate through murder. This makes the value of the peace symbol utterly dubious, a symbol which may only have the right to exist as long as there is no actual peace: something that does not exist can, at most, be indicated and this indication already includes the hidden seed of the opposite of what is indicated.

The general significance of this work with respect to 'the ideal place' is obvious: there is no ideal place and, in a literal sense too, there can never be an ideal place as long as we continue systematically to destroy what could have been the ideal place (the world, each other).

This dimension may be given further depth: the whole concept of the 'ideal' could be suspect in this context. History gives rise to it as well: countless times people have been murdered for the sake of some ideal or other. The ideal as an ideology has become offensive and is associated with propaganda, repression, war and genocide.

This might well be the eventual meaning of this installation: the fact that the invitation to deal with the ideal (here in the form of the ideal place) inevitably results in the opposite and is perhaps suspect in itself, in spite of all good intentions. Not only does the catastrophe continue to be inescapable, it is also coming a bit closer by giving it a socially acceptable touch. The fact that we are talking about 'ideals' when we are surrounded by, or in the vicinity of catastrophe, at best conceals the catastrophe itself which is in progress, perhaps without our realising this and certainly without actively opposing it.

It is therefore remarkable and, whether a coincidence or not, characteristic of the situation, that in the midst of the extreme violence of Rollof's installation there is the beneficient smell of pine-needles. Thus it acquires an additional ambiguity: in a sense, the installation conceals some of its atrociousness by expressing itself in fairy-tale terms of Christmas trees and pine odour. It is a well-known fact that fairy tales are often gruesome and that in order to discover this one should look beneath the surface of the anecdote. In this case, the gruesome facts are already presented to us in that surface, which means that they are close to our skin, closer than we would like at least, for they also point out that we are accomplices or at least that we are present in the catastrophe. We cannot say that we have not been warned, that we did not know it.

PP

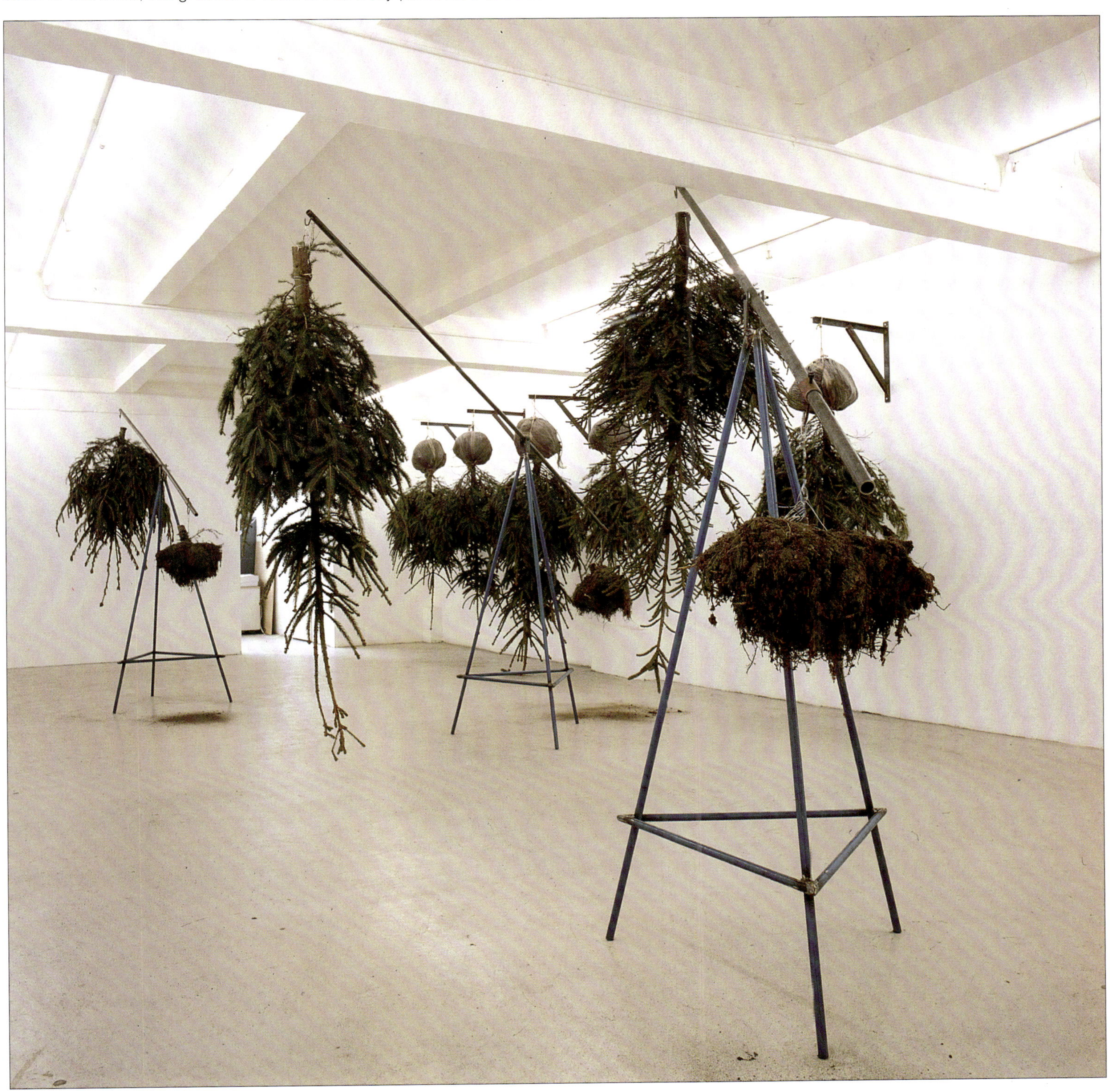

THE IDEAL PLACE: TIME LOST AND WON
JCJ VANDERHEYDEN

To me the painting View of Delft *by Jan Vermeer is an ideal place, when seen at that particular moment of the early morning – the clock in the painting indicates ten past seven.*[1]

On the right-hand side of the painting a small yellow wall is to be seen, described by Marcel Proust [2] *as a precious Chinese work of art ('une précieuse oeuvre d'art Chinoise').*

It is this particular piece of wall in this painting that seems to me to be the ideal place of light, colour, brilliance and atmosphere.

Vermeer worked on View of Delft *from 1655 to 1658; in that same period Velásquez worked on* Las Meninas *in Madrid in 1656.*

A photographic representation of the yellow wall will be applied to canvas according to the scanning ink jet technique. The format of the little wall will be enlarged to the size of the original painting as a whole, that is 117cm.

In order to materialise this image of the wall to a greater extent and to turn it into an object present, the yellow wall will be made in gold and shown in a display case (format: 14.7 x 42 cms).

JCJ Vanderheyden

When I had just started studying history of art, our professor, Hans van de Waal, showed us a Romanesque portrait within the framework of a series of lectures on 'The Portrait'. Before pursuing this matter further, he warned us that naturally we should not look at it 'with 20th-century eyes'. I could agree with that: after all, the work had been made centuries before from a cultural canon in few respects corresponding to ours. Consequently, it had to be looked at 'in its own context'. Without the intention of maintaining now, some 30 years later, that this was complete nonsense (the valid aspects of such an approach remain obvious) I can no longer wholeheartedly subscribe to this utterance. I have no other eyes than 20th-century eyes and everything I see and do will necessarily be coloured by this fact; the time in which you live exercises a kind of inescapable gravitation. How was it possible that Van Meegeren's forgery of Vermeer could pass for genuine among highly estimated scholars at the time, whereas nowadays no one would fall into this trap? This has to do with changes in the norms of a culture (and even simply with visual 'fashion': 'historical' but also science-fiction films from the 50s, for example, in retrospect prove to show the typical clothing and make-up of that time, at which we are now doubled up with laughter, just as in a few decades people will do so with respect to our fantasies on history and the future). At the moment another Vermeer forgery might be invented in principle, which we will not recognise as such right away, because it is likely to meet current patterns of expectation with respect to the missing link in Vermeer's work. And so on, and so forth. Time does not teach us anything, except what time itself thinks about a matter.

View of Delft, although perhaps slightly atypical in the limited knowledge we have of Vermeer's oeuvre, is still a classical icon, not only breathlessly watched by Marcel Proust, although this breathlessness has never been formulated in quite the same way since.

Lastly, but by no means less importantly, Proust's considerations concerned the yellow wall to the right of the canvas. Vanderheyden chose this very spot as a subject to be concentrated upon at greater depth within the framework of his contribution to 'the ideal place'. The manipulations with the wall carried out by him are of a rather special nature.

The work as a whole has the character of, I would say, an exhibition (although today everything is invariably called an 'installation') as was the case with more works by Vanderheyden in the past. This special exhibition largely derives its significance from the fact that with one single existing painting as a starting point, he makes pronouncements, if not on that particular painting, then surely on observation, and more generally, on time and place and present aesthetics of unity and fragmentation.

Roughly put, the exhibition had the following form: it consisted of four components, two of which had been hung on the far wall of the exhibition room in the back and two on the adjoining side walls. The rest of the space had been closed off, so that the actual exhibition space took up just a small part of the total space. For that reason it was a rather intimate exhibition room.

To the left of the back wall was a photographic reproduction of the original work, in a frame similar to the original frame (would it have been even more beautiful if the 'real' work had hung here, which for all sorts of obvious reasons was not possible, or does the very fact that the whole thing starts with a reproduction in this case have a positive meaning, I wondered?) Next to it was a large blow-up, made according to an advanced photographic technique, of the part of the painting on which the yellow wall is so prominently present (or at least, could become prominent by emphasising it to such an extent, for in the whole work it can hardly be regarded as the most immediately striking visual element). This panel is considerably larger than the reproduction of the original painting as a whole, thus in a visual way adding extra stress to what the artist evidently wishes to express. Moreover, the blow-up (and possibly the technique used) results in a much higher degree of abstraction of this fragment than is the case in the original. Moving along to the wall, we come upon a kind of display case of minimal depth, in which the yellow wall is present once again, this time made three-dimensionally in gold and reduced in size again, to approximately the size of the entire 'original' painting. When the observer turns round, he will look into a mirror on the opposite wall, again provided with a similar classical black frame, so that it is clear that we are still dealing with one and the same matter.

These four elements enter into a number of rather complex relations. In the first place there is of course the fragmentation of the whole, almost expressed didactically, and the singling out of a part thereof, which according to the cliché image of the moment, may in a certain respect be considered characteristic of our collapsing or already collapsed culture: the 'View of Delft' is no longer the 'View of Delft'. A 'View of Delft' does not exist anymore, there are only parts, elements, from which once, in the 17th century, an image of that name was made, which can no longer have that original meaning.

Zooming into part of the painting, as it were, the yellow wall (and, I think, not so much because of its conceptual or compository meaning within the whole, but probably more because of its level of abstraction and its typical Vermeer 'light' of which it is an outstanding example, though still a partial aspect) appears again, cut out of the painting as it were, on its own, made out of gold (or a material that looks like gold). A proportionately coarse-grained image is created due to enlargement and change of material, the figurative meaning of which in the original composition can only be of secondary importance at most, recognisable as a frame of reference, as diversion from an image long since left on its way to a meaning of its own, to further autonomy.

Once it has been made, the extra material from the three-dimensional approach (and thus still further removed from the original) produces a kind of autonomous sculpture which rises up in the display case. It is so minimal that, paradoxically enough, it reminds one of the frame of a painting again. It is a manufactured *object trouvé*, for it is a sculpture no one could just invent. It lacks any sense as long as its origin – the whole of the origin – is not involved in the considerations (which also implies that eventually the 'autonomy' of this sculpture is not so far-reaching).

The mirror on the opposite wall is a typical example of the fact that one cannot simultaneously look at and into a mirror, but that both activities are important. In the first place, there is the simple fact that something is mirrored – we already know that when we see the mirror. And then it is a matter of what is being mirrored and what the meaning is. Of course the golden wall is reflected, so that in the work it appears in duplicate (as 'itself' and as its 'mirror image'). One might say that the mirror image (which after all is immaterial and at the same time presents 'another' image than the 'original' image of the golden wall) causes an even greater distance from Vermeer's original with yet another shift in material. On the other hand, this very material, which consists of light (so often painted by Vermeer) in a sense reduces the mirror image to some aspect of the original again. At least it makes it clear that the mirror is not an independent element, not just a capricious addition. This could prove to be of essential importance, which I shall discuss in more depth later.

At the same time the mirror emphasises the factor of 'time', which is a *leitmotif* in this work: whoever looks into the mirror will see the 'present'. Vermeer's painting shows the 17th century and a particular day and point of time (as is indicated by the tower clock of Delft), although this precise point of time should perhaps not be given too much attention – after all, it is not an impressionist, *plein-air* painting, but a canvas at which Vermeer worked in his studio for three years. On the other hand, we may have the point of time play a kind of 'conceptual' role in our considerations. When the clock indicates that it is ten to seven – assuming that the clock indicates

the right time – we should accept that this is indeed correct, a moment like the moment at which, three centuries later, we look into the mirror and see what we see then, be it not 'View of Delft' in the sense composed and painted by Vermeer. At any rate the mirror thus indicates the distance in time between Vermeer's 'View of Delft' and the present moment (and manner) of our observance of this. So the work appears to be about perception in a broader sense, switching back and forth between the literal and the metaphorical.

Naturally, in the course of time the mirror has acquired symbolic meanings that must be considered. In this case I am especially reminded of the fact that those who step 'into' the mirror, enter another (parallel) reality. In a sense one would imagine that one should be able to trace back the image, from the golden wall to the photographic blow-up to (the reproduction of) the original Vermeer – a route which eventually terminates with the 'View of Delft'. What I consider one of the finest aspects of this work is the intrinsic impossibility of such an undertaking, if only because due to the distance in time, one is forced to end up in a mirror image at best, which is *precisely not* (the image of) the original. Attempts at conquering the fragmentation of time and place are doomed to fail and point out 'our place' to us even more. I am not going to discuss mechanisms of memory here, but Proust's search into time lost at best yields a sort of reverse caricature in what could then almost be called Vanderheyden's distorting mirror.

The distance is definitive, and we will have to accept that. The distance between Vermeer and Vanderheyden, which is just as much a distance in time as it is in place (an inseparable couple after all) is not to be bridged. It can be made visible in all sorts of ways and then a work by Vermeer can give rise to a work by Vanderheyden. That is what has happened here and in this respect we can speak of a situation to be defined as 'time won': the past is lost, but the present has been won. Thus the contemporary artist makes use of history, of tradition, not by quoting senselessly (which seems to be fashionable) but by effectively conquering a new place and winning a new time: a place of one's own, a time of one's own.

PP

The following are unauthorised extracts from a discussion at HCAK between Ricardo Brey, Patrick Corillon, JCJ Vanderheyden and an audience. The discussion was chaired by Henk Oosterling.

Vanderheyden: I remember I had an idea about Vermeer's *View of Delft* in my mind for a long time. When I was here about a year ago to discuss participation in this programme, I went afterwards to the Mauritshuis Museum and saw the painting again. I saw the yellow wall which Marcel Proust wrote about and I wanted to try and take that wall out of the painting and reproduce it in a special photographic reproduction technique which seems to be painted. It *is* painted, but by Vermeer, not me. I developed this idea and then recreated the wall in gold, which conveys a more materialistic appearance. So I thought it was the ideal place and also the ideal time, as Vermeer's clock says 7.10am. So that should be the ideal time connected with this painting.

Unfortunately I could not photograph the painting at that time because the Mauritshuis would not give me the opportunity to do so.

But in any case this is not only about the ideal place but also about the ideal moment. Place and time go together. There is no ideal place without time, it exists only in time. This may be a short time – a moment – or it can have a duration of half an hour or a minute or whatever, but there is no place without time. We have no perception or experience of place without being in time.

Brey: When I received the invitation I started to think about what the ideal place could be for me, a human being, an artist. The destination of my work? The destination of my person? Where is the ideal place where I can stay? I think an artist tries to put his work in the right place, like a human being – the place where you can be happy. I thought the best point of view to adopt was that of Baudelaire, who said, 'any place out of this world', because I cannot find any place as comfortable. So my piece is probably only about how uncomfortable many situations are for me. I agree with the poem. Substantially it, and my installation, is against searching for this ideal place. It is not the *paradis artificiel*, which Baudelaire has also written about. I think it is more realistic because in one respect it is not about paradise, but about how we try to find a paradise. We are closing countries and continents and wealth. It is a metaphor for looking at something.

Corillon: I am in agreement about the relationship between time and physical presence. Ten years ago I was in the botanical garden in Paris. It was winter so there were no flowers, just the ground and the signs with the names of the flowers. I saw people walking in the garden and looking at the names of the flowers. The quality of their gaze was very beautiful. They did not need the flowers, only the names; to be in the botanical garden was enough. Another thing I remember was in the metro in Paris where you have the map of the stations which also shows where you are at that moment. Everybody had put their finger on that exact spot, until it had eroded, leaving a hole. All the stations are more or less the same in the metro but you are physically in a hole in the map. For me the installation I made here is like that. I am at all times working with text, with fiction, and I put that fiction in a real place. But you have to be entranced in the fiction to experience the physical reality. It is the same when you read a book. You can physically enter in the book. At the beginning of Mary Poppins there is a pavement painter who is drawing a little kiss and this kiss became reality. For me it is the same. You have to build the ideal place. The ideal place is a process.

I talked to Renzo Piano, the architect of the Centre Pompidou, and he said: 'I use plastic, but if the people who are living in my buidings feel like it they can change the material'. For the ideal place you do not have to choose very strong material. You have to choose a moment to build and this moment can each time build something real. In this case the ideal place is not this specific doormat, it is each doormat. When I have to meet the director of a museum I may be very nervous, so I wipe my feet on the doormat. That is not the same as when I am very tired and enter my house. When you are on a doormat you are never thinking about what you do. That is normal.

Vanderheyden: The time that I am talking about is not the time of the clock or the calender. It is the time of experience. It is the amount of time we use to pay attention. Sometimes this can produce a very heavy experience in an extremely short time. That can vary a lot. In music this is different: there is a beginning and an end and the time inbetween is necessary to experience the music. With visual elements this is unknown. Sometimes I have only 20 minutes to visit a museum, so I always go to the restaurant first and take ten minutes to eat something. Then I have, let's say, twelve minutes afterwards to see a whole exhibition or the whole museum and this *is* possible, I think. Recently I saw three exhibitions at the Stedelijk Museum in Amsterdam in about twelve minutes. I did this several times when I had no more time and I came back at home in the evening and remembered what I had seen in those few minutes and that can actually be a lot. You can see a lot in a very short time and still remember it afterwards. This is only an example. Normally you take much more time for the visual arts or you take a special amount of time to see one particular work of art.

Oosterling: In this work you first see the total view of Vermeer's work (a reproduction of it) and then the whole gets fragmented. Time is fragmented. You take out one thing and give it a different texture through the use of photography. Then you take out one element of this photograph and again give it a different texture: gold. By looking at a coherent image – the *View of Delft* – the coherence is broken up. You change the quality. By changing the quality my experience of time is changing and perhaps this change has been motivated by the different qualities of the materials – the gold shows a different light than the photograph for example, which in itself differs from the light in the reproduction of the whole painting. What is happening to my experience of time when you break up reality by changing the material of reality? Has that something to do with place and time?

Vanderheyden: I think so. Sometimes it is not possible to know the relationship between place and time because it is difficult to analyse. The experience in general is that you sometimes see something in a certain place which transfixes you, and you dedicate more time to it than you would in general. That is a relation in time and place of course. That place on the wall is the place that takes the time you need to see that place. We have the experience of the place but not of the time. What I mean is that we include time because it belongs to the quality of our attention, of our consciousness. It is important to include time in our considerations in order to know more about what place can be and what is ideal and what is fragmented and so on.

Oosterling: In one of your texts you refer to Valéry where he says: 'It's not the difference in sex that matters but the difference in selfhood. Co-existence is something very special. Complete being is in fact double because consciousness implies duplication. Then I speak to myself, answer, am two in one'. So making a work of art must always be a splitting process. Then time is involved because it is a splitting process and space is involved because it is a splitting process. But what you are trying to do is break up space and time by fragmenting reality and changing the materials.

Vanderheyden: I take it apart and bring it together in a new way, and that can be art.

Oosterling: Ricardo Brey, you work in a different way. You are not involved with analysing and synthesising. The materials you use all look worn out. In a sense, of course, an artist is always synthesising by taking out pieces of reality and forming them into a new reality. How do you synthesise your ideal place which does not exist?

Brey: Maybe I can explain this best by talking in metaphors. In the big mythology that the West has about the ideal place, I thought about Gauguin. Gauguin was trying to find his ideal place in Tahiti and I thought of Rimbaud who moved from France to North Africa and became an outsider who wanted to become rich by smuggling weapons. So there is a mythology about finding the ideal place. You could also use Baudelaire as an example in his use of drugs.

I try to create one symbolic place with real things that are dysfunctional. Most of the time I work with things that have been used before because I think that some part of the energy of that passes on to the audience. I also use these things because I feel pity for them. They are lost, they are garbage. People put these things into nature and then they become pollution and nature will not recuperate. So I do not want to create new materials, I can use these 'poor' materials. I recycle them. Sometimes, when you put certain things together, you create something. If you play well, an image will appear; if you play badly, it is only a waste of time and material.

Oosterling: So it has a critical impact. Does it have a political impact?

Brey: I believe that everything is political. When you drink coffee you are in politics, when you drink tea you are in politics. A forest is being destroyed for the production of coffee and tea.

Vanderheyden: Although you are right, of course, I am a bit worried about the trendy way, the terror almost of being politically correct.

Brey: I am not interested in political correctness as a fashion. If the Americans decide to be politically correct, they say we take all the minorities and they all have their rights. But that is besides the point because we live together.

Oosterling: It seems to me, Patrick, that the critical or political impact of your work is at least more implicit, very indirect.

Corillon: I do not speak directly about political subjects. But I have a political point of view on the object. You cannot own my object. It is not to be sold. I would like to make art for everybody, in public spaces or in a museum where you do not have to pay an entrance fee. That is the ideal place for me. You do not have to own the work. But I need people, the work needs interaction with people in order to be able to function. The ideal place for me is a place with people. There has to be a witness, and an active one.

Oosterling: But then the ideal place always has to do with coinci-dence, with the expectations of the spectator. It only happens the moment it happens and then it is gone. You cannot fix it. Neither can you fix objects, as you say. So you cannot own objects because you cannot fix them. We are talking about politics but you can define

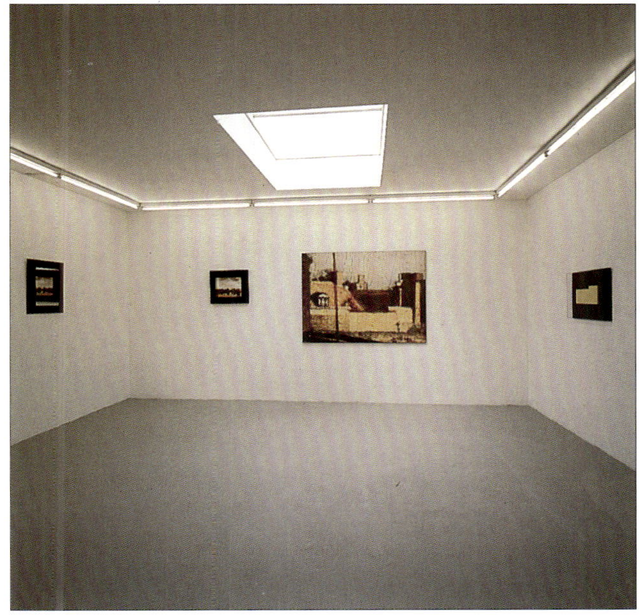

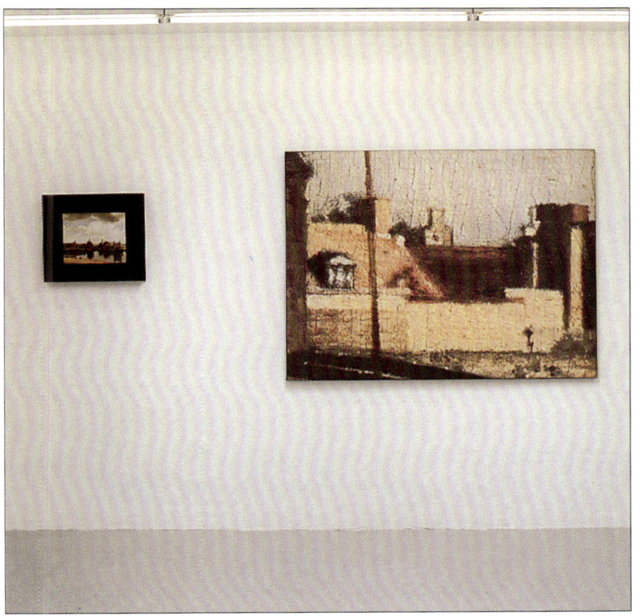

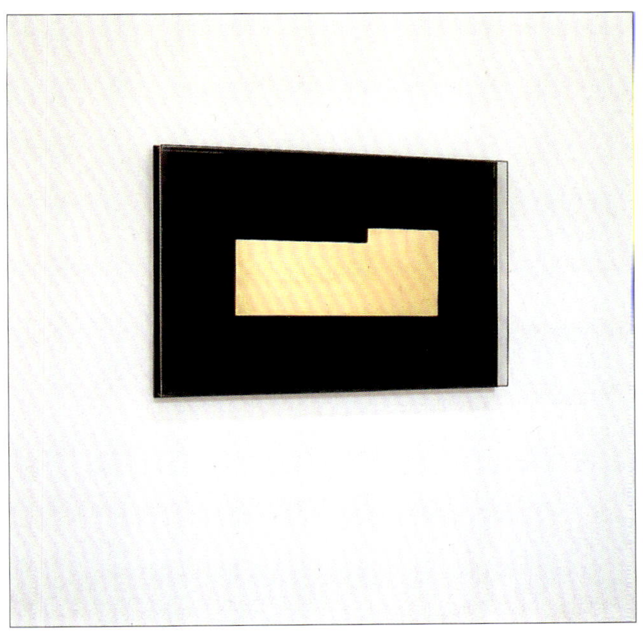

politics in a very narrow way and then you get these fashionable things like political correctness. You can probably widen the definition as Ricardo and you do, talking about tea and coffee, but in reality talking about the exploited. Jacques, when you talk about your art, you are talking about the production rather than the reception of it, as do the other two artists here today. Can work have political impact if you orient yourself only toward production?

Vanderheyden: For me this is no problem. I do not see why not, because art is interrelated with everything. I do not have to think in a specific political way to be political in that sense. I am interested in the world and I am interested in people. It is good that someone comes here to tell us about the coffee and tea thing and the exploitation it involves, because in this country we do not think a lot about these matters because of our luxurious way of life. But there are other levels of social and political thinking. I am interested in that but I do not try to include it in my work. I do not think that this is the work of an artist or the function of art. Art never solves a problem. That is impossible.

Corillon: 'I think it *is* part of the function of art. Art must stay a Utopia but we need a Utopia to be able to live in society. Utopia is an ideal place. I prefer to have an ideal of Utopia rather than the reality of it which can be very dangerous. We cannot live without Utopia. If you read the texts of Malevich and see his work, this is a Utopia you cannot actually enter but if Malevich had been the president of a country that would have been very dangerous.

Oosterling: A very important essay by Walter Benjamin in which he discusses the ability to reproduce works of art ends with a very direct and dangerous statement. He discusses the relationship between politics and art and then says that once art is politicised, ie once it is taken in, as in Cuba, to be a function of politics, it becomes propaganda. But when you aestheticise politics, which is a different movement, then you have fascism. And then he discerns a certain art of the avant-garde which is always critical and emancipatory. Art should develop consciousness. All three of you, I feel, are still within this discourse that art has to be critical and emancipatory. This goes for Jacques' work, too, although in a less direct and strategic way. I am interested in the critical aspect of your work because with Ricardo's and Patrick's it is obvious. What do you expect from your spectators or do you not expect anything at all from them?

Vanderheyden: I expect everything. The difference between the other two artists here at the table and myself is that I distance myself more from what is happening in the world, as well as to what is happening in art and perhaps even to myself. With distance you can sometimes observe and gain perspective more clearly, which can consequently be returned to you work. You give it another kind of attention and that unavoidably enters into your production, whatever you do. For me art is a feedback system. I do not know where it begins and ends. I have my thoughts, I have my mind and I have my work and they are interrelated all the time. I have no special idea about what spectators think about my work or if they look at it anyway. I am the first one to see my own work. Then, like you said about Valéry, I become two persons in one. I go into my room and I

see my work more or less in the same way as a spectator does. Then I can discuss it with myself. That is the basis of everything. You can question and answer yourself – a continuously interactive system. Otherwise I do not worry about being especially social or political. But it is all in there.

Corillon: I think it is too fatalistic to say that everything is political. You can see the enemy. If everything is political you do not know where you are anymore and you need to see who is doing what.

Oosterling: Ricardo, do you agree? If we regard everything as political, are we already defeated before the battle?

Brey: This is a question I have asked myself many times. To my mind and in my life's experience, one of the most horrible things that happened in this century is that people have divided into two kinds. There are those who are very cynical and say that they do not care about anything, and there are those who are the believers. They can be Communists, like in my country, or fascists or whatever. They are the believers who say: 'I am right. I believe in that, I die for that'. Others say, 'I don't care about anything. I live my own life and the rest of the world should take care of itself'. I want to be in a third position. I want to say: 'maybe'. Maybe there is some hope. I do not want to have too much hope because I do not see too much hope, but I want to say to myself: 'maybe it's possible to change things'. I am tired of being politically correct, of being vegetarian, feminist, everything. I am tired of that because I see no solution there. At the same time the bad guys win all the time and that is a terrible thing. The good guys are being politically correct and lesbian and so on and so forth. Why? There is only one problem and that is the bad guys. In the movies the bad guys lose. When you say 'maybe', that just might be one chance for us. In my art there is always this small possibility. The possibility to say 'maybe' in 1994 for me is enough.

Oosterling: You have given up the idea of borders. We are talking here about the ideal place all the time. There seems to be a suggestion that the ideal place has its borders. But is that true? It cannot really have borders, can it?

Brey: We can go back to the Greeks who spoke of the Golden Age. They were trying to find this ideal place. Mankind is always searching for the ideal place. They came up with Pandora's box. Before that it was better and now it is worse. And we construct our Utopias. I find something like Gauguin going to Tahiti to find the ideal place on a poor island most incredible. I come from such a place and there is no Utopia there, I can assure you. On the contrary, it is worse.

Oosterling: We need not care about art history as Jacques has said. But in a contradictory way you are moulded by it in your way of perceiving and in your way of handling materials. Photography for instance is a specific technique within Western art history and now of course there is also television. You cannot deny that. But still you have a kind of universalistic tendency in your work.

Vanderheyden: We are born into that. You cannot deny history, it is in us all. But I do not have to especially care about that. I have my own memory and my personal genetic system. That is what artists work with. This will be more important than history.

Oosterling: Is not the ideal place a function of nations and states with borders? As long as you are in a certain space, within a certain history – say, a 19th-century nation – then you can extrapolate a Utopia. But if there are no borders anymore, how can we think about something outside?

Vanderheyden: Art is making borders. This is a difficult question. If you have borders we do not need to make them and if you have no borders you try to make them. This will be the problem in the next century.

Brey: Imagine we are on one side of the street and the traffic-light is red, and in front of us is a group of people waiting for the light to turn green so that they can cross the road; once they have crossed, they become the others. In the meantime there is some kind of tension. If you have one side and another side there will always be tension.

Corillon: For me the ideal place is to cross the street when the light is red. You need a transgression.

Oosterling: We need a transgression to define the border. Art has been defined by Benjamin as not being propaganda, not being fascist but as a transgression to define the border. So the ideal place perhaps can only be the experience of transgression.

Peters: Ricardo is saying, in the words of Baudelaire, that the ideal place is 'any place out of this world'. This might in a way be true for Patrick's work also. On the doormat, which is the border, Oskar Serti has to wipe his feet clean until they bleed and even then he has to wipe them some more. That is what happens on the border. Could it be, referring back again to the critical or political impact of the work, that this might also be a metaphor for getting 'clean hands'?

Corillon: That will be my next story.

Oosterling: Ricardo's installation, which is very dirty, then tells us about this factual world.

Peters: I do not see why this installation might not be about 'clean hands' as well. And talking about art history and the manipulations with Vermeer's painting which nevertheless remains undamaged, even that work might be about 'clean hands' in a way.

Weiner: A major problem in talking about the ideal place is the ideal place for what? This is essentially a space run by people who either make art or are so involved with the making of art that it is part of their daily existence. What has happened in the artworld as we know it now is that nobody speaks about what is shown – it has no value – but about where it is shown. I think perhaps this question of the ideal place is really a question of contemporary aesthetics. Is art about where you are allowed to come and sit at the table or is art about what you have to say when you do sit at the table? When confronted with this problem, it took me, I think, six months of very persuasive talking by a lot of people to participate in this exhibition and now I am rather pleased that I did. But the ideal place cannot be determined except by what is done in the ideal place. You can have the best bedroom in the world in the best hotel in the world with all of the room service and if you really do not feel like fucking the person that you are with, it is not the deal place.

In talking about the ideal place, you often come up with this idea of what we have been taught from history and what we have been taught from art about the ideal place; you end up looking at somebody like Palladio who was extremely involved with the ideal place. But his ideal place was changed completely by whether the stones he chose had the measurements of 16cm or 19cm. And when they all fell down it was still the ideal place. This is rather interesting because it is about content. And when confronted with this situation I just tried to deal with what at this particular moment I would like to deal with – aesthetics. The essential question then is: how do you determine when what is enough. They used to say that an artist knew exactly when a painting or a sculpture was finished. And that was what being an artist was about because any fool could make things, anybody knows how to do anything. All you need is a little book which you can buy in any language to tell you how to do everything. The trick is to know when the painting or the sculpture is finished. Perhaps that is what I tried to deal with in this room, since the question of the ideal place is a question I hate, because the ideal place is based upon what the generation before you told you. That has nothing to do with us.

Gibbs: You could also interpret this statement GENOEG VAN DIT OF GENOEG VAN DAT (ENOUGH OF THIS OR ENOUGH OF THAT) as being the rejection of the concept of an ideal place.

Weiner: I do not think we have to waste our time rejecting things. Rejection of a previous aesthetic, rejection of what we have been taught that art is, has nothing to do with what art is supposed to be. Art is supposed to be asking questions now, that this generation – and that includes anybody who is alive and functioning at this particular moment – is supposed to be asking at this particular moment. What is the need for art, what questions are we asking about the relationships of human beings to materials and of materials in relationship to human beings? And forget about the accomplishments of other people. I hate to repeat this because I think I have said it too many times, but art should sort of float above the table. And on the table are all the accomplishments of other people – of Van Gogh and Mondrian and so on. But essentially you are still flying. When you stop flying, when the artists at this table stop flying, they enter this history, this table of what people have accomplished.

But art is not about accomplishment. Art is about presenting something that is still a kite in the air, still flying. You do not know if it works or not. So it is not a rejection of anything. In all honesty, I do not really give a fuck whether it fits into the idea of the ideal place or not. That is not my problem. My problem is getting through from waking up in the morning to going to bed at night. Art is supposed to float above what we know is the ideal place. For me today – sitting here, and I am an artist and I made this work – this is the ideal place. I am happy with it. I am not satisfied, I am really happy.

Does not the content of the work determine the context? Do you not believe that the work of an artist is capable of determining a change in the context, rather than that the artist should determine what the context used to stand for? I think this is the issue.

There is no ideal place. I wish I could make art that had an aspiration for the ideal place. I do not have any concept of what would be the ideal place. One of the things that I attempt to do when I make art is to take a position that other people can use to make their own metaphor for their own needs. Therefore there might be an ideal place that is made possible by the work I make, but nobody invites me in once they use the work.

We are always talking in terms of what the public will get from a work of art. And everybody in this room is forgetting that we are also the public. As long as we continue to think of art as something outside the public, the ideal place is always something that people who are not making art will talk about, but artists cannot. They can only talk about the place where work is seen best by the public. But we are the public as well. We pay taxes, we take our children to the dentist, we have the same problems.

The only 'social' artist is an artist who continually tries to present other relationships of materials. The people who spend their time showing how nice they are and taking care of children, washing dishes, being polite, are the parasites. The non-parasites are the doctors, lawyers and artists who do what they are supposed to do. The only reason that I am excited to participate in this exhibition is that maybe it is about time that we realise that there is no ideal place, but any place that lets you in is OK.

Zalme: But the word 'ideal' was not always transcendental. It was simply a standard which was accepted, against which all other things were judged. It did acquire the kind of metaphysical taint . . .

Weiner: . . . because of the impossibility of imposing, once art was no longer imposing. We are talking of a very long time ago. And that is what is so strange: we are still sitting here debating a problem that was solved about the time of Giotto. We are talking about the first times that the so-called public response to art became an important factor. 'That there is an ideal place, this will bring us nearer, my God, to Thou . . .' I think we know that art is really about the aspirations of everybody in this room. It is not about the aspirations of Mutti-Vati Kultur, it is not about the aspirations of other things. It is about what we want to know about our relationship to a piece of stone, to a bottle of beer and that has to be relayed in terms of dialectical materialism (the value of something, its use) so I find myself still wondering why we even ponder the ideal place except to know what other people did before we came along. But in fact it is not going to put a sandwich on the table.

A strange thing happened to me when I had to give one of those compulsory talks to children when I had a show in France. Essentially I found myself at a loss about what to say to them, and when asked why I made art I said, 'because I do think that it can change the world'. And the only way you know the world has changed is through your own perception.

Zalme: I am part of the world. If I change, then I change that part of the world which is me.

Weiner: We are part of the world. It is like Meister Eckhart – when you have a revelation you tell it. Piaget made an amazing discovery with children that were damaged by the Second World War. He asked them a very funny question: why is an apple called an apple? The answer was that the name 'apple' is written down inside the apple. Now as an artist your job and your role and the reason you become an artist is that you discover that the apple is called an apple because the name is written down inside the apple and you want to tell somebody about it. That is the only difference between a practising artist and everybody else in the whole world. You make the decision to spend your life telling people about it, whether they listen or not. The artist is an exhibitionist. They are people who are willing to stand up in public and show how they figured out to put their hands in their trousers. And they are also dumb enough to think they can make a living out of it.

In talking about the ideal, are we talking about a standard as something that we want to attain or are we talking about a standard as something that gives us some sort of driver's licence to keep going, something that will give us the permission to continue? If you can show us that you can do this, then you will be allowed to do something else. Then 'ideal' becomes a terrible word.

Zalme: To me the ideal place means two things that are in direct contradiction to one another: something that I can find evidence of around me and at the same time something that I will never have with me in the flesh.

Weiner: And you would like it to be with you?

Zalme: No, because if I had it with me, I would not have any reason to keep running after it.

Gibbs: It is like desire, like desire running after its own tail.

Zalme: Exactly. I do not want it. I am very happy being miserable. My piece here is about longing and not being able to have. It is certainly not utopian in the true sense because I never tried to actually build it or to actually have it.

Weiner: What happens if you are a real materialist? And you are miserable being miserable and you are happy being happy?

Zalme: I am miserable because I am a human being but I am happy with that.

Weiner: I am trying to push it towards another state. I am trying to say that when we accept the idea of that contradiction and this lack of satisfaction in what we make with our hands and our minds, we accept an idea of society that perhaps I personally (and I cannot speak for anybody else) do not any longer want to accept. I do not want to accept that the inherent contradiction in the problem of being a human being in our society is one of essentially being dissatisfied with it and constantly attempting to satisfy oneself. I am saying that art – maybe without our noticing it – has changed in the last 20 or 30 years to being able to present something which at that particular moment is all right. And in fact, maybe at that particular moment we as artists are all right. That does not mean it is going to be all right next week, but at that moment it might really and truly be all right. In fact you might not be happy being miserable, you are quite happy confronted by the contradictions that your placing this object with that object brought about. The first time I saw a Mondrian or a Pollock or a Carl André, there was a disjunction of my belief with what I was experiencing. Every time I now see a Mondrian on the wall I almost do not see it, I remember it. It is like being a virgin the first time you sleep with somebody. I remember that time when being disjuncted by that object made me feel that I did not know where I was anymore. That is what art does and could do for each generation because each time it is new.

Radermacher: The first time you saw a Pollock or an André was a special experience, where there was quite a gap between what I expected and what I actually saw. Would it not be beautiful – it could even be a goal – to try and keep that quality for oneself in one's own work? Then it would never be a recognition but every time a surprise.

Weiner: That is the problem of every artist. Between 1960 and now, two wars were stopped by people and by artists – the war in Algeria and the war in Vietnam. They stopped those wars with art and literature and music. Artists became part of the populace and are hence in a position to change the way the world was going. That never happened in the history of the world before. Therefore the art that we are looking at, made by the people today, is different from the art made 30 years ago. Perhaps it was a flash in the pan. But it has changed what you consider the ideal of what art can do. Art can in effect change our perceptions of the value of our relationship to an object.

Radermacher: Earlier you said that artists should make art and not programmes. Art is weak, art has absolutely no power whatsoever, art is in its deepest essence powerless. Perhaps that is why it can change something. But art should never be a programme, it should not be terror. The power of art s its lack of power.

Gibbs: We are getting deep into moralistic, ethical issues.

Weiner: When you start with a title like 'The Ideal Place', what else can you expect?

Notes

1 The Mauritshuis is not yet open.

2 *The Lost Time: The Prisoner*, Part 1, p190.

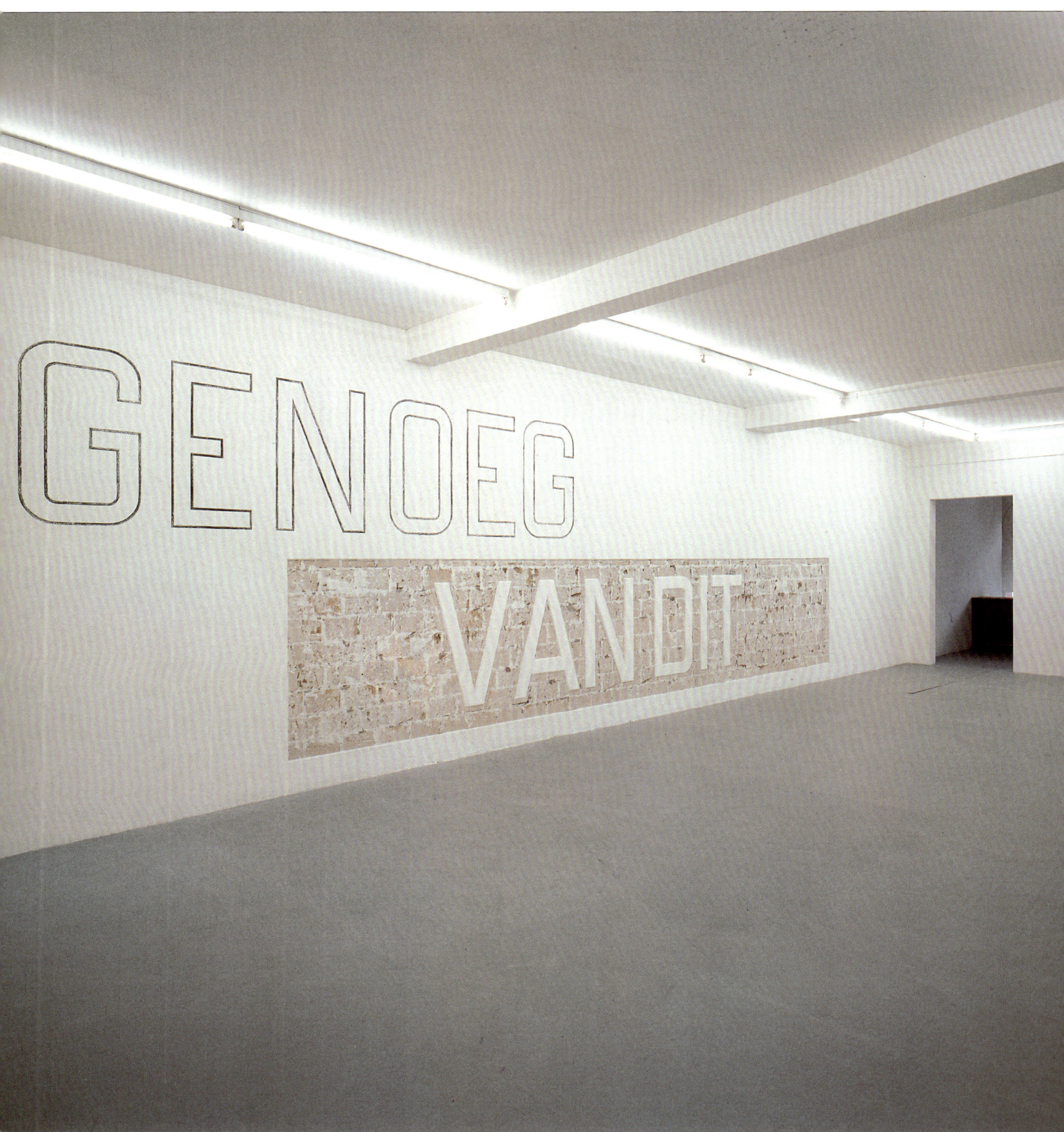
GENOEG
VAN DIT

THE IDEAL PLACE: ENOUGH OF THIS OR ENOUGH OF THAT?

LAWRENCE WEINER

REGARDING THE IDEAL PLACE AS DESTINATION:
THE WORK ATTAINS ITS PLACE. BY BEING PLACED.
IN SITU IS ONLY THE PLACE OF AWARENESS.
IN MOST CASES WHEREVER WITHIN OR ON THE
STRUCTURE WILL DO NICELY.
A PART OF THE MATERIALITY OF THE WORK
ITSELF IS THE PLACEMENT OF THE MATERIALS
NOMERED INTO/ONTO A STRUCTURE AS WELL
LADEN WITH MEANING.
IF THE SHOE FITS – WEAR IT.

Lawrence Weiner

Though it may be so that, apart from occasional trips into the field of video, film and music, the work of Lawrence Weiner usually consists of text, this text is no longer presented so much on its own as it used to be, with the characteristic adhesive letter applied to the wall in a quite impersonal manner. A work like ENOUGH OF THIS OR ENOUGH OF THAT in the HCAK therefore gives rise to more and different considerations.

Of course the art object was never completely dematerialised, as the inventor of this concept during the late 60s, Lucy Lippard, has meanwhile admitted: a work of art needs a medium, whatever that may be, in order to make itself known, and this medium consists of matter, even if it is only an adhesive letter. 'Immateriality' can only be communicated through matter. Moreover, from the start Weiner's work has been explicitly occupied with matter, however minimal this sometimes is. But in a work such as the one we are dealing with here, one can hardly speak of a minimal use of visual means: it is definitely quite sculptural in character (although it is not a classical, freestanding round sculpture). At an earlier stage the work dealt with general conditions in principle to be realised anywhere, and in a sense this still applies here, but on the other hand the specific material presence of this work in this place is so strong that it is hard to get round it. Consequently, it is largely an executed work and not just an indication of something that could be executed. It is explicitly a thing in the world. In other words, it is no longer an indication for a possible sculpture which under the right conditions, in more or less varying forms, could exist almost anywhere ('almost always any-where in or on the structure will be fine'), it is also an object or at least a sculpture having a number of unmistakable aspects directly connected with the object. In my opinion this is a not unimportant difference.

For that reason it is important to look at the execution of the work, involving three of the four walls in the exhibition room. On the left-hand wall, the text ENOUGH has been written in graphite in outline letters with the text OF THIS beneath it – the letters of which have been left open in a sizeable rectangle cut out from the wall. The word OR has been placed high on the crosscut wall written in graphite within a loosely drawn circle and – in the direction of the clock – the second long wall has undergone the same treatment as the former, but this time with the text ENOUGH OF THAT. 'Behind' or 'under' these letters the red-brick structure of the wall is visible.

What is actually being communicated here? ENOUGH OF THIS OR ENOUGH OF THAT seems to be open to various interpretations, the simplest of which (but not necessarily the most unlikely) may be that the artist evidently thinks that there is already enough and hence, there is no need to add all sorts of things to it. Another line of thinking suggested by Weiner himself is that the artist should decide when it is 'enough', when the work is 'finished' and that it is this moment presented here as an 'ideal place', the 'ideal moment' in the existence (or genesis) of a work of art, its 'ideal state'.

But this cannot be the end of the matter. The main problem we come across here is the word OR. For this suggests an alternative: (there is) enough of this *or* enough of that, but obviously not enough of both, for then the word *and* would have been used here instead of *or*. Or could it be that this does not matter, just as, by analogy, the manner of execution does not matter either – in this case partly in outline letters, partly in densely written letters and partly in letters left out from the wall. The almost arbitrary change within the method of execution itself might bring up the unexplicit but evidently suggested possibility that any other manner of execution could also be satisfactory, as long as the text remains unchanged. In that case we will have to conclude that none of it matters, which on the other hand seems to be somewhat in contradiction with the elaborate execution: why then go through all this trouble? Moreover, one would ultimately have to conclude that nothing matters anyway which seems not what art or Weiner's work is about. Besides, the word OR has been given a clearly visible accent: it is enclosed by a kind of circle, thus being further isolated from the rest of the communication and at the same time being given extra stress, being situated at the centre of the installation. It may even be the crucial word. An alternative may be indicated by it or a certain indifference, or perhaps doubt. Of course doubt is justified, it is an unavoidable part of artistic existence: the decision arises from doubt and one may also make the decision to doubt. When we interpret the work in terms of the ideal, which after all is the theme of this project, it may be conceivable that an alternative is presented between 'material' and 'immaterial' – enough of either is sufficient for indicating the ideal place. One may choose whether the ideal place is a concrete or mental place. Either one is possible, but it is not necessarily required to have both. Knowing Weiner's ideas, I think he would opt for the material aspect ever while refusing to acknowledge that there is or should be such a thing as the ideal place.

At any rate, even if the present execution does not wish to be more than one of the numerous possible forms of the work, there is a remarkable field of tension between the literal materiality of the work and the metaphorical meaning of the text. As a comparison, there is a work by Weiner which – I describe it here from memory – proposes the possibility of removing a rectangle of accurately defined measurements from a wall. This work has also been put into actual 'execution' at least once, in the sense that from a particular existing wall a rectangle of those measurements has been cut out. A photograph of it exists. One may therefore state that these two works are in the same way related, as a score is related to an execution of that score (which of course does not change the fact that the score itself represents the music just as much). I think this possibility applies to much of Weiner's more 'classical' works.

But does it also apply here? Are we still dealing with a score or rather, maintaining the analogy, with a score which in a partial form as score is at the same time partly made to actually 'sound'? Although this score can be executed anywhere given the right conditions of the space it finds itself in, it is still already partly executed here in this place. So we may have a moment of doubt after all, or to put it differently, with something that could almost be a contamination of two decisions, or a hybrid between score and actual execution. Or should we, all this notwithstanding, regard score and execution as one undivisible whole: ENOUGH OF THIS OR ENOUGH OF THAT?

Another consideration forces itself when observing the material form of this work: the words OF THIS and OF THAT, although prominently visible, are in reality the residue (or part) of the wall: the space around it has been cut out. This implies that these words are not there at all, they only exist by virtue of the absence of the counterforms in the wall. Thus there is more ambiguity to be found in this work than appears to be the case at first sight. Reasoning *ad absurdum* along these (admittedly) somewhat unlikely lines, the following text might arise: ENOUGH OR ENOUGH, thus ending up suspiciously close to the familiar tautology again. Then this definition of the ideal place may just be: ENOUGH.

PP
(with acknowledgement to MZ)

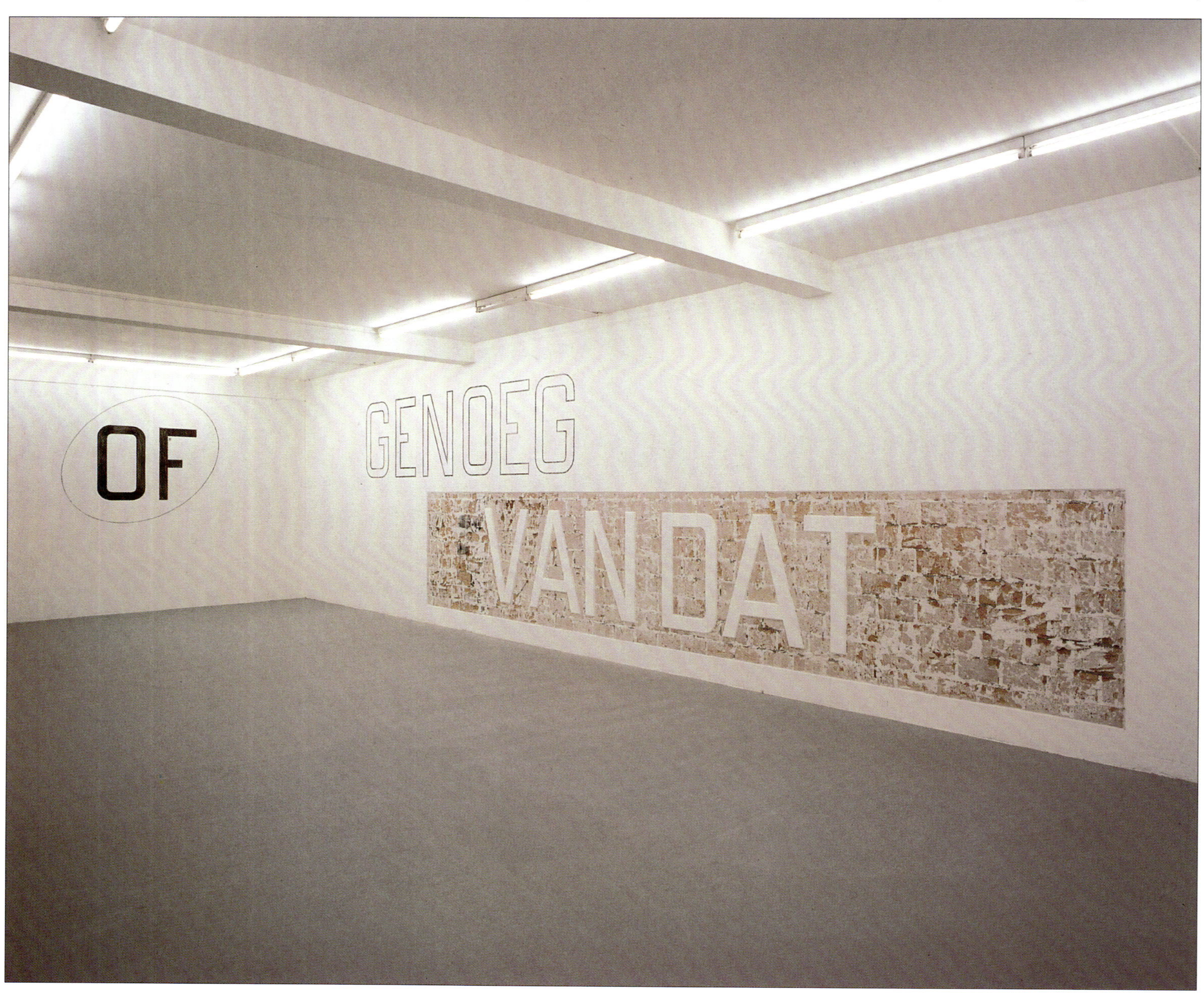

THE IDEAL PLACE: IDEAL SOCIETY
STEPHEN WILLATS

Democratic Model is an expression of the basic society of consensus between people, and as such is also an ideological statement that acknowledges the importance of fluidity and relativity in people's perception of what constitutes their culture.

In the work 32 men and women, who have not met before, and who are representatives of diverse social groupings, nationalities and ages, come together in a community room in The Hague for one day. The objective of them coming together is to participate in the construction and expression of a collective perceptual model of the ideal society and of the physical, social space in which it may be manifested and facilitated. The work is the vehicle for externalising this expression.

A sequential structure forms a time-based process that enables the group to formally work, step by step, towards 32 individuals becoming one group of 32 members, there being six stages to the progression, each one built around a problem situation presented as a question. The question/problem asks participants to form a consensus in their response to the idea of how they see themselves relating to each other in the ultimate living space, a dice being thrown at each point to generate random combinations of participants in ever larger groupings. The sequence of groupings is as follows. Problem One: 32 individuals; Problem Two: 16 pairs of participants; Problem Three: eight groups of four participants; Problem Four: four groups of eight participants; Problem Five: two groups of 16 participants; Problem Six: one group of 32 participants.

The work is an open channel, and all participants' expressions are made on response sheets consisting of an open frame which does not seek to influence the articulations made. All participants' responses are considered equally valid and are all displayed later in an installation that is formed from the sequence of six problems, situated at the HCAK, The Hague. The response sheets progressively enlarge in surface area to reflect the bigger groupings of participants, starting with Problem One: a 15cm square space, progressing to 22.5cm² space, 30cm² space, 60cm² space, 120cm² space, and finally to 240cm² space.

The outcome of this work cannot be known, and the interpretation of the ultimate living space is completely relative to the models held and expressed by the 32 participants. However, the structure of the work from the individual towards forming progressively larger groups ensures that the participants will interact with each other, and at some undetermined level influence each others' perceptual models in the drive towards consensus. The group disbands as Problem Six has been completed and then the response sheets are grouped together into six stages, and publically displayed as a testimony and expression of the potential of this event.

The notion of the ultimate living space is considered relative, transient, and illusory in the conception of Democratic Model, being thought of as an ideal that can create a mental buffer to release people from the pragmatics of their actual daily reality. This release enables people to engage in the pursuit of projecting themselves into normally difficult imaginative speculations. Democratic Model demonstrates the actual fluidity of cognitive models, that nothing held as social representation is absolute, especially in the dynamics of interpersonal exchange when searching for a consensus. In a parallel way, in that Democratic Model is a statement about the way social models are formed and re-formed as a constantly changing state, it also concerns the nature of art practice.

Democratic Model as an essentially social experience is seen to be a demonstration of a model art practice that is in cultural opposition to the monumentality of recent art embodied in the permanent, immortal object. While the outcome of Democratic Model cannot be known or even predicted as a planned event structured in time, it embodies relevant heuristics for the future interactive communication based culture that is now emerging.

Stephen Willats

Democratic Model by Stephen Willats is a perfect exponent of his manner of working, in which design is dependent on the contributions of the participants: 32 people were asked to indicate or visualise their 'ideal living environment' on a square sheet of paper. Subsequently, they were arbitrarily divided into pairs, who were asked to do the same thing, but now on a larger sheet. After this, eight groups of four were formed, then four groups of eight and two of 16, until eventually one group of 32 was formed, who had to try and make a joint statement on their views on 'the ideal place', by mutual consultation and on a much larger sheet of paper. As regards background, age and gender the participants were more or less a cross selection of the population of The Hague. The results of the process were exhibited in the HCAK.

Although the eventual images could not be predicted, it was to be expected that initially various visual idioms would come up, which could later be traced back in the joint products. This turned out to be more or less the case: the individual persons had largely remained recognisable from beginning to end.

This is not the place to enter into the various interpretations of 'the ideal place' which this abundantly diverse work has resulted in. They ranged from an idyllic landscape to an abstract construction mainly consisting of arrows.

What is more remarkable and relevant, is how the interaction developed: this can be clearly traced from the results and also proves to correspond with the participants' experiences. The first stages did not present any problems, the original statements, part of them splendidly negotiated, recurred in the subsequent stages. But

"

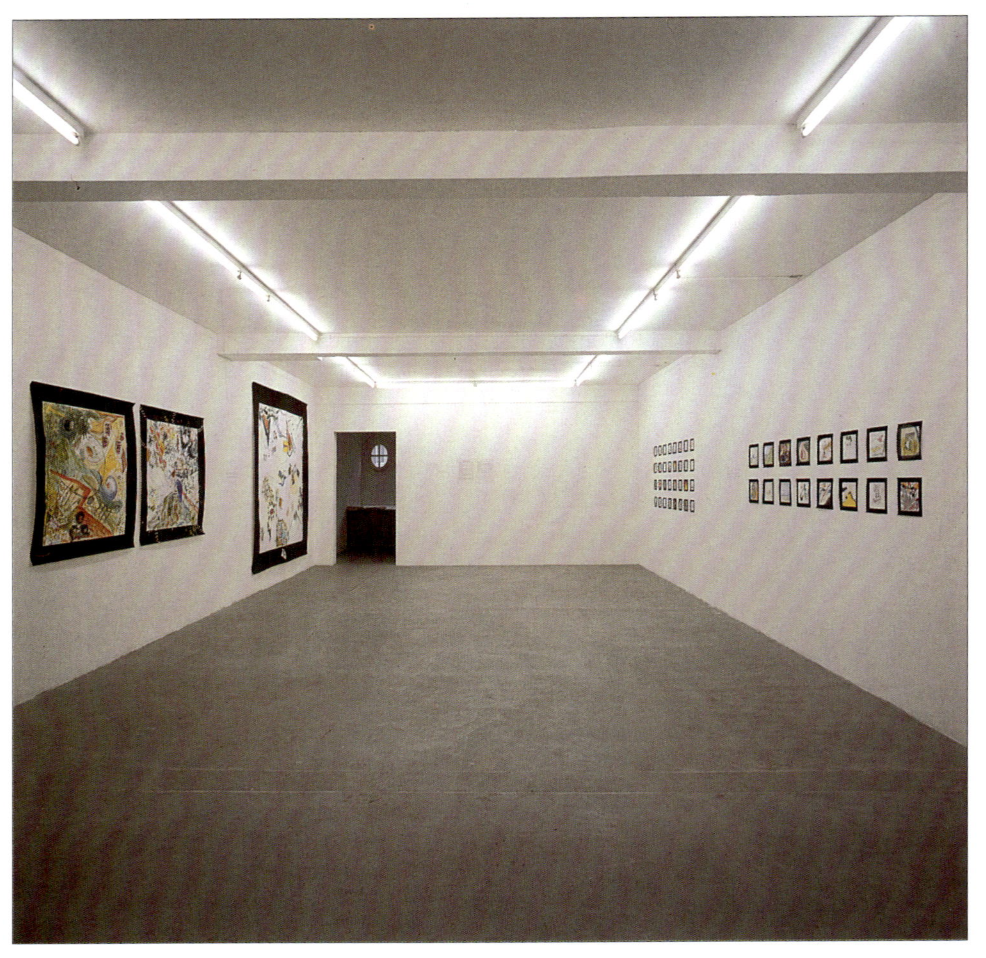

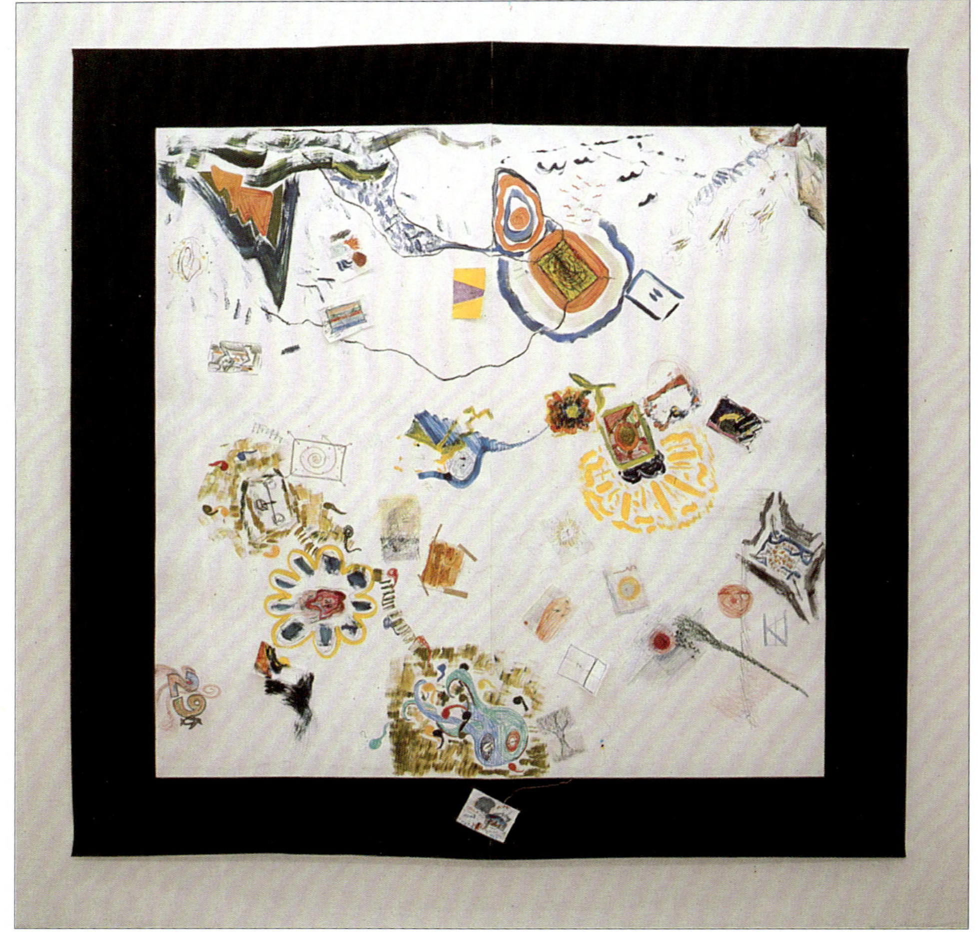

when the group consisted of 16 people it had evidently become too large – instead of the fairly articulate previous statements, an image was now created which looked a bit like the sort of pleasantly 'expressing yourself in paint' sometimes practised in creativity centres or creative therapy. Individual opinions had here been drowned in an orgy of stripes, smudges and so on, which had little to do with the theme. What would the groups do later on, when they had eventually been combined to a group twice as large? The result was surprising: on the last sheet the tendency of 'free expression in paint' had not continued, but neither had the thread of combining ideas really been resumed. Instead, there was a return to the initial situation (directly opposite which this last product was hung at the presentation) but now on one sheet – whereas in the penultimate stage not a single spot on the sheet had been left blank, now large parts of the sheet remained empty. The participants had withdrawn to little islands, and in a sense, more loosely connected references to the original images recurred on this last sheet. The group which had to be welded together kept this up until there were four groups of eight people, but after that the process tailed off.

I do not know what exactly is to be learned from this. Surely after one experiment it cannot be concluded that a group of eight people can still communicate in visual images on a theme like 'the ideal place' and a group of 16 people can do so no longer – for such a conclusion, the experiment would have to be carried out more often and probably in a different way. But of course we were not practising science here. This was not an attempt at advancing or proving a hypothesis. The aim was to give a number of people the opportunity to work democratically in groups at formulating 'the ideal place'.

In a work like this it is the process that is most important. This manner of working deliberately turns its back on the aspect of the work of art as object. The final result (or results) is only interesting as the outcome of the process, in which people present their dreams and desires. It is their experiences that are the issue here and that give the work its meaning. In that sense the result somewhat spoils the effect of the process, of which it is a souvenir.

The position of the artist, the special vision on what being an artist means, is essential for this manner of working. The artist is not prominently present in his work; he allows others to speak on his behalf. This does not mean that he is completely absent as he writes the scenario and acts as a director. But within this context, the work is almost entirely composed of variables: the actors are free to fill in the theme as they consider fit. It is their experiences that are actually concerned here – they take up the central position in the work. The artist functions as a catalyst in a process that is probably in the first place social in character, he creates conditions and offers means. The utopian aspect of this view of the artist is obvious: by taking up the function of an intermediary, the artist wants to give people material for the purpose of gaining insight into their living environment with the ultimate aim of finding the means to change their situation wherever this should be unsatisfactory and alienated. Thus, each work by Stephen Willats (including, of course, this one) can be seen as a step on the way to the ideal society in which everyone is subject to equal opportunities and can fulfil his or her personal needs in a non-hierarchic structure.

PP

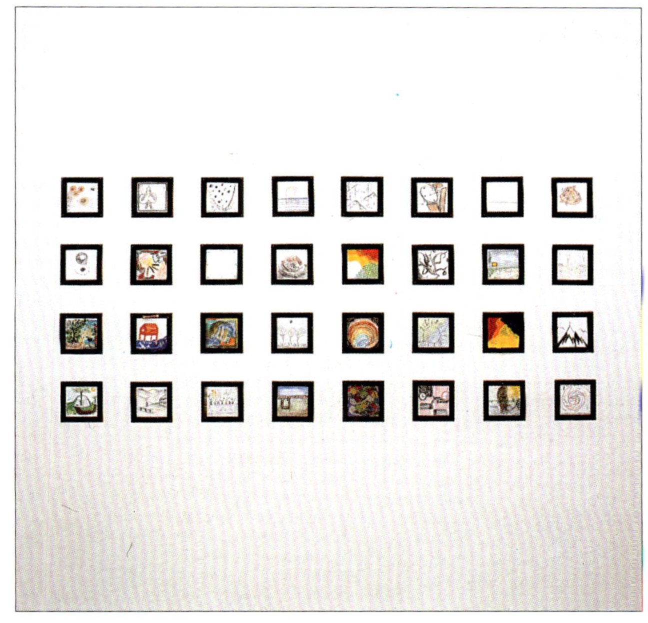

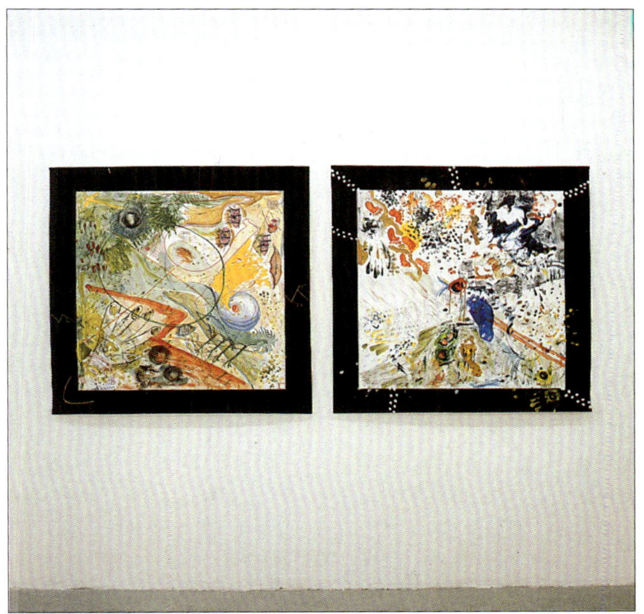

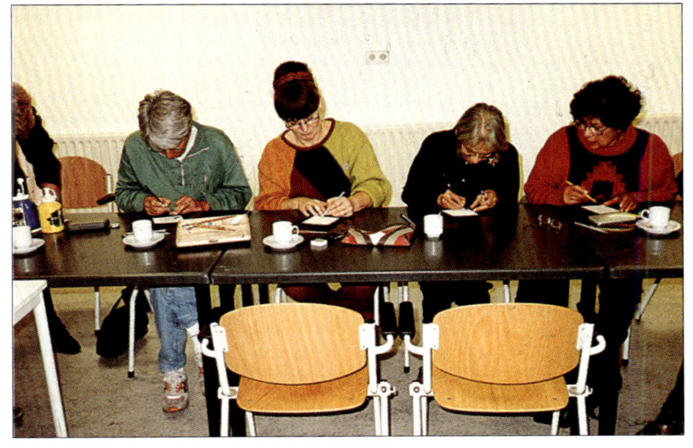

BELOW: Individuals drawing in response to the first question, HCAK, 1993-94

THE IDEAL PLACE: LOOKING AT THE ESSENCE
ROBIN WINTERS

WE ARE BUT RAGS TO WASH THE FEET OF HUMANITY

I opened my mail and received my HCAK invitation to participate in 'The Ideal Place'. The other letter I received the same day was an invitation from Trinity Church to buy a plot of ground for a gravesite. Trinity Church listed many famous people who were buried there and offered me a discount price.

We all have the same destination in life. Our common destination is Death. How we go from point A to point B is what is important. All places being the same, my living destinations have been equally ideal. I think my exhibitions in public schools, libraries, prisons and mental institutions have been as important as my exhibitions in the Stedelijk Museum, the Whitney Museum or the Museum of Modern Art although the general art discourse seems to make it all a money, career, popularity contest.

During the 80s when someone would ask, 'How did your show go?' it generally meant 'Did you sell it all?' – a sad fact of the marketplace being the determination of so-called good art. If you show at X gallery, suddenly everyone is interested in the work, while the same work in Y gallery is completely dismissed. The artists are as responsible for this as the critics and curators. The collectors are the ones who control production and exposure. Money talks. Suddenly everyone is interested in B because C, D and E have purchased his work for $ 150.000. B is now on the cover of every art magazine and curators are now including B in every exhibition. For same artists, this is the ideal destination – to be talked about and consumed. A history made by the conquerors.

For my work at the HCAK, I will come with some cardboard and paint. I will write some words which I will intuitively pick in relation to the context. Placement will be visual. I may or may not write in complete sentences. I hope that my choices will relate in some significant way to the community I have been invited to engage with.

It is always a question for me when invited to participate in an exhibit, what the sponsors want from me. Usually if I ask, no one will tell me. They always say that I can do what I like. I guess this freedom is a form of Ideal Destination, although sometimes it would seem more clear if I was actually given an assignment, a job description to fulfill.

The extension of one's self into a realm of non-belonging by being public domain; the domain of the senses; the visual, verbal, actual actualisation of one's dreams, if not some exquisite adventure or some well worn trail to the campfire burning on the edge of an immortal tribe eternal. We shall cook and be together, and so on. Am I venting longing or inventing platitudes? Latitude is what I give. Permission to adventure, experiment and play seriously. What else is there? However, the clowns and devils tempt the angels. The agreement is unbroken but it is always a marriage. Fashion and

death, youth and old age – we are but a summation of our follies.
When man and woman are one
When the heart and the mind are one
When the eye and the hand are one
Then you will enter the Kingdom.

(The Gospel according to Thomas)

There can be no understanding between the heart and the brain unless the heart works as a mediator.

(Fritz Lang, Metropolis)

Serene Marine – A soldier in the eye of the storm, holding fast to the rigging of life. Laughing as they go 'ho ho ho', the bozo troops go marching on. Bend the line, but don't break it. Do we see the light at the end of the tunnel? Only twilight gleaning the omnipresent future which in the past was an event to be looked forward to. Hopefully we will again be onward and upward and out of the trenches and onto a higher ground, tranquility base, to face the moral issues of the day.

My Creed is to remain alive in mind and body, to deliver to the world my gift in as sensitive and powerful a fashion as I can.

No fascism, no Napoleons, no Hitlers, no Elvis Presleys, no Walt Disneys. Only heartbeats on paper drums with the loaded instrument being the viewer's view of the moment noticed. This is The Ideal Place.

Robin Winters

Robin Winters' version of 'The Fabric of Life' is a representation of a 'genuine', decorated fabric on paper in a number of vertical strips. The almost airy, apparent casualness evoked by the way in which it has been made definitely sets the tone of this work, which on either side had already started with a present: dishes with sweets, cigarettes and the like.

The entire work can be interpreted as a present and in a sense this is an important option of art. The artist takes up a position through which he creates a place for himself in the history of ideas. All kinds of positions are possible. I think Robin Winters is a person who wishes to share his 'positive' attitude to life with his public.

Such an attitude has almost disappeared from art. The predominant norm is the norm of postmodernism with all its negations of centre, construction and meaning. But the inaccessible monumentality of classical modernism and its late offshoots are also denied here, as it were. It may be true that criticism is intrinsically linked up with its subject (just as postmodernism as criticism of modernism is in itself a modernist variant: how can one escape from gravitation with the aid of means which are themselves derived from gravitation and comply with its laws?) the work of Robin Winters wishes to place itself beyond any category, it seems.

This installation is at the same time playfully graceful and sacral. A small, white ceramic human head is placed on a pedestal, accompanied by a number of incense sticks. On the one hand, it is clear that a cult moment has been suggested here; on the other hand, the deliberate lack of pretension of the statuette is an indication of relativisation or a 'human dimension'.

Thus the dice cups with minuscule fortune-telling letters in them can also be seen in these two ways, just as the dishes with sweets, which are vaguely reminiscent of voodoo-like rituals. Then there are also somewhat larger cardboard letters in various colours lying on the floor, from which words can be formed as one chooses.

Besides graceful and sacral, this installation is therefore also interactive. One can intervene in the work so as to give the exhibition room a personal character, to make the work come alive, as it were. Or to put it differently, to use the work as a medium in the fulfilment of personal desires.

The HCAK simultaneously presented the work of Art & Language, which also explicitly communicates with the visitor, but in a way that is almost in contrast with it – their installation makes demands of the observer and then makes him lose his footing, whereas Winters' work, on the contrary, wishes to put him at his ease. The work of Art & Language commands intellectual reflection, Winters' work invites play: the concept of *homo ludens*, playful man, is here brought up. This work is explicitly at the service of the public.

Grace does not imply depreciation. For reasons unknown to us, in culture ponderous statements are ranked higher. It even seems as if a hierarchy of emotions is adhered to, in which the smile/laugh are less highly regarded. There is no valid reason to defend this.

The work of Winters evokes a smile and this smile is a smile of contentment. This contentment is not a sleepy confirmation of the status quo, but a sense of well-being, of being in the right place, in other words: in the ideal place.

In this view his work is no longer merely charming, but touches upon essential human needs and possibilities. In addition, the words 'specere' and 'eidos' on either side of the installation indicate once again that important issues are concerned here: 'looking at the essence'.

The smile evoked by the work is not just an ordinary amused smile: it is the cosmic smile of the Buddha, of the sense of harmony and unity of which the work is a representation and which the observer/participant can identify with through his own contribution to the work.

A work creating this opportunity is entitled to be called 'The Ideal Place'. For those who interpret it right.

PP

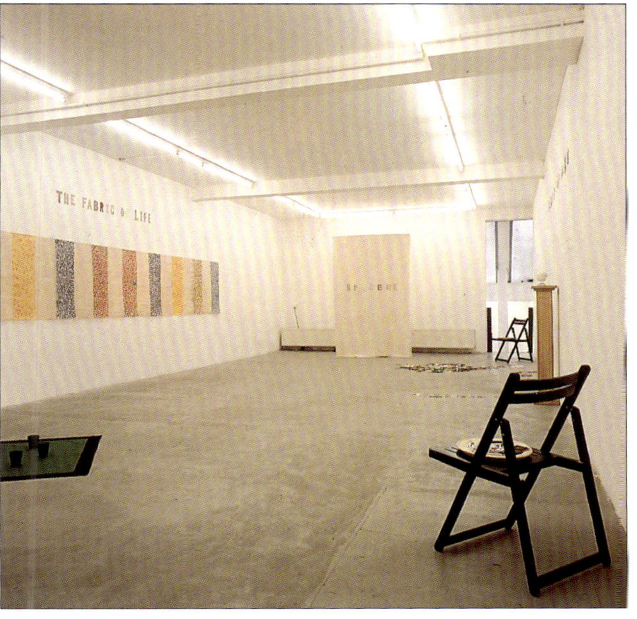

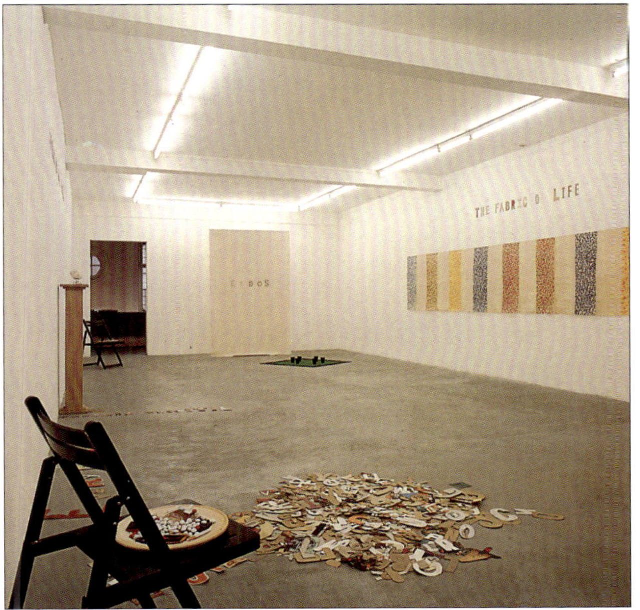

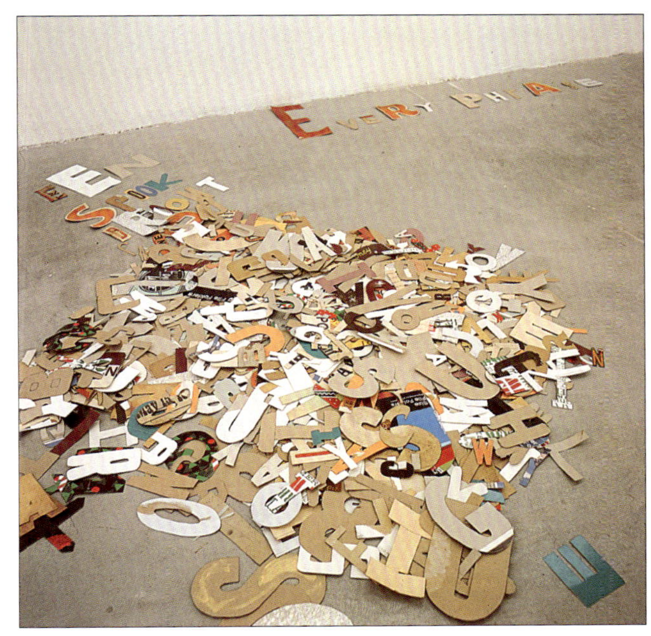

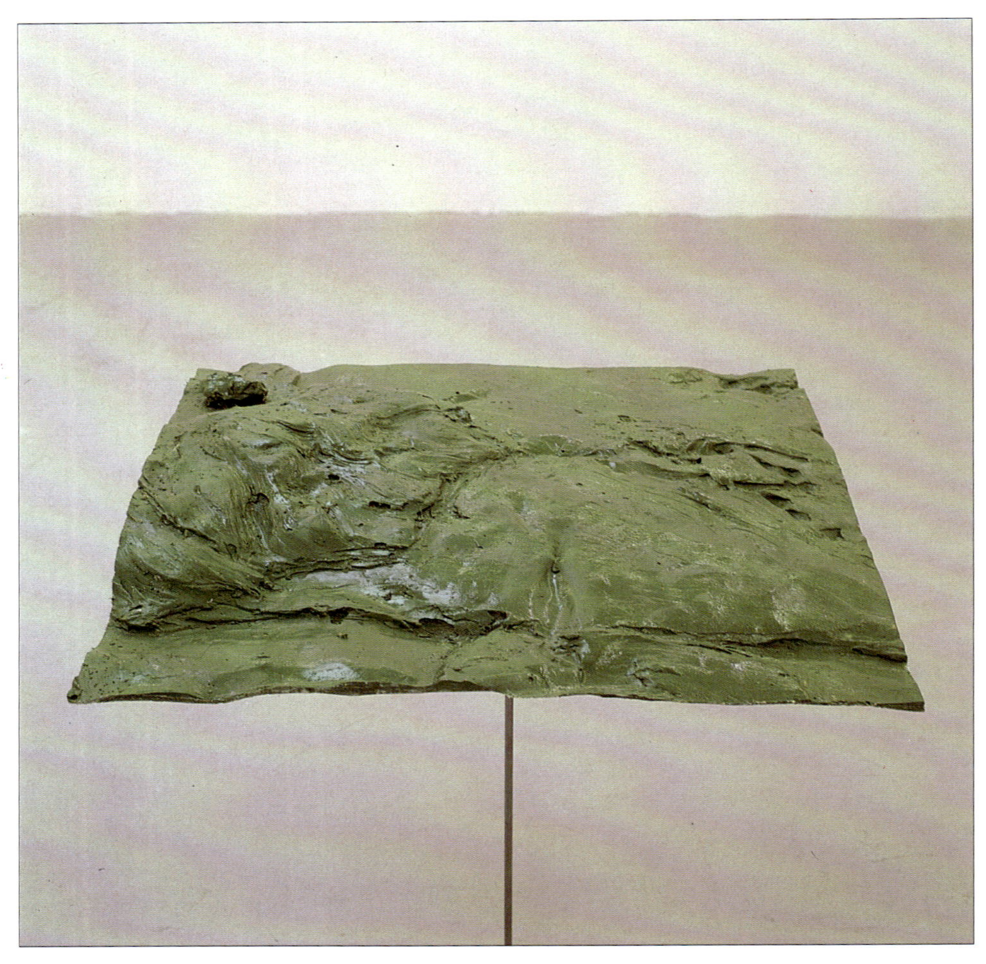

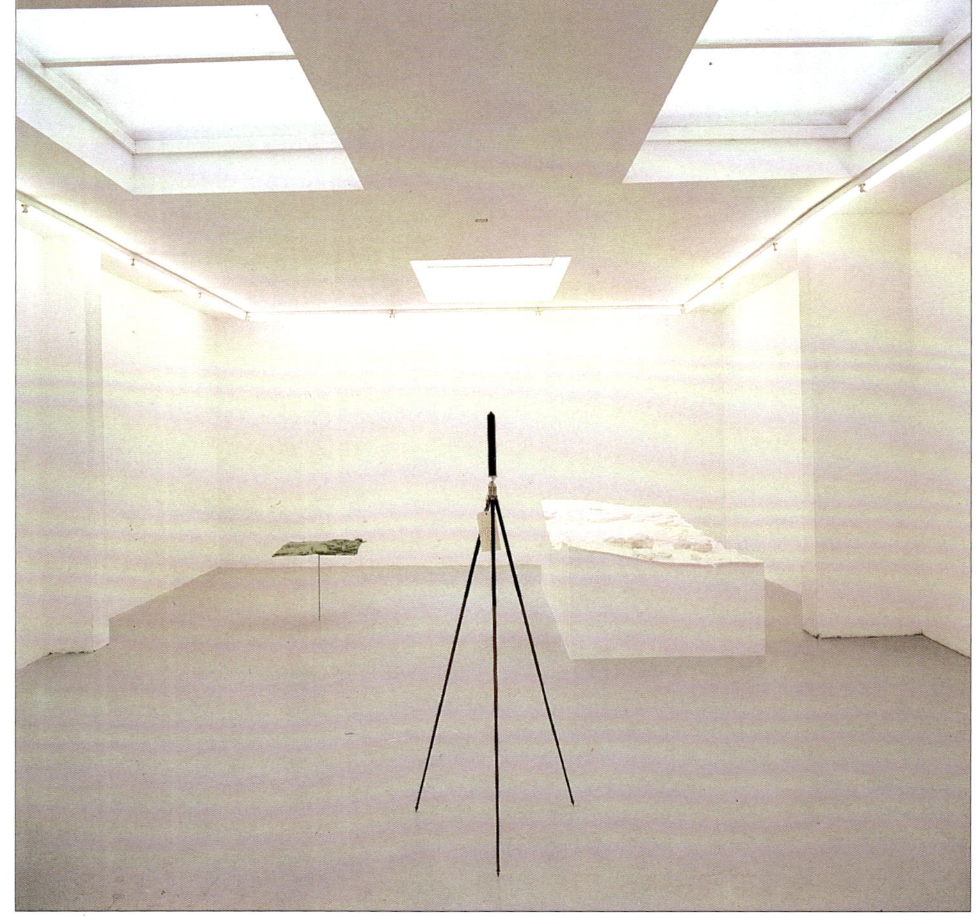

THE IDEAL PLACE: BETWEEN DREAM AND REALITY

MARCEL ZALME

The Place of the Ideal

It was not what I had hoped for, but thinking about 'the ideal place' has driven me to a conclusion that on the surface sounds fairly pessimistic. I find myself in a position that seems a betrayal of optimism: namely that I will never be happy with any solution to the proposition that I could formulate.

Perhaps this is because, to begin with, my work carries in it a broad negation of the world as I find it. This was a mixed blessing from the beginning. I have created a country which provides me with the means I need to make any work at all, but it is not a place, nor does it refer to a place that anyone can visit.

A time arrived not so long ago that I became desperate to escape from this country, so that the relief was very great whenever I thought I had found a means. Except that this has always turned out to be an escape on a purely formal level. In fact, it was always just another branch in the same road. A mild horror with the idealised state of my desires has always had a certain effect on my work, and the prolonged concentration on it begun by this project has, indeed, led me not only to 're-examine the basis of my practice', but also the word 'ideal' itself. If I accept the word on the terms laid down by others before me, then it seems to be something from which there is no escape – except downwards. In that case, we are doomed as a race to improve. The dilemma carried by the word is clear: complete submission to an ideal seems like an appalling form of slavery, whereas life without passion is a sleep worse than death. So I feel compelled at the very least to pay lip service to the idea, or the ideal, for fear of having nothing if I accept the full consequences of freedom. The word demands we make a choice, and all choices disappoint.

The Genesis of the Standard

The necessity of a project like this one within the context of the HCAK was clear once all of our earlier projects had been laid end to end – it was simply the next logical step. The programming could be seen as a registration of the progress of an idea from conception to inception. The only step that seemed to be missing was the arrival of the idea at its most perfect place of rest.

When speaking of such a place it is difficult not to fall back on 'idyllic' terms. Yet the word 'ideal' was chosen and now we have to deal with the consequences. A word like this was felt to be necessary for the sake of our proposition, ie that the perfect place of rest is a thing with enough reality to be seriously discussed, yet we are aware at the same time that the word implies more than merely a standard against which to judge a thing's success or failure. It seems to imply an unreachable standard. 'Ideals' have always been used and understood in terms of projection, either as visions which transcend reality or as part of a social agenda. The methods invented to make the word functional instead of merely luminary

have always had this in common, that they were formed within a model which had to be achieved before it could be lived in. The direction we faced was unconditional, it could not be anywhere but to the front, with eyes fixed on the horizon. History was useful because her mistakes were a means of adjusting the compass to point 'true north', if you like I do not think we have stopped entirely trying to improve as navigators, but the idea of the ideal as a destination seems to have fallen out of favour. The object of divinity which encouraged the quest is a sham, or at least not representative of true divinity. The fashion has turned from the good and true destination to mere 'context' as the 'place' towards which we work. The degree of liberation this has given is obvious when we see the grip it has on the artistic community: it has become an endless source of fascination. We feel that the freedom it gives from utopian fixations allows us to see the relationship between object and subject more clearly. Their place and shape are no longer as distorted as they were by a desire to see them somewhere else, newer and improved. The pressure to pinpoint a meaning (or an ideal) as being somewhere 'there' has shifted to somewhere 'here'. This is also clearly noticeable in the way artwork is intended to be received. There is no longer any question that reception must be transcendent, but that it can be immanent, or local, completely in the hands of the observer. Within this context it is hard to see why anyone would still wish to discuss a work of art in terms of an ideal, as long as the word implies transcendence.

If this is true, what trick of thinking do we use when we apply the word 'ideal' when we have really come to think of 'the goal' as less interesting than 'the means'? Apparently, the word 'ideal' still stands for something. At the very least it is convenient, a word which I can deploy to do work for me I rather not do myself. But are we hypocrites who use it without really believing in it? It is a case of belief being less important than the desire. If we look no further than the word's semantic value we see a contradiction. The title of this project is a place I can name, but which cannot exist, at least not if you accept that imperfection is an inescapable norm, and that the word 'ideal' is about perfection. Yet the semantic trap becomes superfluous once you admit that the word is based on a sentiment, and that sentiments do have a tangible reality. It is almost a case of language trapping us into the denial of such a sentiment, of the heartfelt desire that ideals should have relevance. As confusing and dated as it is, the strength of the word in its decline is still sufficient to stir longing. Well, if the shell of the word denotes a thing which is lacking, at least not present in its complete form, then we are free to see its objective as not necessarily being 'ideal', although having it may seem to be. For good or ill, the word has digressed from its status as a universal standard in order to survive as some other form of mythology: it is obvious from the devotion of the artists working on this project, that all the denials that there is such a thing or place are not preventing them from offering a catalogue of descriptions of it.

The Place Dreamt of Before Experience is Acquired

It was obvious from the outset that the 'place' we are looking for could be anything: actual or mental. A point that still might be made is that a 'resting-place', whether realisable or not, can only be completely understood if examined in relation to its forebear in the mind of the artist. Never mind that this might be impossible, we are speaking of ideals here. And though I am not even sure that a forebear exists for everyone, I am certain that it did for me. By it I mean the insubstantial image of a 'place' which arrived with the idea, appeared with it in the doorway, so to speak, and left an impression of itself to be used thereafter as the standard against which the rest might be judged. Far from being 'ideal' in the philosophical sense, this first image might be arbitrary, may derive its power simply from being the first strong emotion of a creative life. It might even be displaced by stronger emotions which follow, so that it might be better to say that the standard is the feeling which survives. The most important thing about it is its transience, so that it becomes the thing we want at all costs to have again: it becomes the basis of a passion. I am convinced that in my case this emotion had the qualities of a 'place' since its recurrence since then has always been strongest when placed in in a physical context. At least, if a place did not have those qualities itself, it could mirror them perfectly. The ideas which have followed have always passed this 'place' like a parade, and those found lacking in comparison have been discarded. What comes next is probably a kind of incestuous pairing between the 'winners' and the original emotion, each gener-ating fresh variations of each other, to the point that distinction between the two becomes almost impossible. The final step of translating the resulting germ of an idea into the visible world must be so somplex that it cannot be an accident that those who do it well often end up doing little else. In other words, though we all make comparisons between what we see and what we feel, only a few of us manage to communicate it.

For the artists who have made this activity their profession, one of the consequences of long practical experience might be that this first intergenerational activity, something a child may enjoy without realising it, suffers a continually shorter life-span. For the child the place dreamt of before (wordly) experience is acquired is not yet qualified by the physical struggle with resistant matter, which must follow. The mature practitioner, on the other hand, leaps with an idea into the branch of practicality almost at the moment of conception. I can imagine that a moment must arrive for these people that the two things aquire such an interdependence, ie that practicality actually becomes a prerequisite, that the time before this was so, takes on the status of a myth and is lost from sight. Most of us live with the sense that materials have a banality which our imagination does not. Or, if not the materials we use, then our own limited capabilities when using them. How could this be unless we had a basis for comparison with something ulterior, our ultima thule? Our ideal place.

Reconciliation with the Ideal

I began by saying that the project had led to disappointment. I went on to explain where I thought the ideal stood in a modern context, and where I thought my own conception of it came from. Now I have to explain how I think the two can be reconciled.

One of the nice things about the new physics is that it tells us that we are able to dictate terms to reality. Whether this is true or not, the idea has interesting biblical precedents: something I would be tempted to call Lucifer's fall into happiness. Being bereft of angelic substance, the dreams that Lucifer touches turn into their opposite, or matter. His joy is the discovery that matter has beauty, and his joy is our joy. (We cannot resist redirecting our gaze every now and then to that dream before the fall, perhaps because we grow tired of the things which can be possessed. The obvious beauty of the whole set-up is that we never grow tired of Heaven, since we never arrive: the dream need never be infected with its realisation.) It is because matter has that beauty that I need not place my ideal on a metaphysical level. The only advantage of metaphysics is their timelessness; the things which I decide are there are out of reach because of my own mortality. And we come to the reason that new physics has made it so interesting to be a human being again – I can decide that my perception of Time has been incorrect, or at least incomplete. When I shift my perception of Time like a carpet from under Creation, I can shift my ideal with it, from being beyond the metaphysical curtain, into my own 'time'.

Seeing this involves, I think, only a slightly different assessment of the time and place I am in. That I think I am able to do this may sound like subjective bunk, especially when I add that I love the past more than the present, yet physicists tell me that my subjectivity has more power over the way things are, than I used to think.

The technique is quite simply to acquire a feeling about time which is different from the apocalyptic edge that it has had, especially when the point we call the present is the leading point, and the collective consciousness a ragged forward line or a front – as though this were a Great War, and Time the enemy. A 'front line' may not be incorrect as a metaphor, except that it needs to be followed quite literally: the landscape a battlefront stretches across is known to carry on beyond it, and as something we can still recognise as a landscape. We know this because we can see it, even though the greater part of it may be unknown in the way a strange country might be. I know myself, therefore, to inhabit a point deep in a territory, and not on the thrusting point, over the edge at the end of the world. I am 'in' Time as though it were a country. The idea is obvious, yet reassuring (even while being aware that my actions might one day make my presence there precarious).

And there again is that 'place': by converting time into a place, we have a stage where forward, backward or lateral movement are possible. The distance is narrowed down – at least psychically – between myself and the things I desire. The dead (or dying) generations that I considered unreachable seem close enough to be contemporaries. Time is restored to being a process, a spring in various stages of tension, instead of a line which is static because of its inevitable 'forwardness'. It could even be described as a 'state', just as susceptible to influence and change as any of the other (physical) elements.

One definition of Utopia might be a place where we finally and constantly live at the climax of processes, instead of waiting for them and having them for just a few moments, which is the way we generally characterise living, having time. We cannot stomach the idea of a passive 'holiness'. A common joke about Heaven is that we would all like to arrive there, but nobody would want to stay. (Being in Heaven might be like living in the prettiest house in the street: the only problem is that you have the worst view of anyone from your window.) Which is another good reason for examining the place we are in for symptoms of being 'ideal', whatever that means. In a sense it carries on being a destination since we are searching for it, only it is not 'there' somewhere, it is 'here' somewhere. Only now the finding is not so much a journey as an alteration in perception: it was here all along. An ideal place might be nothing more than a flickering in our line of sight.

Marcel Zalme

My best childhood memories lie in Tilburg, a provincial town in the south of the Netherlands. My grandparents lived there and I went there every summer to stay with them for about a month. I had friends there, there was no school, there was nothing to worry about, the weather was always fine. When I was two years old I fell in love there for the first time, with a girl in a white dress. I was looked after and pampered. Grandpa read to me and we went for walks in some kind of wood on our way to a farm where I could collect eggs. Grandma called me 'little lad' and made the tastiest meat balls, the recipe of which she took with her to the grave. It was the early 50s. The deep voice of the newsreader came from a creaking radio.

In the mornings, when I woke up around 6.30, I looked out of the window of my room which overlooked the garden and there was Grandpa in his dustcoat his arms spread out, feeding the pigeons. He looked like St Francis. The pigeons perched on his arms and shoulders, his head even. The pebbles of the garden path creaked under his slippered feet.

Years later, not so very long ago, I went back there. I had to give a lecture in Tilburg that evening and for the afternoon I had planned a few studio visits. I had some time left inbetween. So I went back to that street which had been the paradise of my youth. It was spring, the sun had set, but it was still not dark – that mysterious gap in the day, when everything is quiet, but also sharply defined in contours, a moment of reverie and reflection, a moment of openness. Castaneda calls it a *moment of power*. I was about 40 at the time, I think, but gradually I was turning the clock back to the age of seven: in one's memory several moments, several ages, several stages in one's life exist side by side and mixed up. Proust based his life's work on this fact. After a while a little boy of my age (which is to say, of about seven years old) came skipping around the corner. He was skipping along the garden path and rang the bell of the house where I had been so happy. The door opened, he went in, the door closed again. I was standing across the road, consumed with jealously: I was no longer permitted to go back in there.

Let us assume, somewhat one-sidedly, that at his birth man is more or less *tabula rasa*. At any rate, impressions absorbed will penetrate an untrodden or hardly trodden breeding ground. That is why these (first) impressions are so strong and so important. They may determine (parts of) one's entire life, even or particularly when the original impression has evaporated into something we call 'memory' for want of a better word. That is what this work of Marcel Zalme deals with, this tension between numinous experience and looking back in remembrance.

It consists of two parts: a white plaster rectangle, the upper side of which has been modelled into a landscape, not on a reduced scale, but in a proportion of 1:1. On its left there is a comparable but much smaller square piece of polyester, this time in green, placed on a stake. A few metres to the front of these two constructions there is a kind of pole. Those who stand close to it and focus their eyes on the highest point of the pole (approximately at eye level), will see the two landscapes in the distance, the green one and the white one, moving over each other; briefly they melt together but without completely losing their separate identities.

The pole in front of the landscapes reminds one of the kind of vantage point to be found here and there. Usually one can throw coins into them and overlook the wide surroundings through a kind of telescope. That is also the function of this vantage point, but although it presents a special outward view it is a view which is in fact turned inwardly, not towards something actually existing, but towards a mental image in our own heads, corresponding to the landscapes in front of us. They are the means to achieve this.

For Zalme's landscapes are no existing landscapes, they are mental constructs which have taken on the form of landscapes. This suggests that they are places which we *inhabit* as it were: the (memory of the) ideal place manifests itself in the shape of a landscape without wishing to be an existing or even possible landscape.

Of course this work stands for the lost innocence of a child, for paradise lost if you like, of which the residue observed in a state of (no longer innocent) adulthood is a pale and bare reflection, which under special circumstances (if one focuses sharply on the point of the pole in front of it, on a point which is *deliberately* not part of the landscape) can for a moment be observed and experienced in something like its original glory.

Here lurks the paradox of the human condition: the ideal place does exist, but can only (and just briefly) be observed when we *do not* focus on it. The ideal place *is* there, right in front of us *in* ourselves even, but we cannot touch or enter it. It is, as Zalme says, no more than a 'flickering in our field of vision'.

The 'innocent' ideal place and daily adult reality seem to merge for a moment, but this is mainly a matter of longing, for *never the twain shall meet.*

PP

THE IDEAL PLACE: THE ACT OF SEEING
REMY ZAUGG

The ideal place is that place where there is an ideal relationship between the theme and the artist's proposal. But because no such ideal relationship can be expected, there is no ideal place; every place can be ideal.

Rémy Zaugg

I have the feeling that 'seeing' is one of those words we like to use because of the illusion it gives of precision. In a written text I can give the word nuances for example by italicising it. This way I am doubly deluded that I am being precise. But when I try to explain just what it is that I detect beneath the outward appearance of things I am confronted with the imprecision of the word. The closest I can come is that my imagination takes leaps and bounds because I *see* more than I am looking at.

To 'The Ideal Place' in the HCAK have come 24 different ways of seeing the ideal place, all of them different. Some so different from one another that you wonder if they can possibly be speaking about the same thing. Yet if there is any kind of symmetry behind these ideas from which we can deduce something shared, then it must be in the 'simple' act of *seeing*. They are all a response to something seen, or *seen*, or experienced, though I will leave it to someone else to sketch out the differences between them.

I think it would be fair to say that seeing, or sight, has been one of Rémy Zaugg's favorite preoccupations. So it was not a surprise to find small grey paintings scattered at various points throughout the HCAK with the following text screen-printed in a lighter grey on them: BUT I WORLD I SEE YOU, although this is the first direct reference to seeing as such that he has made to my knowledge.

How should the sentence be read? Even before examining what it seems to suggest, the reader has to decide who is speaking, since the 'I' is ambiguous in the very first instance: either the 'I' or the 'world' can be interpreted as being the subject of the sentence. Either I am a person seeing the world, or I am the world seeing, what? Whichever reason you choose, the sentence seems on the face of it a pretty standard example of a reflexive idiom; I, or I-the-world see you seeing me seeing you etc, and since 'I' or 'I-the-world' am of the world (even when I am 'art' since 'I' am a painting) it is myself I am seeing. Yet the sentence is a bit trickier than that, since it is stated in the form of a rejoinder: 'BUT I WORLD I SEE YOU'. Why would Zaugg wish to complicate an already complex sentence? It looks very much as though the sentence is not so much a simple confirmation of (reflexive) observation as a plea that 'I' be seen to be seeing. By marking it as a rebuttal, I the reader am introduced into a 'discussion' of an unknown length and quality, with an emotional tone or temperature I can only guess at.

Because of the 'but' I find I want to indulge briefly in the game of guessing at the conversation, or context, which preceded the statement. At this point I can only imagine three possibilities: either a direct dialogue with 'the world', or an internal conversation with the world as the subject, or even a response to how others think about her. But why should 'I' lay such a stress on the accomplishment of seeing the world? Does she ignore me? Or overlook me? Does she despise the littleness of my intelligence? Perhaps I feel that others misunderstand her. Or perhaps I am answering my own question, whether I think she is real, or just a dream. Guessing games are amusing but whichever you choose (why not all of them?) the tenor of the statement is unmistakable: 'I' am saying my vision has validity. It adds that little extra to the classic pairing of the observer and the observed. The 'but' underscores the inimitable, the individual, or even the summit of individuals, the consciousness attached to a distinct entity, which is unique to that entity. Others may think they see you, but I see you in a way that no one else can or does.

Speculations aside, Zaugg's manner of speaking makes me lean towards the conclusion that his sentence is meaningless, in the way that water is colourless. In a normal conversation we know who we are speaking to. The theatricality of naming the interlocutor leads me to think that the statement is rhetorical: I know the world is unaware of me and will not answer. This reading gives the words an air of futility. In fact, to register the act of seeing itself with words is either a deed in itself sublime in its positivism, or the act of a desperate man trying to fabricate the proof of his existence. If Zaugg's exacting description of Cézanne's paintings are a confirmation that they are 'real', and the paintings themselves proof that the landscape was 'real', then perhaps he hopes that the panels in the HCAK are proof that 'seeing' is real. Before a canvas became a Cézanne, there was a Cézanne that *saw*. And since seeing is almost literally the registration of that which passes before our eyes – I mean which passes and then is gone – then it is easy to sympathise with an artist who craves it with such passion that he wants to freeze it in mid-motion. Besides which, a concrete registration of our 'sight' is the best monument to our having passed here ourselves. What is frozen by Zaugg in his panels is the *seeing*, and not the seen. Which brings me to the 'greyness' of the paintings.

Seeing, Zaugg seems to be saying, aside from being paramount, is of itself impartial. He seems to be speaking about seeing before it becomes *seeing*. Seeing has no value until it is transformed into deeds. The *place* where seeing happens has no value until *seeing* has occurred there. And this, as we all know, can happen anywhere. Zaugg's panels are scattered seemingly at random around the HCAK, even where they seem to interfere formally with the work of other artists. They could apparently take any conceivable position that you or I could. They represent potential.

If the vantage points from which to look are too many to count, so are the reasons for stopping at one. It is down to what I desire, or fear, or what interests me that I stop where I do, and see what I see. But one of the things that make the equation between being a person with eyes, and the things there are to see so unpredictable and so wonderful, is that each can be said to have a degree of self-determination. Not the eyes alone, but the place as well. A point of view, or vantage point is not chosen by the volition of the spectator without the uniqueness of its position among things helping him to. These two variables allow for an infinite number and combination of meetings between us and the things around us. The uniqueness of the viewer and the unreproductibility of a place (and vice versa) since no two are alike, combine and combust in a way which is anything but 'grey'. If Zaugg meant us to feel his longing for the image with his *Tableau Aveugle* (Blind Painting), then perhaps he means us to feel his passion for the *potential* of sight in the HCAK. But if sight is essentially neutral, grey, and the place *of itself* arbitrary, one in a multitude, at what point in their meeting do they become 'ideal'?

It is as if Zaugg wishes me to think that seeing is ideal as long as it remains a potentiality. It is true that once the seen has passed into action (or even inaction) it is somehow altered. I believe that it is that moment of innocence, before my mental make-up alters what I see that I long for and keep hoping to repeat: the moment before the inevitable disappointment in which the unexpected can happen and the world could change for me. The moment in which meaning is seen. Zaugg leaves unanswered what might happen when the thing seen has been appropriated by a response. The ideal place is perhaps wherever the gaze has been fastened before my response has infected it, and made it complicit in a process. It is where a pure, uninhibited perception of things occurs before judgement is passed. As such it is an impossible state for me to sustain. Zaugg's words may have no real precision to speak of, but is that any different from our desire to see the world?

MZ

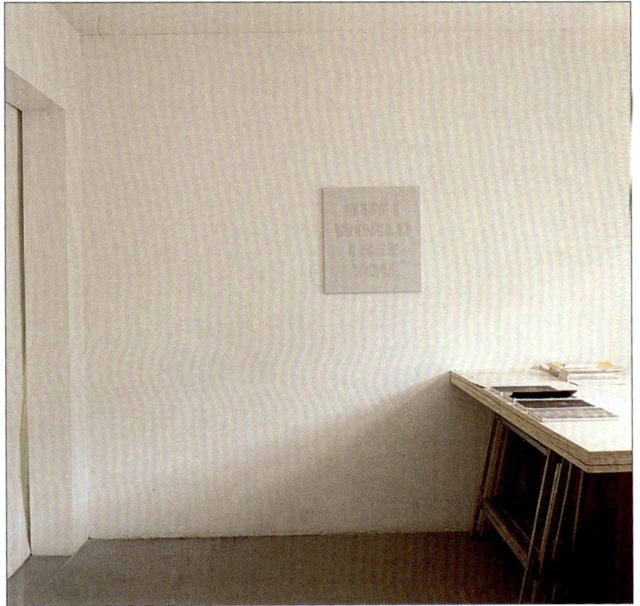

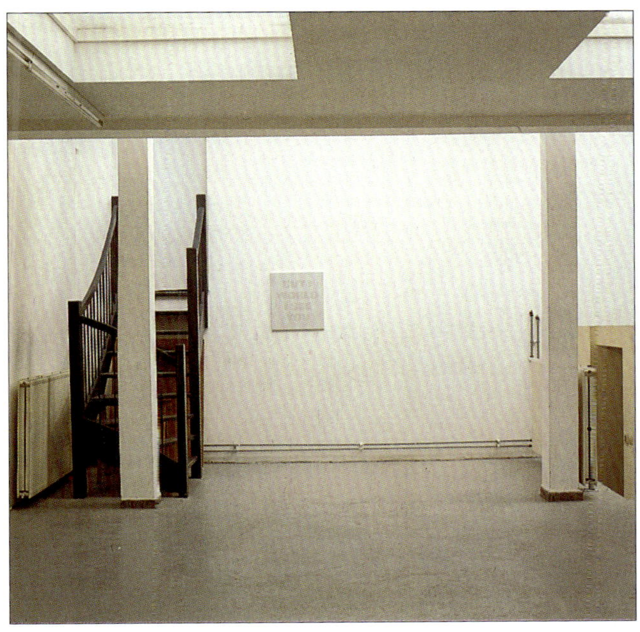

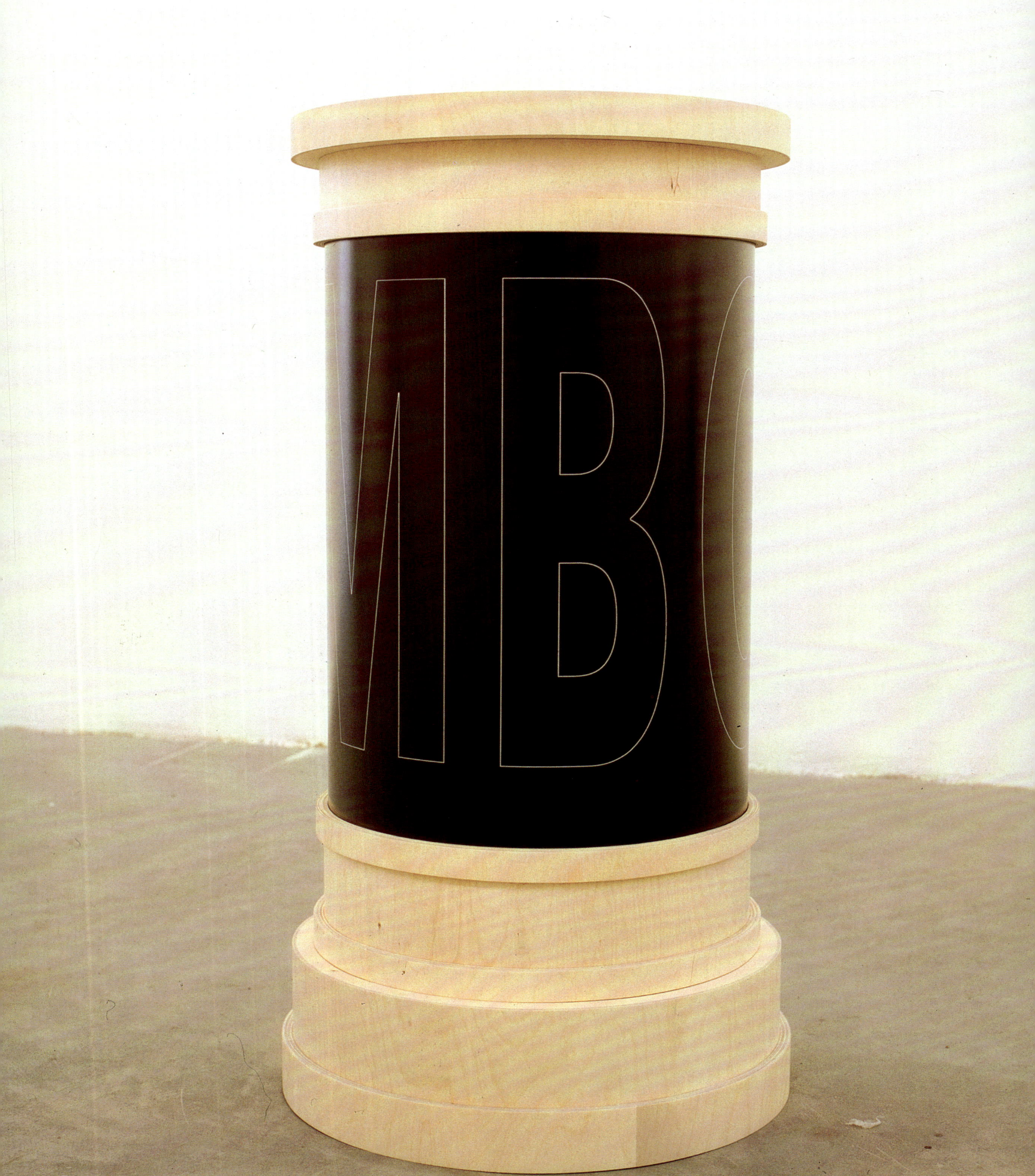

THE IDEAL PLACE AS DESTINATION: FINGERS POINTING AT THE MOON

MIRJAM DE ZEEUW

An ideal place is an interaction between two factors:

• A recognition: analysis of impressions in a new formation.
• An acknowledgement: to openly show the meaning of that place.
Mirjam de Zeeuw

Mirjam de Zeeuw presented five small columns placed independently in the exhibition room. Each column bore an inscription in a different language.

The use of columns as bearers of meaning at once reminds one of 'the classical ideal', of which the column in itself may already be a symbol. Here the distance between status quo and ideal is immediately felt: the classical ideal is an ideal belonging to another time, no longer valid now. Evidently, even indicating the ideal place is no longer possible in our time without borrowing visual means from another cultural period, when the spiritual ideal still had a more or less unambiguous meaning, when at least it was not uncommon to discuss the ideal, it was a current concept. Consequently, borrowing such a vocabulary also tells us something about the evident unattainability of 'the ideal place' in our time, or at any rate about the absence of a terminology of our own to deal with the concept.

On account of their small height, the columns can also be interpreted as pedestals. In that case something ought to be standing on them, a statue, which in this context, should be viewed as (the visualisation of) an ideal. Or, since there are five columns, as a place created by the installation as a whole, where the ideal is given shape.

But there are no statues on the pedestals. There are inscriptions instead, again a form of indication. 'The ideal place' is here filled in by text. 'The ideal place' is therefore not presented but represented.

In random order the inscriptions are: sinnbild (symbol), symbol, onderscheidingsteken (distinguishing mark), alegoria (allegory) and embleme (emblem).

Symbol, allegory and emblem: these were the terms used to define the ideal (but not exclusively) in former times. They are categories according to type, which in themselves need to be filled in, in order to give them a specific meaning. The use of different languages, all of them European or of European origin for that matter, emphasises the exemplary character of this work. In a sense one could maintain that not only the pedestals are empty, but the inscriptions as well. Both indicate (archaic or anachronistic) methods to come to a definition of 'the ideal place', but they do not result in an actual 'ideal place'. They are fingers pointing at the moon.

It is only the word 'onderscheidingsteken' (distinguishing mark) that does not belong in the 'classical' list. It is typically a concept of this time, a message from an individualised culture, where no central norms operate and where recognisability has been replaced by (and in another sense, is paradoxically based on) distinction; a culture without unity, not aspiring after similarity and harmony, but on the contrary, after difference and conflict.

Could it be so that the 'distinguishing mark', the individual moment, is the ideal? Or is it no more than a comment on the status quo: a 'new' concept nestling among and surrounded by a mass of tradition? Perhaps the 'distinguishing mark' is also a finger pointing at the moon.

There are five columns and a hand has five fingers. Continuing the metaphor, human powerlessness with respect to the spiritual ideal, consequently with respect to 'the ideal place' is here brought home to us very pregnantly indeed: in this work not just one finger is pointing at the moon, but a whole hand.

PP

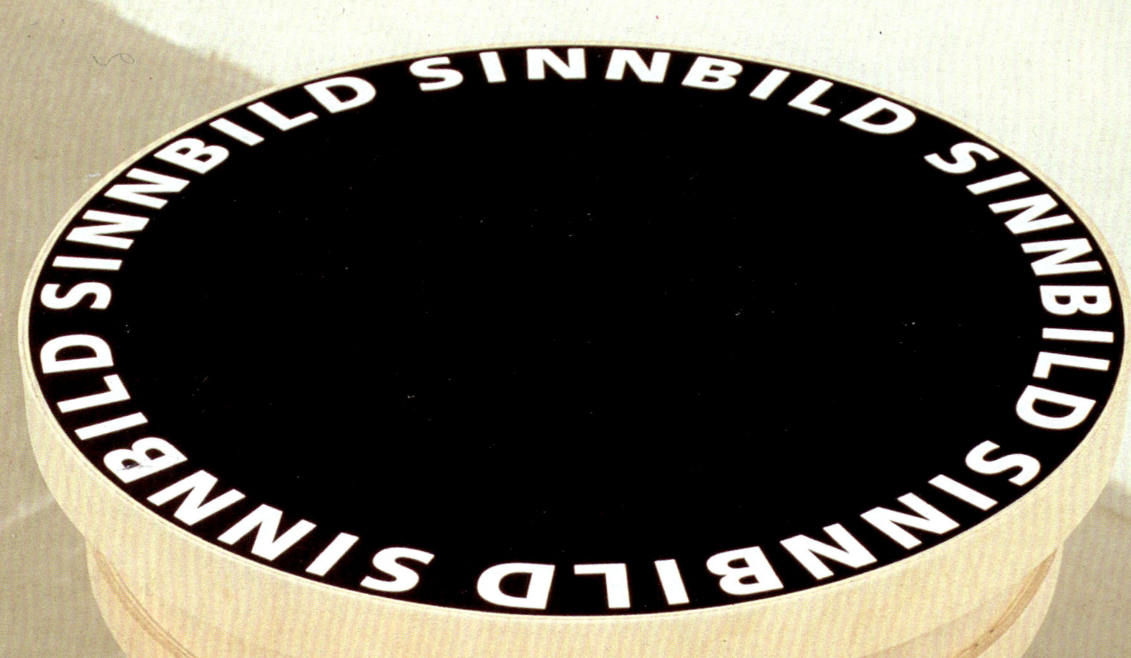

SINNBILD